A TIME FOR GIANTS

A TIME

FOR

GIANTS

POLITICS OF THE
AMERICAN HIGH COMMAND
IN WORLD WAR II

BY D. CLAYTON JAMES
WITH ANNE SHARP WELLS

FRANKLIN WATTS ★ NEW YORK ★ TORONTO ★ 1987

Photographs following page 190 courtesy of:
(top) U.S. Navy, (bottom) U.S. Army Signal Corps;
(top) MacArthur Memorial, (bottom) Navy Department;
(top) U.S. Army, (bottom) U.S. Army;
(top) U.S. Army, (bottom) U.S. Air Force;
(top) U.S. Air Force, (bottom) U.S. Marine Corps;
(top) U.S. Army, (bottom) U.S. Army Signal Corps;
(top) Department of Defense, (bottom) U.S. Navy;
(top) Department of Defense, (bottom) U.S. Army.

Library of Congress Cataloging-in-Publication Data

James, D. Clayton.
A time for giants.

Bibliography: p.
Includes index.
1. World War, 1939–1945—United States—Biography.
2. Generals—United States—Biography. 3. Admirals—
United States—Biography. 4. Command of troops—
History—20th century. I. Wells, Anne Sharp. II. Title.
D773.J36   1987   940.54′0973   87-16041
ISBN 0-531-15046-1

**BOOKS BY
D. CLAYTON JAMES**

*A Time for Giants
Politics of the American High
Command in World War II* (1987)

The Years of MacArthur
Volume III, *Triumph and
Disaster, 1945–1964* (1985)

The Years of MacArthur
Volume II, *1941–1945* (1975)

*South to Bataan, North to Mukden:
The Prison Diary of Brigadier
General W. E. Brougher* [ed.] (1971)

The Years of MacArthur
Volume I, *1880–1941* (1970)

Antebellum Natchez (1968)

TO DORRIS BANKSTON

CONTENTS

★ IX ★

★ X ★

FOREWORD

When George C. Marshall was elevated to Army chief of staff, he had never commanded troops in battle. When Dwight D. Eisenhower assumed command of the Allied invasion of Northwest Africa, he had never been under enemy fire. Of the seven generals and admirals promoted to five-star rank in 1944, only Douglas MacArthur had ever personally led forces in combat. Without distinction in battle to recommend them, how did America's high commanders of World War II attain their lofty positions of authority?

This book is an introduction to the military leaders and the manner of their selection to the high command of the United States armed services during the Second World War. A considerable body of literature exists on the achievements of these men during the war years, but little attention has been directed to how they acquired their positions of power and leadership.

The organization of this book is based on a tripartite division of each chapter (except the final one), with the first section of the chapter constituting an overview of the framework and evolution of certain aspects of the high command, particularly during a given time span in a specific theater of operations. The first sections of the chapters, in brief, deal with the following topics: first, the development of the Joint

Chiefs of Staff and the Combined Chiefs of Staff, together with the main American and Allied commands they controlled (Chapters 1–2); second, the global crises faced by the American high command, December 1941–May 1942 (Chapter 3); third, the evolution of the high commands of American officers who headed major United States or Allied forces and theaters in the war against the European Axis, May 1942–May 1943 (Chapter 4), May 1943–June 1944 (Chapter 6), and June 1944–May 1945 (Chapter 8), as well as in the war against Japan, May 1942–May 1943 (Chapter 5), May 1943–June 1944 (Chapter 7), and June 1944–August 1945 (Chapter 9). Chapter 10 consists of concluding observations on the politics of the high command and on common threads running through the selection of the featured senior officers.

The second and third sections of each of the first nine chapters introduce the eighteen members of the high command selected by the author as the most significant. The emphasis in each essay is on how the officer rose to his position of high command in World War II. Attention is devoted also to the circumstances surrounding his transfer from one post to a higher one in the top echelon, his movement downward from the high command to a lower level, or the factors involved in how he almost moved up or down the chain of command to another position, if, of course, any of these conditions prevailed after his initial entry into the high command. Except for one army-level commander, General George S. Patton, Jr., the author has chosen officers who attained posts during the war at levels higher than those of commanders of numerically designated armies, fleets, or air forces.

The distribution by services roughly follows the strengths of those services during the war. Thus seven Army generals, five admirals, four Army Air Forces generals, and two Marine generals are included, while in 1941–45 the peak strengths of the services were approximately 5.9 million personnel in the Army ground and service organizations, 3.5 million in the Navy, 2.4 million in the Army Air Forces, and slightly less than a half million in the Marine Corps.

The criteria used in selecting the eighteen officers from an original list that exceeded fifty were many but not altogether explicable nor measurable. They included the following: wartime positions held, achievements or successes in those roles, evaluations by contemporary peers and superiors, maximum strengths of their services, theaters of operations, ranks, fame, seniority, significant honors and decorations, postwar professional recognition and leadership, existence of reliable published writings by or about them, availability and accessibility of manuscript sources relating to them, and, most important, the author's personal judgments based on over two decades as a military historian. The author readily grants that it is unlikely that any two dozen established scholars on World War II could agree on the eighteen most important leaders of the American high command in that conflict. Indeed, the author himself easily could have substituted a number of other top-level commanders.

The sources on which this book is based include some personal and official papers, interviews, and other unpublished materials but consist primarily of the many published works of biography and autobiography that reveal the eighteen featured commanders, along with their superiors and their subordinates. The notes have been kept to a minimum and largely refer to quotations. The select bibliography has been confined to the author's choice of the best or standard books on the American high command during the Second World War.

Acknowledgment is gratefully given for the help provided by the staffs of the following repositories: the Hoover Institution on War, Revolution, and Peace, Stanford University, Stanford, California; the Manuscript Division of the Library of Congress, Washington, D.C.; the U.S. Marine Corps Historical Center, Washington, D.C.; the U.S. Naval Historical Center, Washington, D.C.; the U.S. Army Center of Military History, Washington, D.C.; the Military Archives Division of the National Archives, Washington, D.C.; the Washington National Records Center, Suitland, Maryland;

the Albert F. Simpson Historical Research Center, Maxwell Air Force Base, Alabama; the MacArthur Memorial, Norfolk, Virginia; the Franklin D. Roosevelt Library, Hyde Park, New York; the Harry S. Truman Library, Independence, Missouri; the Dwight D. Eisenhower Library, Abilene, Kansas; the Manuscripts and Archives Department of the Sterling Library, Yale University, New Haven, Connecticut; and the Mitchell Memorial Library, Mississippi State University, Mississippi State, Mississippi.

Collaborating invaluably on all aspects of this project was Miss Anne S. Wells, who has been assisting me since 1974. As in the past, the skill, time, and interest that she gave were crucial to the completion of this book. During the critical phases of research of all six of my books, my wife, Erlene, has made important contributions; her work, advice, and supportive spirit have been of immeasurable worth. Students who helped part-time were Miss Terri F. Lacey, Miss Cindy M. Greiczek, Miss Chirá A. Wadsworth, Mrs. Melinda G. Brand, Mr. Altaf Hossain, and Miss B. Yvette Rishel. I am grateful also to Professors Charles D. Lowery, Edward L. McGlone, George R. Lewis, Frances N. Coleman, and Martha B. Irby, all of Mississippi State University, for the various ways in which they assisted me. My appreciation is expressed, too, to Mr. Fred Faulk for his photographic assistance. In addition, my thanks go to Mrs. Ellen Joseph, my editor, for her excellent counsel and encouragement, and to Mr. Gerard F. McCauley, my literary agent, for his fine efforts on my behalf.

Mississippi State University   *D. Clayton James*
February 1987

A TIME FOR GIANTS

ONE

PREPARING FOR
WARTIME COMMANDS

THE TOP ECHELON

At the Quebec Conference in September 1944, the strategy makers of America and Britain interrupted the conference to pose for group photographs outside the Citadel, their imposing meeting place on the bluff above the St. Lawrence River. The occasion's best-known picture is of President Franklin D. Roosevelt and Prime Minister Winston S. Churchill, their hats nearly touching as they talk briskly. Around them are the Combined Chiefs of Staff, the Anglo-American officers who advised the president and the prime minister on the direction of the global war against the Axis nations. While Roosevelt and Churchill would be recognizable to most of their countrymen four decades later, the uniformed men beside them would be familiar to few citizens of their nations then or now in spite of their lofty positions. Much has been written about the achievements of the Joint Chiefs, the American members of the Combined Chiefs, as well as about some of the other high-level American commanders of World War II, but the manner in which most of them were selected has received scant attention. The story of the selection of these wielders of great military power begins in Washington, D.C.

★ 1 ★

When World War II's early flames swept over North China in July 1937 and Poland in September 1939, the War and Navy departments in Washington accelerated their contingency planning for vast expansions of the armed forces should the United States be caught in the spreading conflagrations. Few planners imagined that the United States citizens who donned uniforms in 1941–45 would number fifteen million, or more than the grand total of Americans who had served in all the nation's prior wars. The number and nature of the high military positions needed during the impending emergency could not be foreseen in the late 1930s, but it was expected that the demand for senior-level generals and admirals would be unprecedented. Over the nearly four years of American involvement in the Second World War, the enormous responsibilities of commanding huge forces, the truly worldwide scope of the conflict, and the desperateness of the terrible struggle for survival against powerful adversaries made it a time *for* giants. Whether the American high command's responses to the awesome challenges made it also a time *of* giants is not easily determined. At the outset, however, it is noteworthy that of the eighteen senior officers whose wartime appointments are featured herein only one was relieved of his command—and the justification for that action is moot. The system that produced the American high command of World War II, though seldom consistent and never formalized, seemed to prove its adequacy for the duration of the crisis by the performances of the officers at the top.

Between the world wars the Army, Army Air Corps, Navy, and Marine Corps had developed personnel advancement programs that, while differing by branches and services, all appeared on paper at least to provide orderly systems for promoting and assigning officers. Exhibiting trends away from seniority and toward merit as the principal criterion, they included efficiency (fitness) reports, selection boards, and personnel sections that determined officers' futures until they reached the two- or three-star ranks of general and flag officers. In the past, when the officer corps had been small, most field-grade and higher officers knew their peers, making extensive records-keeping unnecessary in recommending officers for promotions or assignments. With the huge growth in officer strength in World War II, it was imperative to have a rationalized basis for ratings since personal dealings were not practicable in most cases. But the efficiency, or fitness, reports of the 1920s and 1930s were largely uncritical, with a sizable proportion of officers in all the services receiving high ratings. Thus on the eve of America's entry into the Second World War the personnel bureaus of the War and Navy departments could not readily identify from their records the nucleus of field-grade officers most likely to succeed if elevated to major wartime commands. The service secretaries and military chiefs found themselves relying upon personal knowledge, not only in recommending officers for high-level responsibilities who were already seasoned at the lower general- or flag-officer levels, but also in identifying officers farther down the ladder for assignments that would prepare them for eventual succession to important commands. The leniency in ratings continued throughout the war, nevertheless, so that by 1945, for example, 95 percent of the Army's captains were rated "superior" or "excellent" overall and 60 percent of its colonels were judged "superior."[1]

The final decision in selecting the top commanders lay with Roosevelt, because, as provided in Article II, Section 2, of the Constitution, the president is commander in chief of the nation's military services. With war clouds growing during his second presidential term, Roosevelt increasingly exercised his authority as commander in chief. Perhaps because of his experience as assistant secretary of the Navy between 1913 and 1920 and his lifelong interest in things nautical, he was most interested in developing a two-ocean navy and tended to meddle more in Navy Department matters than in affairs of the War Department. Yet he became an enthusiast of air power between 1939 and 1941, and, thanks to the tactful educating efforts of General George C. Marshall, the wartime chief of staff of the Army, Roosevelt gradually began to appreciate the role of ground forces. The president wielded his military powers in sundry ways during the ensuing war years and with an aggressiveness unprecedented among presidents. Indeed, he became engrossed in problems of strategy, logistics, and command and, not unlike Churchill, came to fancy himself as a grand strategist and master of war, if not of battles. He took his role as supreme war leader so seriously that he asked his cabinet officials to address him as commander in chief instead of as president. It nettled him that Admiral Ernest J. King also used the title of commander in chief when he became head of the United States Fleet in late 1941.

Subject to the advice and consent of the Senate, the president is empowered under the Constitution to appoint all officers of the armed services. That authority extends to all commissions, promotions, and assignments in a de jure sense, but because of his great wartime responsibilities, Roosevelt's de facto practice was usually to approve the recommendations of the War and Navy departments, including the filling of senior commands. As their personal and professional ties deepened during the war, Roosevelt came to rely heavily in selecting key commanders on the views of Marshall; King, who also was chief of naval operations by March 1942; and, to a lesser extent, General Henry H. "Hap" Arnold, commanding general of the Army Air Forces. Surprisingly, he seldom sought advice on command appointments from Admiral William D. Leahy, who served as chief of staff to the president and as acting chairman of the Joint Chiefs of Staff (ultimately, Marshall, King, Arnold, and Leahy). "It was very pleasing to me that the President did not make it a habit to discuss command assignments with me," remarked Leahy, who felt that the chief of staff to Roosevelt ought to "remain as neutral as possible in matters of this nature" and, besides, President Roosevelt was "very well informed" about his high-ranking officers, especially the admirals.[2]

Roosevelt went against the counsel of his military chiefs sometimes on issues of grand strategy and high command, but such instances were exceptional (especially after 1942), even if attracting much attention in writings on the war. No consistent pattern can be delineated as to his support of, or his contrary action on, command recommendations sent up to him. But several of his decisions that went against his chiefs' views involved American officers who were serving in or were under consideration for significant Allied leadership roles. On such occasions crucial Allied political or diplomatic issues were at stake from the White House viewpoint, and apparently the president decided that his chiefs' opinions were of limited value in weighing the nonmilitary elements in the particular situations.

Roosevelt issued an executive order in July 1939 that required the Joint Army-Navy Board, which consisted of the Army chief of staff, the chief of naval operations, and several of their senior assistants, to report directly to him, bypassing the service secretaries. In executive orders authorizing administrative reorganizations of the War and Navy departments in the spring of 1942, the president again jealously guarded his authority as commander in chief by establishing direct relations with the military chiefs of the services on the strategic and operational aspects of the direction of the war and relegating the War and Navy secretaries largely to administration of their departments. Secretary of War Henry L. Stimson and Secretary of the Navy Frank Knox found that Roosevelt solicited their views on high command selections often with more politeness than earnestness, for the president heeded more frequently the advice of Marshall and King regarding their top generals and admirals.

Of great influence on the president in deciding matters of diplomacy, strategy, and command, particularly for the European and Mediterranean theaters, was Harry L. Hopkins, Roosevelt's brilliant, tough-minded, and enigmatic confidant. To a man, the military chiefs were wary of "Harry the Hop" at first, perhaps because of his long prior association with relief and reform programs of the New Deal; but each officer eventually was persuaded of his invaluable assistance to Roosevelt and to the Allied war effort. In White

House discussions, according to Leahy, Hopkins "would usually be the first man to put a finger on the essential element of a problem."[3] Arnold and Marshall were convinced that Hopkins was instrumental in their appointments and in the naming of other key commanders. His impact was especially strong in cases of Allied command selections in the war against Germany and Italy. Churchill, who greatly respected his perceptiveness, nicknamed him "Lord Root of the Matter," and later praised him as "a crumbling lighthouse [referring to Hopkins' serious wartime illnesses] from which there shone the beams that lead great fleets to harbours."[4]

The president and his chiefs used different criteria and sources of counsel in almost every case of picking officers to fill high command slots in World War II. The naming of commanders of large units within a service was the responsibility of the military head of the Army, Army Air Forces, Navy, or Marine Corps. Normally he might solicit advice from the theater commander, the branch chief, the service secretary or his assistants, the personnel section chief, the officer immediately superior to the position, the officer who previously held the position, and other officers who knew the candidate and whose judgments the service chief had come to trust. Both Marshall and King became known for the confidential written or mental notes they had made earlier in their careers regarding colleagues whom they noticed as unusually able or inept leaders. Arnold and Generals Thomas Holcomb and A. Archer Vandegrift, the successive wartime commandants of the Marine Corps, submitted their command recommendations through War and Navy department channels respectively since their services were not autonomous. Of course, Arnold remained an Army officer subordinate to Marshall throughout the war, though he was granted membership on the Joint and Combined Chiefs of Staff and enjoyed cordial, supportive relations with the Army chief of staff.

If the service chief determined the final recommendations to the president regarding commands within his service, the Joint Chiefs, usually by informal concurrence, decided the recommendations for joint commands, that is, those involving more than one American service. Selection of officers to head combined commands, which were made up of more than one Allied nation's forces, differed widely according to the coalition members engaged, but it often brought the heads of state more actively into the process, as earlier mentioned.

Five days after the Japanese attack on Pearl Harbor, Churchill and his principal military and political advisers left by sea for Washington, where for several weeks in late December 1941 and early January 1942 the Anglo-American heads of state and their assistants conferred on common war problems in the Arcadia Conference. Advising Roosevelt on the military side were Marshall, King, Arnold, and Admiral Harold R. Stark, who was then chief of naval operations. Among the Arcadia decisions, surely the most far-reaching was the creation of the Combined Chiefs of Staff, which was to consist of the British Chiefs of Staff Committee and its American counterpart, at first informally called the U.S. Chiefs of Staff. The British chiefs would maintain representatives in Washington to serve as a liaison committee with the American chiefs. The Joint Chiefs of Staff as a corporate entity evolved from the Arcadia Conference as a belated American effort to match the impressive interservice high command system of the British. The Joint Army-Navy Board had never been suitable for trying to achieve unity of command or better interservice cooperation, and by early 1942 it seemed obsolete in the face of the intense pressures and baffling complexities of worldwide warfare that hit the American defense establishment. Actually the first formal meeting of the Joint Chiefs of Staff did not take place until early February 1942, several weeks after Arcadia adjourned.

The Joint Chiefs as a command agency grew out of two needs that became apparent to Roosevelt and his military advisers during the Arcadia talks: the necessity for better coordination between the American services, including the creation of joint commands; and the need for an American high command body to counter British efforts to dominate Anglo-American strategy making. Interestingly, Roosevelt never issued a specific directive or charter validating the establishment of the Joint Chiefs of Staff; its statutory basis would not be provided until the National Security Act of 1947. King maintained that "this informal character gave great flexibility to the organization," which later in the war enabled it to set up a large committee structure and extend its influence in a number of areas not foreseen in early 1942.[5] On the often complex issues of service, joint, and combined commands, however, the Joint Chiefs, as individuals and as a body, soon found their lines of interest entangled as they tried to function as advisers to Roosevelt, as heads of their respective services, and as the American representatives on the Combined Chiefs of Staff.

The later portions of these first two chapters will be devoted to the manner in which the four highest-ranking American commanders—Arnold, Marshall, King, and Leahy—obtained the positions that earned them membership on the Joint Chiefs of Staff.

THE LESS TROUBLESOME
MAVERICK: ARNOLD

Flying was very dangerous for the few daring young men who were pilots when Henry H. "Hap" Arnold, a twenty-five-year-old infantry lieutenant, learned from the Wright brothers at their Dayton, Ohio, school in 1911. Lessons were limited to short periods at dawn and dusk when the wind was calm enough for the flimsy, weakly powered Wright aircraft. Often the local undertaker parked his horse-drawn hearse beside the fence at the end of the field until the student pilots had landed safely or the opportunistic entrepreneur had some business. After crashing into the ocean on a flight along the Massachusetts coast in 1912, Arnold developed a fear of flying that took him many agonizing months to overcome.

By the time the United States entered World War I, however, he had risen to assistant chief of the Army Air Service. He efficiently administered its wartime training programs, which grew to include 140,000 officers and enlisted men. During the interwar years he won esteem in the Army Air Corps as a flyer, administrator, and innovator, winning the coveted Mackay Trophy twice for record-setting aerial feats, successfully heading key field commands, and pioneering in techniques such as mid-air refueling and air supply drops. He strongly backed Brigadier General William Mitchell's crusade for air power and became an ardent advocate of strategic air warfare and the need for long-range bombers. Impatient, enthusiastic, stubborn, and mischievous, he irritated some War Department superiors, but he did not hesitate to stay in the Army when the presidency of Pan American Airways was offered to him. By early 1935 he was a brigadier general and commanded the First Wing of the General Headquarters (GHQ) Air Force, the newly formed air strike arm headed by Brigadier General Frank M. Andrews.

Before retiring as chief of the Army Air Corps in December 1935, Major General Benjamin D. Foulois recommended Hap Arnold as his successor. Foulois was convinced, says an authority, that "the commander of the west coast wing [Arnold] was an excellent administrator, a diplomatic yet dynamic airpower advocate, and the Air Corps' senior active pilot . . . the right man for the job."[6] But on Christmas Eve, Secretary of War George F. Dern announced that the new Air Corps chief was Brigadier General Oscar Westover. It was said that Westover's candidacy had been pushed mainly by Assistant Secretary of War Henry H. Woodring, who would succeed Dern in less than a year, and by General Malin Craig, who had replaced General Douglas MacArthur as Army chief of staff in October 1935. Woodring and Craig wanted an air chief who would adhere strictly to War Department lines and not push aggressively for more Air Corps funds, especially for strategic bombers, as Andrews and Arnold had been demanding. Promotions to major general were shortly forthcoming for Westover, the new chief, and, surprising to some, for Andrews, the latter advancement bestowed because of his position as commander of the GHQ Air Force.[7]

Flying from his wing headquarters at March Field, California, to Florida for GHQ Air Force maneuvers in December 1935, Arnold received word soon after his arrival that he was to report to the Army chief of staff, General Craig. Arnold was informed when he met with Craig that Westover had requested him as assistant chief of the Army Air Corps and that the chief of staff had already approved it. To Craig's astonishment, Arnold objected: "I protested with all my heart that I would rather stay on the Coast with my silver leaves back; really, would rather be a lieutenant colonel running my present command than a staff general in Washington! No use." From past tours of duty in the national capital he had developed a deep dislike for Washington, and he was gloomy for a long while about giving up his wing command for a staff job. Later Arnold recalled, "If I had realized then that I would stay in Washington for ten consecutive years, right up to my retirement, I would almost have dared to turn my overloaded car around and drive straight back to California."[8]

After moving to his office in the Army Air Corps headquarters, located in the Munitions Building in Washington, Arnold worked industriously to build up American land-based air strength. Much of his energy went to selling the importance of preparedness and aerial defenses to the General Staff, Congress, and the Bureau of the Budget. But isolationism was still strong in public opinion and on Capitol Hill, and despite the best efforts of the New Dealers the Great Depression had not loosened much of its grip on the nation's economy. So appropriations for military aviation remained parsimonious, and by early 1938 the Army Air Corps had less than 18,000 officers and men. Its bombers and fighters were few and mostly obsolete, with only thirteen of the new B-17 "Flying Fortresses" in service or due for delivery soon. Meanwhile Andrews and a coterie of air of ficers close to him had become increasingly insistent on a higher priority for the GHQ Air Force, particularly for more heavy bombers.

As Air Corps chief, Westover enjoyed flying around the country to visit air bases, training schools, and aircraft plants. During his many trips Arnold served as acting chief of the Air Corps and gained much experience in the duties of the office. On September 21, 1938, Westover was piloting his single-engine AT-15, accompanied by a crew chief, when he ran into turbulence during his landing approach at the Lockheed airfield in Burbank, California. The plane stalled, spun briefly, and crashed in flames, killing both men.

Several candidates may have been under consideration briefly for chief of the Air Corps, but the principal ones were Andrews and Arnold. Since 1926, the assistant chief had always become the next chief of the Air Corps. Arnold expected to be Westover's successor, yet time began to pass with no indication from the War Department. Andrews, however, was summoned from his GHQ Air Force headquarters at Langley Field to meet in the Army chief of staff's office with Craig and his five assistant chiefs of staff. Craig stated bluntly that the War Department was prepared to recommend him to the president for the position of Air Corps chief, but first "we would like your assurance that you will give up these ideas about large bombers and conform to the policies of the War Department." Andrews refused to compromise, emphasizing that if he were chief he would perform his duties *as I see them* to the best of my ability." Craig responded curtly, "Thank you for coming; that is all."[9] A few months later, after further collisions with Woodring and Craig mainly regarding the need for strategic bombers, Andrews was reduced from major general to colonel, relieved of the GHQ Air Force command, and sent into a Mitchell-style exile at Fort Sam Houston, Texas.

Andrews' session with Craig was confidential, so Arnold, who was a great admirer of Andy Andrews and would have been pleased to serve under him again, became more restless as the days went by with no announcement from the War

Department about Westover's replacement. Then rumors began to circulate in Washington, supposedly leaked by a White House staff member, that the president hesitated to appoint Arnold because the general was reported to be an alcoholic. Allegedly Arnold had been seen drunk in public while on duty in Hawaii. It was obviously a smear campaign because Arnold had never served in Hawaii. "Further, as my friends knew," said Arnold, "I hadn't had a drink of hard liquor since 1920."[10] He talked the matter over with Colonels Carl A. Spaatz and Ira C. Eaker, two key members of his staff and his oldest friends. Spaatz proposed to get Arnold's efficiency reports covering the period in question into the hands of Roosevelt's main confidant, Harry Hopkins. Spaatz and Eaker also urged Arnold to talk with Hopkins, whom he had not met. Arnold reluctantly went to Hopkins and, to his pleasant surprise, found him sympathetic and also interested in Air Corps problems. Hopkins promptly went to the President and corrected his misconception about Arnold.

Exactly one week after Westover's death, Arnold was invited to a meeting at the White House. The fateful Munich Conference of Hitler with the French and British prime ministers was getting underway, and top leaders around Roosevelt were edgy about the possibility of a European war. Those at the session with the president included the secretaries of War, Navy, and Treasury; Stark, Marshall, and several of their senior officers; and Hopkins. Roosevelt expressed alarm over the European situation and proposed that a large air force might deter Hitler more effectively than expansion of ground or sea forces. He asked Arnold's opinion, and the general responded with a spontaneous but convincing brief presentation. He stressed the fact that air power involved far more than just large numbers of aircraft, pointing out the need for more pilots, crews, maintenance personnel, bases, training programs, and equipment stocks. Whether won over by Arnold, Hopkins, or others supporting the assistant chief, the president announced the next day,

September 29, 1938, the appointment of Arnold as the new chief of the Army Air Corps.

The following day, without firing a shot, Hitler took another step toward World War II with the signing of the Munich Pact that gave western Czechoslovakia to Nazi Germany. From his first day in office as Air Corps chief, Arnold faced the prospect that someday his fighters and bombers would have to challenge Hitler's vaunted Luftwaffe.

Among leading airmen the choice of Arnold was well received, and long after his wartime leadership he would be highly regarded. General James H. Doolittle, for instance, said he was "a remarkable character, a truly great man" who was, more than anyone else, "responsible for the excellence of our aviation effort" in World War II.[11] General Thomas D. White, Air Force chief of staff from 1957 to 1961, was on Arnold's wartime staff and remembered him as "a very dynamic, a very positive sort" of commander.[12]

Arnold displayed degrees of tactfulness and patience unusual for him in trying to restrain his friend Andrews and other such dedicated air officers from challenging War Department authorities further on issues of funding priorities, strategic forces, and Air Corps autonomy. The new chief favored all three but believed his corps had to work through its Army superiors for the duration of the approaching emergencies over aggressions in East Asia, Africa, and Europe. But, unfortunately, he was not able to contain his well-known tendency toward outspokenness in the relationship most crucial to his job tenure, namely, with the president. In view of the alarming shortages of planes in his Army Air Corps, Arnold was outraged when he learned that Secretary of the Treasury Henry Morgenthau, Jr., was negotiating secret deals with the British and French for the purchase of a significant proportion of new combat aircraft production in the United States. During his testimony before the House Military Affairs Committee in March 1940 regarding Air Corps problems, he was blunt in his criticism of the big orders the British and French were allowed to place with American aircraft manufacturers. When he heard of the air chief's remarks, Roosevelt summoned him to a meeting in the Oval Office which also included a group of top-level officials of the War, Navy, and Treasury departments. Angrily the president lashed out at those who would obstruct his program to aid embattled France and Great Britain; he expressed great displeasure over irresponsible remarks made recently by War Department representatives before congressional committees; and, looking directly at Arnold, he warned that officers who did not cooperate with his policy would be sent to Guam.

Arnold was not relieved of his command, but it would be nine months before he would be invited again to a White House meeting or social. By then the air battle of Britain had been decided in the Royal Air Force's favor, and the president was obviously relaxed when Arnold entered the room. His first words to his Air Corps chief since the previous spring were: "Good evening, Hap. How about my mixing you an Old Fashioned?" Undoubtedly recalling the rumor that almost cost him his chance to head the Air Corps, Arnold replied: "Thanks, Mr. President. I haven't had one for about twenty years, but I assure you I will enjoy this one with you tremendously."[13] Until the president's death four and a half years later, he and Arnold would cultivate a growing admiration and liking of each other.

Fortunately for Arnold's formative period in heading the Army Air Corps, three key changes occurred in the War Department's leadership that brought in able men who would become strong supporters of him and of air power: Henry Stimson, who took over as secretary of war in July 1940; Robert Lovett, who became assistant secretary of war for air in April 1941; and, most important, George Marshall, who was elevated from assistant chief of staff, War Plans Division, to deputy chief of staff of the Army in October 1938 and to chief of staff the next summer. According to Arnold, Marshall "needed plenty of indoctrination about the air facts of life," but he would "become one of the most potent forces behind the development of a real American air power" because of "his ability to digest what he saw and make it part of as strong a body of military genius as I have ever known."[14] In the summer of 1941, Arnold discussed the setting up of the Army Air Forces with Andrews and said of Marshall's part: "The Chief of Staff has been with me 100 percent in creating this organization. It is not a separate Air Corps, but we are no longer the fifth wheel of a wagon."[15]

Marshall helped to get Andrews' rank restored to major general and later, despite stormy opposition from some War Department leaders, chose him as his assistant chief of staff for operations and training (G-3), an unusually important role for an airman to hold at that time. Thanks to Marshall's influence, too, Arnold was given the additional title of deputy chief of staff for air in October 1940. In the War Department reorganizations of June 1941 and March 1942, Arnold became the chief and then the commanding general of the Army Air Forces, as the Air Corps was renamed. Elevated to the permanent rank of major general in May 1941, he was given increasing responsibilities in War Department administrative planning, but he was still surprised when Roosevelt included him as a participant in the Arcadia Conference in the winter of 1941–42 and as a member of the Combined and Joint Chiefs of Staff. In sessions with the British he at first tended to speak out only on air matters, but later he was outspoken on some strategic issues, especially in defending the priority of the cross-channel invasion of France. In December 1944, he would become the first and only American air officer to attain the rank of five-star general.

During the course of the war, as he organized and managed the greatest air force ever assembled—2.5 million officers and men and 63,000 planes—Arnold's job security was not threatened again by Roosevelt, but it was challenged by his poor health: four heart attacks struck him between March 1943 and January 1945. He recuperated quickly from the first coronary occlusion, but when he returned to work after two weeks of rest in Florida he was anxious about his professional future. Army regulations, if strictly interpreted, did not leave him much hope of continuing on active duty, but Roosevelt, as commander in chief, could rule otherwise.

Arnold got his physician to help persuade Stimson and Marshall, who, in turn, urged Roosevelt to keep him as head of the Army Air Forces. After personally discussing the general's condition with Arnold's physician, the president approved his continuation in the pressure-laden post. Following each of his subsequent heart attacks, Arnold somehow managed to rebound with amazing speed, to display new surges of energy in directing his global air organization, and to convince his superiors that he was well nigh inexpendable. Of course, in his favor was the fact that Roosevelt, Stimson, and Marshall all were holding high-tension positions despite moderate to serious health problems and warnings from their doctors about work loads and stresses beyond normal endurance capacities. Though his recuperation from the fourth attack was slower than from the others, Arnold stubbornly continued to shoulder the additional burden of serving as the Joint Chiefs' executive agent in commanding the Twentieth Air Force, the B-29 "Superfortress" commands in China and the Marianas.

Arnold did not yield his position as commanding general of the Army Air Forces until early 1946 when his closest friend, General Carl "Tooey" Spaatz, succeeded him. But, according to his biographer, "the dynamic drive for which he had become famous began to diminish soon after Germany and Japan surrendered. He was a tired man, his energy drained by seven years of unremitting effort to build the Air Forces," his health in worsening condition, and his marital life badly upset by the tribulations of the war years. "By any reasonable measurement, he was a casualty of the war."[16]

PERSHING'S MOST VALUABLE
PROTÉGÉ: MARSHALL

For over two decades after World War I, General of the Armies John J. "Black Jack" Pershing wielded incredible influence in sponsoring for top positions the best and bright est of the young officers who served under him during the 1918 campaigns in France. The one whom he foresaw as the greatest of the lot was George C. Marshall, a thirty-eight-year-old colonel in the operations sections of his American Expeditionary Forces and First Army. Pershing and several of his senior commanders were impressed by his integrity and judiciousness, as well as the mastery of logistical and operational planning he demonstrated in the massive AEF offensives of September–November 1918. Earning the nickname of "Wizard" from combat correspondents, Marshall performed superbly in overseeing the rapid, orderly movement of over 600,000 troops from the St. Mihiel area—once the German salient there had been eliminated—to the northwest for the beginning of the Meuse-Argonne drive nine days later, involving 1.2 million AEF soldiers. After the war it seemed natural when Pershing selected Marshall as his senior aide, a post he held for five years, including the period when Pershing served as the Army's chief of staff. The friendship between the two men grew deeper, and for many years after his retirement in 1924 Pershing reminded officers in senior slots, many of whom had served under him in the AEF, that Marshall was one of the few who had his special blessing. While Marshall was not a West Pointer, usually favored in the severely competitive route to the rank of general officer, he did possess three great assets: Pershing's support; a distinguished record in World War I, though in staff positions; and, most significant, his growing reputation among peers as an unusually gifted professional soldier.

An appointment important to the careers of Marshall and many other commanders of the Second World War was his five-year tenure as assistant commandant in charge of instruction at the Infantry School, Fort Benning, Georgia. Developing personal knowledge of promising officers, Marshall knew more than 160 future generals as students, instructors, or staff officers during the years 1927–32 at Fort Benning. Among the group were Omar N. Bradley, Courtney Hodges, and Joseph W. Stilwell, then at field-grade level, besides a number of other men who became commanders of armies, corps, or divisions during World War II or chiefs of staff after the war.[17]

What seemed to be a career setback lay ahead for Marshall, however. In September 1933 he was promoted to colonel but was stunned the following month when, in spite of his protest, Chief of Staff Douglas MacArthur upheld his orders to report as senior instructor of the Illinois National Guard. Marshall regarded this post as an impediment to future advance and confided to a friend that "it looks now as if I never will" become chief of staff of the Army, an ambition he nourished but rarely admitted. He added, "If I don't make Brigadier General soon, I'll be so far behind in seniority I won't even be in the running."[18] That promotion came in October 1936, and he was assigned to head the 5th Infantry Brigade at Vancouver Barracks, Washington, where he remained for twenty months. This command proved to be the last one in his career in which he would have the opportunity to lead soldiers, an activity which he performed well and thoroughly enjoyed.

In a strange turn of events, Marshall in 1938 moved in short order from Pershing's side in Arizona to an office in the War Department in the national capital. That spring Pershing, aged seventy-eight, was felled by what Army physicians diagnosed as probably a terminal illness. At Pershing's request, Chief of Staff Craig ordered Marshall to go to Tucson to make preliminary arrangements for the funeral of the country's only four-star officer. By the time Marshall arrived, however, Pershing had rallied; he greeted his former aide warmly and assured him, "George, they're not going to kill me off until I've seen that you've got your second star."[19]

After a brief visit Marshall left for troop inspections and maneuvers, but he shortly received a message from Craig announcing that his new assignment was to be in the War Plans Division in the War Department. When he reported for duty in early July, he learned that Brigadier General Walter Krueger, the assistant chief of staff of the Army in charge of that division, had been transferred to a brigade command and he was Krueger's replacement. Thus Marshall began his War Department tour of duty as one of the five assistant chiefs under Craig, but, as chief of war planning, in the best position of the group to move upward. In fact, Major General Stanley D. Embick, a former head of the War Plans Division and currently deputy chief of staff to Craig, had long admired Marshall and reportedly wanted him to be his successor. Secretary of War Woodring liked the idea of making Marshall the next deputy chief, according to Marshall's principal biographer, because he wished "to build up an alternative to General Drum for the Chief of Staff's office."[20] Major General Hugh A. Drum, deputy to MacArthur when he was chief of staff and an unsuccessful contender in 1935 for the higher post, was campaigning unabashedly to become Craig's successor in 1939. Although he agreed with Woodring on little else, Assistant Secretary of War Louis Johnson also supported Marshall after his earlier visit to Vancouver Barracks where he was impressed by his performance in troop command.

When Embick left Washington in late September to assume command of the IV Corps Area, rumors circulated that Marshall would replace him. But Craig hesitated about the appointment, in part because Marshall would be in a position over many officers senior to him. The chief of staff intended to postpone the decision for several months, but intercessions by Pershing and Johnson brought the matter to a head much sooner. Pershing paid a visit to the White House where he allegedly advised Roosevelt: "Mr. President, you have a man over there in the War Plans Division who has just come here—Marshall. He's Chief of Staff material. Why don't you send for him and look him over? I think he will be a great help." Roosevelt apparently did not send for Marshall until later, but he may have contacted Woodring, Johnson, or Craig, and undoubtedly Pershing made his sentiments known to them during his Washington visit. As acting secretary while Woodring was out of town in early October, Johnson called a meeting of senior officials of the War Department, a group that usually included the deputy chief of staff. He abruptly asked Craig if Marshall was going to be named as the new deputy chief. When the startled Craig answered evasively, Johnson stated that the meeting would be adjourned "until that thing is worked out." Craig quickly left the session, returning a few minutes later to announce, "The orders have been issued."[21]

Marshall became deputy chief of staff of the Army in mid-October 1938, but the prospects for satisfaction in his new job were dim. The strength of the Army (including the Army Air Corps) was only 185,000 officers and men in 1938; it would grow by merely 5,000 the next year, remaining seventeenth in size among the armies of the world. Secretary Woodring and Assistant Secretary Johnson were locked in bitter feuding that involved personality differences as well as clashes over military policies. Chief of Staff Craig was caught in their crossfire, his influence negligible on defense matters and his staff officers handicapped by declining departmental morale. Moreover, Marshall had to face the reality that of eleven deputy chiefs since the position was established in 1921, only one had become chief of staff.

After his first three months as deputy chief, Marshall was upset over the widespread public speculation about the next military head of the Army, Craig's retirement at the end of August being common knowledge. Marshall wrote Pershing in January, "I was very sorry to see the New York papers starting discussions as to the next Chief of Staff, in which my name was mentioned. I suppose this is inevitable but it certainly is distasteful to me—and I think not at all helpful."[22] Traditionally no one had been named chief of staff unless he had at least four years of active duty left before reaching the statutory retirement age of sixty-four. Although thirty-three of the sixty-seven generals then on active duty outranked Marshall, the age criterion eliminated all but four of those ahead of him.[23] Three of the eligible officers, including Krueger, did not want the job, leaving only Major General Drum among the four as a serious competitor to

Marshall, a brigadier general. A New York columnist reported that Roosevelt received "tremendous pressure" to choose Drum. Among his supporters was the president's longtime friend and powerful Democratic leader, Postmaster General James A. Farley. The president also had the option of selecting a general junior to Marshall, such as Brigadier General Daniel I. Sultan, who was believed to be favored by Roosevelt's aide, Brigadier General Edwin "Pa" Watson. On the other hand, Pershing, who had backed Drum in 1935, now lobbied for Marshall, and Hopkins, the president's most trusted adviser, "strongly recommended" Marshall.[24]

In early April the president asked Woodring for the records of officers eligible for chief of staff and received the files of seven generals. The selection, made primarily by Craig, included several inexplicable choices: Drum and Krueger, but not the other two eligible major generals; Marshall; and four brigadier generals junior to Marshall, but excluding Sultan. Woodring and Craig had come to favor Marshall but not with the same fervor as Hopkins, Pershing, and Johnson.

On Sunday afternoon, April 23, without informing in advance the secretary of war or the chief of staff, Roosevelt summoned Marshall to a private meeting at the White House. In a forty-minute conversation that Marshall found "interesting," the president informed him that he would become acting chief of staff on July 1, when Craig's terminal leave began, and he would be sworn in as chief of staff on September 1, 1939, immediately after Craig's formal retirement. "I told him," Marshall recalled, "I wanted the right to say what I think and it would often be unpleasing. 'Is that all right?' He said, 'Yes.' I said, 'You said *yes* pleasantly, but it may be unpleasant.'" Roosevelt grinned and remarked, "I know." On several occasions as deputy chief, Marshall had accompanied Craig to the White House and had spoken frankly in disagreeing with the president, who had told him he was "pleased to have someone who will speak an honest opinion."[25] Indeed, in spite of all the advice he had received about candidates for the post of chief of staff, Roosevelt may well have been influenced most in his decision by the wise counsel, confidence, and moral courage he had already observed in Marshall.

Before dawn on September 1, Marshall received a call from the War Department notifying him that German forces had invaded Poland. The long-expected European stage of World War II was beginning. At nine that morning Marshall was sworn in by the Army adjutant general as the new chief of staff; also he was promoted to the temporary rank of four-star general (and the permanent rank of major general). Because of the ominous news breaking in Europe, the ceremony was brief, and the rest of his first day as military head of the Army was filled with somber high-level meetings.

A week later he visited Uniontown, Pennsylvania, where he was born fifty-eight years earlier. He was the guest of honor at a round of festivities, including a parade, banquet, and reception. Marshall treated the experience as "almost a ceremonial return to the wellsprings of his youth, as if renewing his strength in preparation for the future," states his main biographer. In his speech before the Uniontown citizens he provided a glimpse of the calm determination that would characterize his leadership during the years of war that lay ahead: referring briefly to national defense, he observed that "the importance of this matter is so great and the cost, unfortunately, is bound to be so high, that all that we do should be planned and executed in a businesslike manner, without emotional hysteria, demagogic speeches, or other unfortunate methods which will befog the issue and might mislead our efforts."[26]

During the next six years Marshall became the dominant force in the transition of the American Army from inexperienced, poorly equipped ground and air forces numbering 190,000 personnel in 1939 to powerful units deployed worldwide with a total strength of 8.3 million soldiers and airmen by 1945. Churchill praised him as the principal Anglo-American "organizer of victory," while President Harry S. Truman said, "He was the greatest of the great in our time," and statesman-financier Bernard M. Baruch saw him as "the first

global strategist," to cite a few of his more prominent prais-
ers.[27] As he grew in stature as a leader during the period
1939–45, he became the most respected and influential member of the Joint Chiefs and eventually of the Combined Chiefs,
in addition to earning the esteem of Roosevelt, most congressmen with whom he dealt, and nearly all the senior
American Army officers in various theaters whose careers
were shaped largely by his sagacious decisions or counsel.
Although he made his mark as a manager rather than as a
warrior, Marshall has been increasingly acclaimed by military historians as the greatest American general not only of
World War II but also of the period since the Civil War.

When asked near the end of his life who was the greatest
commander he ever knew, Eisenhower responded quickly,
"I would rank General Marshall foremost without a doubt."[28]
General Thomas T. Handy, wartime Operations Division
chief and deputy chief of staff, commented, "I worked for
'the Old Man,' General Marshall, for quite a long time pretty
closely. For my money, he is in a class by himself as a leader.
. . . He was very objective about people and everything
else."[29] General Harold K. Johnson, who was in the war
against Japan and later rose to chief of staff, said that Marshall's service was "the epitome of the kind of selflessness
that is the hallmark of a really great commander." He noted,
too, that in running the Army's global operations of 1941–
45 "Marshall put it all together and had the iron will to hold
it all together."[30] Churchill described Marshall in mid-1943
as "a tower of strength and sagacity."[31] Brigadier General
Frank McCarthy, General Staff secretary and a staff officer
close to Marshall, was impressed by the careful attention the
Army chief of staff devoted to "appointments of division
commanders and above." He seriously weighed "the recommendations of the superiors involved" and then thoroughly went over the cases "with the Deputy Chief of Staff,
the Chief of Operations, and the G-1. . . . One thing is
certain, though. General Marshall was so well acquainted
with so many—if not all—of the senior officers of the Army
that his imprint was very strong on the promotion system

and, of course, on all major assignments."[32] Mrs. Katherine Marshall observed about her husband's technique "in choosing his higher commanders. He has always said that he possesses a wicked memory; and this is true—he never forgets a brilliant performance and he never forgets a dullard."[33]

Because of the excellent relations he established with Roosevelt, Truman, Hopkins, Stimson, and other key leaders in Washington and London, Marshall was secure in his position throughout the war. The ugly search for scapegoats in the press and in the sundry official investigations following the Pearl Harbor disaster led to command upheavals, including the removal of able Admiral Harold R. Stark as chief of naval operations. But Marshall escaped any serious harm to his career during the Pearl Harbor recriminations, though he and Stark bore about equal responsibility at the Washington end for their respective services' preparedness on Oahu. Many senior naval officers concluded, as expressed by Admiral Richard S. Edwards, "that the President had decided that Stark must go because there was a better man available for the high naval command [King] and that he used Pearl Harbor as an excuse for easing him out." Marshall reportedly was retained as chief of staff "because the Army had no one qualified to replace him."[34] (As evidenced by the continuing torrent of writings about the Pearl Harbor episode, the controversy over individual responsibility remains far from settled. Fortunately for America and her allies, Marshall was spared during the terrible struggle of 1941–45 to contribute immeasurably to the final victory over the Axis.)

Sometime later, there was a real possibility that Marshall would be appointed supreme commander for Operation Overlord, the Normandy invasion. By August 1943, Stimson thought he had convinced the president to choose Marshall, and Churchill had been persuaded by Hopkins to support Marshall, thereby breaking his promise to Field Marshal Alan Brooke, chief of the Imperial General Staff, that he would get the coveted Overlord command. The other Joint Chiefs, together with General Dwight D. Eisenhower and various high-ranking American and British officers of the

European and Mediterranean theaters, all expected the appointment to go to Marshall. But Roosevelt decided in early December 1943 to choose Eisenhower instead. He endeavored to explain his decision to Marshall by telling him that he was so indispensable as chief of staff that "I didn't feel I could sleep at ease if you were out of Washington."[35]

The selection of Marshall to serve as the military head of the United States Army during its critical buildup for war and then during its far-reaching ground and air operations against the Axis powers was the most important command appointment of the war in protecting American strategic interests. With the surrender of Germany in early May 1945, Eisenhower, commander of the victorious Anglo-American forces in West Europe, wrote Marshall, who he knew had longed to hold a great field command:

Your unparalleled place in the respect and affections of all military and political leaders with whom I have been associated, as well as with the mass of American fighting men, is so high and so assured that I deeply regret you could not have visited here after this army had attained its full strength and before the breakup necessarily begins. Our army and our people have never been so deeply indebted to any other soldier.[36]

TWO

ADJUSTING TO COALITION WARFARE

ALLIED COMMANDS

At the Arcadia meetings in early January 1942 the first Allied command was created—ABDACOM, or the American, British, Dutch, and Australian Command—to defend Southeast Asia. Neither the Americans nor the British were eager to sacrifice one of their top officers to head ABDACOM, obviously doomed in view of the weak forces available. For supreme commander they chose General Archibald P. Wavell, an apt British leader in the North African campaigns who had lost favor with Churchill. In a sense, his selection was a setback in British one-upmanship, since the ABDACOM area was overrun shortly by the Japanese and Wavell was identified henceforth with the defeat. But the Americans' success in such maneuverings was to be short-lived, for Churchill and his well-organized chiefs would get their way on many future Allied appointments. If not typical of later Anglo-American dealings on Allied commands, the ABDACOM decision was characteristic of their relations with lesser partners: Roosevelt, Churchill, and the Combined Chiefs established ABDACOM without even consulting the Australian or Dutch authorities. A War Department historical study frankly states that the ABDACOM directive "demonstrated that the British and American Governments were ready and willing to take bilateral action in the field of military affairs, in spite of differences in national policy and notwithstanding the embarrassments they might incur in the fields of domestic and foreign policy."[1]

With the aplomb of the Spanish and Portuguese monarchs dividing the world between them in 1494 for colonization, Roosevelt and Churchill reached an agreement in March 1942 whereby they marked off huge areas of the globe as spheres of strategic responsibility under the executive direction of their separate or combined bodies of military chiefs. The United States Joint Chiefs of Staff would exercise strategic control in the Pacific area, with Americans to be supreme commanders of the theaters to be established there. The British Chiefs of Staff Committee would be responsible for strategic direction in the Indian Ocean and Middle East regions, where British officers would continue to command theaters set up there. The Combined Chiefs of Staff would exercise strategic responsibility in the Atlantic and European areas. North Africa and the Mediterranean would be interpreted as regions of Anglo-American combined responsibility, too. Selection of Allied high commands in these areas of combined jurisdiction would provide some serious challenges to Anglo-American cooperation.

Unity of command in the Battle of the Atlantic was not easily achieved. Differences over command organizations, patrol and detection techniques, and combat tactics, along with logistical problems, led to allocation of national responsibilities by geographic divisions, the Americans being assigned primarily the Central Atlantic. In the early stages, when U-boats were sinking Allied ships faster than they could be built, sharp clashes occurred within the American camp between the Army Air Forces and the Navy over jurisdictional issues. After Ernest King gained principal authority over American antisubmarine operations in early 1943, he created the Tenth Fleet as a centralized command to cope solely with the U-boat threat. King designated himself as fleet commander but turned over operational control to Rear

Admiral Francis S. Low, the fleet's chief of staff and a submarine veteran who, remarked a colleague, "probably knew as much about King's way of thinking as anyone." That fall King announced the Atlantic turning point with the cautious statement that German submarines "have not been driven from the seas, but they have changed status from menace to problem."[2]

American troops first went into action against German and Italian armies in the North African and Mediterranean theaters, where Britain's imperial interests ranged from Gibraltar and Malta to Cyprus and Egypt. Churchill and his chiefs appeared willing to compromise on theater command positions but, in actuality, got their candidates into virtually all the key field commands. When Roosevelt overruled the Joint Chiefs and concurred with Churchill on launching Operation Torch, the North African invasion of November 1942, the prime minister and his military lords agreeably went along with the appointment of General Ike Eisenhower as commander in chief, Allied Expeditionary Force, North Africa. They did so for two apparent reasons: first, Eisenhower, already in Britain as head of United States Army forces in the European theater, had proven to be strongly pro-British and committed to Anglo-American teamwork; and, second, the Torch campaign that culminated in victory in Tunisia had British officers as heads of the Allied naval and air forces, as leader of the army group, and as commanders of the two armies. Although American, as well as British, army commanders participated in the subsequent invasions of Sicily and Italy, the London chiefs were not dissatisfied with the arrangement, for Anglophile Eisenhower stayed in the top post and General Harold R.L.G. Alexander, the British leader from the African operations, was retained as army group commander.

In an administrative reshuffling in December 1943, Eisenhower became commander in chief of the new Mediterranean theater, a position he held only a month before moving back to London to head Operation Overlord. The Combined Chiefs chose British General Henry M. "Jumbo"

Wilson as his replacement and Lieutenant General Jacob L. Devers, an American, as deputy commander in chief. Henceforth Churchill and his chiefs would demonstrate much greater interest in operations in Italy than would the American leaders, who were more attracted to the possibilities of Overlord. In late 1944 the Combined Chiefs continued the British hold on the Mediterranean theater command, selecting Alexander to succeed Wilson. Lieutenant General Joseph T. McNarney, of the American Army Air Forces, was named deputy theater commander, and for the first time an American, General Mark W. Clark, was given the theater's one army group command, then directing Allied operations in North Italy. By then, however, the slow-moving war in Italy had been overshadowed by the Western Allies' offensives from France and the Soviet drives from East Europe that were penetrating the borders of Germany.

Nearly a year before an Overlord supreme commander was named, the Combined Chiefs set in motion certain prerequisite projects to the cross-channel invasion of June 1944, the principal ones being Pointblank and COSSAC. The former was the Combined Bomber Offensive against Germany, under the general direction of Marshal of the Royal Air Force Charles Portal, chief of the British Air Staff. He would be retained as the Combined Chiefs' executive agent over the strategic air war even after American air power over Europe had grown much stronger than that of the British. The Combined Chiefs also established in early 1943 the office of chief of staff to the supreme Allied commander (designate) for Overlord and chose Lieutenant General Frederick E. Morgan, of the British Army, for COSSAC, as his post and the new agency both were called. He was provided with a staff of British and American officers to conduct the preliminary planning for the Normandy invasion. When Eisenhower arrived in London in January 1944 as the newly appointed Overlord supreme commander, he found the COSSAC preparations to be invaluable, made Morgan deputy chief of staff at his headquarters, and incorporated most of the COSSAC group into his Overlord planning staff. Morgan was respected by Eisenhower and became his fast friend, but Eisenhower decided to retain as chief of staff the American officer who had served him well in North Africa, Major General Walter Bedell "Beetle" Smith.

Despite the fact that by the summer of 1944 the majority of ground, air, and sea forces committed to Overlord were American, with their proportion of the Allied strength on the Continent increasing in ensuing months, Churchill and the British chiefs proved to be so shrewd and persuasive in dealing with their American peers that they landed an impressive share of the high command posts in Overlord for British officers. Employing tactics not unlike those used in determining the North Africa-Mediterranean senior positions, Churchill told Roosevelt at Quebec in August 1943 that an American should get the Overlord command. While disappointed at the time at not getting the post himself, Field Marshal Alan Brooke, the British chiefs' chairman, undoubtedly admitted to the prime minister later that the British were well represented in the high levels of the Allied Expeditionary Force for the invasion of Northwest Europe. With Eisenhower, the American officer most dedicated to Anglo-American harmony, as supreme commander, the top four command positions under him in Overlord went to British officers: deputy supreme commander, naval commander in chief, air commander in chief, and de facto commander of the Allied armies until Eisenhower set up his headquarters in Normandy and assumed the role of ground commander in chief (while continuing as supreme commander). Much hostility and misunderstanding would grow out of Eisenhower's reserving the ground command to himself, especially since the position was coveted by the volatile British army group commander, Field Marshal Bernard L. "Monty" Montgomery.

Under the terms of the Anglo-American strategic spheres agreement in early 1942, the British Chiefs of Staff Committee served as the executive agency for the Combined Chiefs in directing the war in the Middle East and Indian Ocean areas. In the latter region the Southeast Asia Command was established by the Combined Chiefs in August 1943, with British Admiral Louis Mountbatten appointed supreme commander. Mountbatten's headquarters staff was heavily British, and the commanders of the ground, air, and sea forces were British, as expected. But Americans were allotted several roles in the nominally Allied command, notably the position of deputy supreme commander, which was held by General Joseph W. Stilwell and later by Lieutenant General Raymond A. Wheeler, and the post of deputy chief of staff, held the first year by Major General Albert C. Wedemeyer. As will be expounded more fully later, Stilwell and Wedemeyer also served as successive chiefs of staff to Generalissimo Chiang Kai-shek in the China theater. But the recalcitrance of the Chinese high command and the low priority accorded the theater in official Washington meant for the American generals there a paucity of United States forces, confusing directives, and disappointingly little impact on strategy, command, and operations on the battlefronts of China and Burma.

In late March 1942, less than a week after the Combined Chiefs' directive designating the Pacific as an American sphere of strategic responsibility, the Joint Chiefs, with the president's approval, created two Pacific theaters: the Southwest Pacific Area, with General Douglas MacArthur, recently rescued from the beseiged Philippines, as commander in chief; and the Pacific Ocean Areas, commanded by Admiral Chester W. Nimitz, who also headed the Pacific Fleet. MacArthur set up an American Army-dominated headquarters, though his new command depended heavily, especially until late 1943, on Australian Army units. Titular command of Allied ground forces went to Australian General Thomas Blamey, prominent earlier in the North African desert war, but he was often circumvented by American Army commanders. Allied naval and air forces in the Southwest Pacific theater were led by Americans, Admiral Thomas C. Kinkaid and General George C. Kenney (both preceded by officers whom MacArthur dismissed). Besides an Australian army, MacArthur's ground forces eventually included two American armies, which became the main offensive force of the theater by 1944. Except for New Zealand air and naval units used sparingly in the South Pacific subtheater, as well as some British ships employed in Central Pacific operations in 1945, Nimitz's Pacific Ocean Areas was not an Allied command, and his headquarters and key field leadership positions were filled largely by American Navy and Marine officers.

Compromise and cooperation were common ingredients in Anglo-American decision making on strategy and command in the war against Germany and Italy. They were evident to a limited extent even in the Southeast Asia and China theaters, where the British and Chinese authorities, respectively, allowed some participation by Americans and other nationals in the command echelons. But in the Pacific the Joint Chiefs, MacArthur, and Nimitz excluded Allied officers from strategic planning and selection of commanders. Thus MacArthur received his directives and orders from George Marshall, the Army chief of staff, who also assigned his commanders down to the division level, usually after message exchanges regarding assorted candidates. Nimitz and Ernest King, the Navy chief, developed a much closer personal and professional relationship, meeting many times at San Francisco or Pearl Harbor to discuss personnel and other matters.

The tight American hold on strategy and command in the Pacific war produced tensions in American relations with the other twelve Allies engaged in the conflict with Japan. The most aggrieved were the leaders of Nationalist China and Australia, whose contributions to the ultimate triumph over Japan were invaluable. Roosevelt paid lip service to the important postwar friendships the United States wanted with China and Australia, but both were treated as quite unequal partners with America and Britain during the war. Indeed, during the final year of Pacific hostilities the British position in the Pacific had become so subservient that only after lengthy, sometimes humiliating negotiations by Churchill and his military leaders did Admiral King yield under pressure from Roosevelt to permit British naval participation in the "American theater."

The zenith of Western Allied harmony in deciding issues of strategy and command occurred during the West European operations of 1944–45. The exception in that theater usually involved General Charles de Gaulle of the Free French. By V-E Day, American and British leaders had ample reasons to be annoyed with the haughty Frenchman, but, in turn, he and his French colleagues harbored some understandable resentments, especially when Free French forces had to serve under American or British army group or army commanders who had been selected without French advice. Despite the remarkably good relations developed between the American and British leaders, however, Roosevelt, Churchill, the Combined Chiefs, and Eisenhower and his commanders engaged in some acrimonious sessions, particularly over Allied ground and air command issues and strategic plans for the final defeat of Germany.

All four of the Joint Chiefs were involved in the decision-making process when American officers were candidates for high-level Allied posts, though the two admirals of that body may have been the most distinctive in their influence: Ernest King, whom the British found rancorous and rude, but whose views they listened to respectfully because of his unusual sharpness and candor, as well as his often thinly veiled threats to shift more American ships to the Pacific; and William Leahy, who spoke for the president in his absence, possessed considerable experience in diplomacy, and was believed by many Allied leaders to influence Roosevelt significantly on matters of both military and foreign policy.

MASTER OF NEW DIMENSIONS
IN NAVAL WARFARE: KING

Ambitious and opportunistic, Ernest J. King began his naval career impressively. In his first sea duty, at age nineteen, he earned a medal for action in combat aboard a cruiser in the

Spanish-American War. Three years later he graduated from the Naval Academy with high academic marks and holding the top cadet post, lieutenant commander of the battalion of cadets. His sponsors later included Admirals Hugo Osterhaus and Henry T. Mayo, two of the most powerful leaders of the early twentieth-century Navy. In World War I, King served in the European war zone on Mayo's staff when the admiral headed the Atlantic Fleet. During the period between the world wars he achieved distinction in the submarine service and then became a naval aviator in 1927, at the age of forty-eight, subsequently excelling as a carrier commander and rising to chief of the Navy's Bureau of Aeronautics. By the mid-1930s, few, if any, American naval officers could match King's distinguished record in all three of the naval forces that would prove dominant in the Second World War: destroyers (his commands before World War I), submarines, and aircraft carriers. A prize-winning essayist and former editor of the Naval Institute's *Proceedings,* he was also known as one of the Navy's most articulate thinkers, becoming a brilliant student of strategy and employing a "conceptual, almost intellectual, approach to naval problems."[3]

While attaining flag rank in 1933 and building a solid reputation as a sagacious sea dog, King became notorious for heavy drinking, temper explosions, extramarital affairs, and unabashed ambition to become chief of naval operations. A noted naval historian maintains that "he seemed almost to pride himself on the fact that he had earned his rank solely on his merits as a professional naval officer, rather than as a result of the friendship of others."[4] As the time neared for Admiral Leahy to retire as chief of naval operations in the summer of 1939, King, who had won his second star in early 1938, proudly refused to exploit several chances to curry the president's favor, yet he did not hesitate to push his candidacy among his naval superiors and peers. When a list of recommended officers was sent to Roosevelt by William Leahy, the secretary of the Navy, and the chief of the Bureau of Navigation (renamed Bureau of Personnel in 1942),

King's name was excluded. His biographer argues the principal reason was probably the feud between battleship and carrier admirals, which had strategic, tactical, budgetary, and personal ramifications in the Navy Department: "Of the seventy-four flag officers then in the Navy, only three were naval aviators: King, [William F.] Halsey, and Charles A. Blakely. Clearly, the surface ship hierarchy would select one of its own."[5]

Vice Admiral King was with Rear Admiral Harold "Betty" Stark at the Guantanamo, Cuba, naval base in mid-March when they learned that Roosevelt had chosen Stark as the new chief of naval operations. Hiding his "keen disappointment," King offered his congratulations, and Stark responded that he was, of course, pleased to be selected but believed "King ought to have been given the position." Facing mandatory retirement in November 1942, King privately concluded that "his remaining prospect was three years of honorable routine obscurity before being beached for life."[6]

His fear seemed confirmed when he shortly learned that his next tour of duty would be on the Navy's General Board. He was so upset that he wept as he told a friend about it. "This dignified body," he later said, "then seemed to be a bourn from which no traveler returns."[7] Having been reduced to his permanent rank of rear admiral, he despondently moved his family to Washington and joined the General Board in August, only days before the outbreak of war in Europe.

His luck began to change in March 1940 when Roosevelt suggested to Secretary of the Navy Charles Edison that he take King along as his "tour guide" on his six-week visit to installations and ships of the Pacific Fleet. Impressed on the trip by King's professionalism and versatility, Edison later asked him to develop a plan for increased antiaircraft defenses on fleet ships. Again, he was highly pleased by the admiral's performance. In a final memorandum to the president before he was succeeded by Frank Knox as secretary of the Navy that summer, Edison strongly recommended King for commander in chief of the United States Fleet.

Allegedly Roosevelt did not choose him because of rumors about his excessive drinking. In September 1940, however, Admiral Harold Stark and Rear Admiral Chester W. Nimitz, the naval personnel chief (Bureau of Navigation), agreed that King should be given another opportunity for sea duty. He was offered command of the Atlantic Squadron but with no promise of regaining his rank as vice admiral. King happily jumped at the chance to have a sea command again.

By the time King assumed command in mid-December, the Atlantic Squadron had been redesignated the Patrol Force of the United States Fleet. It had only a small number of ships, all quite old; in fact, his flagship was one of the most ancient major American vessels, the battleship *Texas.* His situation had improved, but the United States Navy's most powerful and newest ships were in the Pacific Fleet, which Washington planners expected to be America's offensive spearhead if war with Japan occurred. As in World War I, however, strategists did not expect the Navy to play a major offensive role in case of war with the European Axis.

Suddenly, in January 1941, the president decided to place a higher priority on the security of the sea lanes to the British Isles, probably in connection with his impending lend-lease program and plans to increase covert shipments of war material to the British. Surprising leaders in the Navy Department, he ordered the re-establishment of the Atlantic Fleet, a buildup in naval strength in the Atlantic, and the elevation of that fleet command to four-star rank. And, upon the recommendations of Knox, Stark, and Nimitz, he appointed King, the officer who only a year and a half earlier had gone ashore, apparently never to command again, as commander in chief of the Atlantic Fleet.

On February 1, 1941, King's new four-star flag was raised on the *Texas,* and his ambition was surging again. That summer his Atlantic Fleet, now reinforced by a carrier, three battleships, and more auxiliary ships, became the center of a growing storm in relations between the United States and Germany. On Roosevelt's order, his ships began escorting Allied convoys across much of the submarine-infested waters of the North Atlantic, besides transporting American troops to newly acquired bases in Greenland and Iceland. He was pleased with his greatly augmented responsibilities and especially with the president's growing esteem. In August, Roosevelt included him, along with Stark, Marshall, and top Navy and War department officials, in his delegation at the Atlantic Conference, strategic talks held aboard ship off Argentia, Newfoundland, with Churchill and his advisers. Beginning in early September, King's fleet was often in the headlines as battles and near-confrontations took place between his convoy-escorting destroyers and German U-boats. He was delighted to be commanding the first American naval forces to go into combat in the Second World War. The resurrection of his career even inspired him to stop his heavy drinking—for the duration of the war.

The morning after the Pearl Harbor attack, Stark called King to come to Washington. Leaving his flagship, now the heavy cruiser *Augusta,* at the Newport, Rhode Island, naval base, he and an aide traveled by train to the capital. For the next four days he was engaged in emergency meetings at the White House and Navy Department, while on Capitol Hill declarations of war against the Axis powers were passed by nearly unanimous votes. When Knox returned on December 14 from a quick trip to Pearl Harbor, he summoned King back from Newport. The Navy secretary informed him that the president had approved his recommendations that Nimitz replace Admiral Husband E. Kimmel as head of the Pacific Fleet and that King become commander in chief of the United States Fleet. King suggested that command of the whole fleet should go to Stark, but Knox was insistent. On the sixteenth, King discussed the matter with Stark and the president. Before finally agreeing, King, never known for timidity, wrung concessions from Roosevelt and Knox that (1) his headquarters would be in Washington "where the power is"; (2) he would not have to deal with Congress or the press; (3) the lines of authority between him and Stark would be clarified; and (4) his title acronym would be COMINCH rather than the old CINCUS (pronounced "sink us"), in view of the recent incident at Pearl Harbor. King audaciously asked for command over all the bureaus of the Navy Department, but since that involved changing a federal law, Roosevelt pledged that any bureau chief whom King declared uncooperative would be replaced.[8] On December 18 the president issued an executive order appointing King as the head of the entire American fleet and making him directly responsible to the president. King actually assumed command of the United States Fleet on December 30, 1941.

It was soon found that Roosevelt's order had not delineated adequately the scope of King's jurisdiction in relation to Stark, the chief of naval operations. The basic problem lay not in their personal relations, for the two admirals were friends and tried to make the arrangement work. But there were too many responsibilities and functions that overlapped. At a White House meeting with the president and Knox, King explained that "a definite relationship" between him and Stark needed to be defined and that he was "perfectly willing" to be under Stark and "in fact thought that the logical arrangement."[9] Roosevelt responded, "Don't worry. We'll take care of that."[10]

King later maintained that he "had neither sought to bring about nor anticipated" the solution Roosevelt found: on presidential orders, Stark was transferred to London as commander of United States Naval Forces in Europe, and on March 12 Roosevelt issued an executive order appointing King chief of naval operations as well as commander in chief of the United States Fleet.[11] As his biographer states, "King now had complete military control of the Navy." It was the first and only time the two positions were combined. The president's action "made King the most powerful naval officer in the history of the United States."[12]

King's strong personality made an indelible impression on his contemporaries. Best known is the prewar remark of unknown origin that was used by Roosevelt, Secretary Charles Edison, and others to tease him: "He's so tough he shaves with a blowtorch."[13] Another that has been quoted widely appeared in the published version of Eisenhower's diary;

then the Army's war plans chief, Ike wrote in March 1942: "One thing that might help win this war is to get someone to shoot King . . . a deliberately rude person . . . a mental bully."[14] Vice Admiral Richard L. Conolly said he had "a frosty, forbidding presence" but was "the brainiest man I ever knew."[15] Turner Catledge of the *New York Times* found him to be "very articulate, with a well-ordered mind, resolute and confident, and a bit wily."[16] Vice Admiral Alan G. Kirk remarked succinctly, "He was difficult."[17] On the other hand, to Admiral Thomas C. Hart "the man for the job" was King. "His determination, his ruggedness, his inflexibility . . . were very much needed. His wisdom was a great asset."[18] Admiral Leahy observed: "He was an exceptionally able sea commander. He was also explosive. . . . The President [Roosevelt] had a high opinion of King's ability but also felt he was a very undiplomatic person, especially when the Admiral's boiling point would be reached in some altercation with the British."[19]

Writing in his diary after a session of the Cairo Conference of November 1943, General Stilwell said: "King almost climbed over the table at Brooke. God, he was mad."[20] In pushing their own strategic interests, the British leaders found King the most obstructionist of the Americans. Yet Alan Brooke, whose diary is known for acerb comments about peers, was relatively moderate on King, calling him "tough and stubborn" but lauding him as "the ablest strategist on the American Chiefs of Staff."[21] General Hastings Ismay, Churchill's chief of staff, described King as "intolerant and suspicious of all things British" but added that he "was almost equally intolerant and suspicious of the American Army."[22]

When Congress approved the so-called Five-Star Bill in December 1944 authorizing the president to appoint four fleet admirals and four generals of the Army, it was no surprise in naval circles when King was named. He well deserved the five-star rank, as did Leahy and Nimitz, all three being confirmed that month (and William Halsey a year hence).

In truth, King had been lobbying hard since late 1942 for the creation of the new rank, believing it was essential in Combined Chiefs' dealings since a number of British and other Allied officers outranked the top American commanders. (Getting passage of the bill did not appear as difficult as deciding the wording of the new titles. At an early stage King liked "arch admiral" for the new naval rank and others favored "field marshal" for the army officers, but both proposals were dropped because "Arch Admiral King" and "Field Marshal Marshall" evoked chuckles when pronounced aloud. After the titles were finally decided and the appointments made, King was delighted while Marshall, as from the start of the issue, seemed to care little about the honor—one of the many differences in outlook between the two chiefs.)

Despite his abrasive, intimidating manner, King was firmly backed by Roosevelt, Hopkins, Leahy, Nimitz, and most other senior admirals. His position was never in serious jeopardy as head of the wartime Navy, but, says one source, his relations with Frank Knox were "cool, sometimes excessively formal."[23] The loudest noises in protest against his power stratagems in the Navy Department came from James V. Forrestal, who succeeded Knox as secretary of the navy when Knox died in April 1944. King's persisting efforts to reform naval administration and to centralize his authority had led to skirmishes with Knox, but they turned into bitter battles when Forrestal became secretary. After Harry Truman moved into the White House in April 1945, it was said that Forrestal and his supporters gradually prejudiced Truman against King; whatever the case, King never became close to the new president.

In October 1945 King abolished one of his own positions, commander in chief of the United States Fleet, on the grounds that the lines of authority between that post and the post of chief of naval operations were still unclear. Despite Forrestal's support for another admiral, King persuaded Truman to appoint Chester Nimitz as the next chief of naval operations. Forrestal won two final rounds against King, however, limiting Nimitz to a two-year term and disapproving King's recommendation of a medal for Harold Stark for his European record since 1942. In a very brief ceremony Nimitz relieved King as chief of naval operations on December 15, 1945, and King departed, musing morosely about the nation's lack of need for his type except in war and about Forrestal's obvious relief in watching him leave.

It was not the most appreciative of farewells for the admiral who had commanded the greatest navy in history, totaling 3.5 million officers and enlisted men, 8,100 ships, and 24,000 aircraft. Surely he had been blunt and impatient in fighting for the interests of the American Navy and in pushing for a higher priority on the war against Japan, especially Nimitz's Central Pacific offensive. But his ideas on strategy in the Pacific war had proven wise, particularly on the cardinal importance of the Marianas, on bypassing as many other Japanese-held islands as possible, and on relying heavily on naval power—surface, submarine, and air forces—instead of on ground forces. King's constant pressing for more attention to the Pacific contributed toward ensuring a quicker defeat of Japan.

Besides earning his place among the foremost strategists of the century, King made an invaluable contribution by selecting many of the officers who would prove aggressive and successful in naval commands in the European, Mediterranean, and Atlantic theaters, as well as in "the Navy's own theater, the Pacific." When he left the post of chief of naval operations, one of his most eloquent tributes came, ironically, from the British Chiefs of Staff: "We are anxious that you should know how deeply we have appreciated, throughout our association in the higher direction of the war, your keen insight, your breadth of vision and your unshakeable determination to secure the defeat of our enemies in the shortest possible time."[24] They declared their great admiration of him, but they did not say they liked him. That was fine with King, for he valued candor and, after all, he had never been much concerned about his popularity.

THE PRESIDENTS' ADMIRAL: LEAHY

The most important friendship of William D. Leahy's professional life began in 1913 when he was on duty in the Navy
Department and got to know the thirty-four-year-old assistant secretary of the Navy, Franklin D. Roosevelt. Leahy
described him as "a handsome, companionable, athletic young
man of unusual energy, initiative, and decision," who had
a sound knowledge of naval history and was "a highly competent small-boat sailor and coast pilot." When Leahy, a
lieutenant commander and forty years of age, was transferred to command of the secretary of the Navy's dispatch
boat in 1915, he found himself not only transporting government dispatches but also carrying high-level officials to
locations from the Caribbean to New England. A frequent
passenger was Roosevelt, who enjoyed chatting with Leahy
and sometimes insisted on taking the helm himself. Roosevelt occasionally used the vessel to go to his residences at
Hyde Park, on the Hudson, and Campobello, in New Bruns-
wick; Leahy was included in many activities with the Roosevelt clan. "There developed between us," said Leahy of
his friendship with Roosevelt, "a deep personal affection that
endured unchanged until his untimely death."[25]

Upon America's entry into World War I, Leahy was
transferred to sea duty with the Atlantic Fleet. He commanded a troop transport on numerous Atlantic crossings
in 1918 and earned the Navy Cross. After the war he achieved
a distinguished record in staff and command positions of
increasing responsibility, and by 1936 he had risen to the
rank of four-star admiral and commanded the Battle Force
of the United States Fleet. Shortly after his reelection that
autumn, President Roosevelt chose Leahy to be the next
chief of naval operations, beginning in January 1937. The
admiral was no stranger to the politics and administration
of the Navy Department, having earlier served as chief of
the bureaus of Ordnance and of Navigation. In fact, he was
the only officer to head both of these important bureaus and
also to become CNO.

Leahy stated that he and Roosevelt "held many conferences on America's need for an adequate defense" during his tenure as chief of naval operations, a critical period for the Navy as it began to gird for war. Because of Secretary of the Navy Claude A. Swanson's frequent absences due to illness, Leahy assumed many additional responsibilities, which meant more trips to the White House and Capitol Hill than the chief's job normally entailed. When he stepped down as chief of naval operations in July 1939, replaced by his nominee, Harold Stark, Leahy was awarded the Distinguished Service Medal by Roosevelt. At the end of the ceremony Roosevelt solemnly remarked to him in private: "Bill, if we have a war, you're going to be right back here helping me to run it." Leahy's biographer observes, "In Leahy, FDR found a man of integrity, sound judgment, and common sense." He also points out that Roosevelt had a penchant for filling posts with friends from his early career: not only Leahy but also his predecessor as CNO, Admiral William H. Standley, and his successor, Stark, had known Roosevelt well when he was assistant secretary of the Navy during the Woodrow Wilson administration.[26] Leahy retired in August at the mandatory age of sixty-four, but with Europe exploding a few days later in a new world war he firmly believed that he would be "called to new duty" by his friend in the White House.

The president made sure that in the meantime his favorite admiral had a sinecure that would broaden him in diplomacy and civil affairs: he appointed Leahy as governor of Puerto Rico. Because of the mounting threat of German aggression outside Europe during his governorship, September 1939–November 1940, Leahy was busier than he had expected in defense preparations for the entire Caribbean area as well as for Puerto Rico.

On short notice Roosevelt called him to Washington and gave him the sensitive and significant post of ambassador to Vichy, France. Arriving at Vichy in January 1941, Leahy held the difficult position for the next fifteen months. He won the confidence of aged Marshal Henri Pétain, the head of the Vichy regime, and helped to prevent the Germans from gaining control of the French fleet, which was a serious concern especially to Churchill. He was valuable also in administering American food relief and assisting American intelligence activities in France and French North Africa. Because of his decreasing influence as the French government at Vichy succumbed to German control, Leahy asked to be recalled in the fall of 1941. But Roosevelt decided to keep him there a while longer, partly at the behest of Churchill. Finally, the president issued orders recalling him to Washington, but Mrs. Leahy died in a Vichy hospital in April 1942 on the eve of their departure. Admiral Leahy's first task upon returning to the States in June was her interment in Arlington National Cemetery. When he reported for duty at the State Department, he was provided with a tiny office while he completed his reports on the Vichy situation.

As early as March, George Marshall began to discuss with Roosevelt, Henry Stimson, and members of the Joint Board the need for a chief of staff to the president as commander in chief who would also serve on the Joint Chiefs of Staff. According to the official JCS history, Marshall maintained that such a position would contribute some needed assets to the top echelon of the high command:

> *As a representative of the President rather than of one of the services, such an officer might have a peculiar effectiveness in expediting business and would operate as a moderator at times when the interests of the Army and Navy appeared in conflict. He might also be able to remedy the serious difficulties that had arisen from the lack of an orderly system for keeping track of papers sent to the White House for approval. General Marshall's interest in having a disinterested person to serve as chairman of the JCS meetings had been further enhanced by the departure of Admiral Stark, since he then found himself in the rather awkward position of presiding over discussions in which he was himself a major participant. Finally, in accordance with his*

fundamental conception of the constitutional duties of the President, General Marshall seemed to feel that such an appointment would be the most fitting and timely answer to the proponents of a single military department.[27]

At first Marshall argued the case for the new post on theoretical grounds without having in mind a specific officer. When he learned in April, however, that Leahy would be returning from France, the Army chief of staff nominated him for the position. Of course, Leahy was already held in the highest regard by the president. For a while King would not agree to the idea because, according to the JCS chronicle, he feared "the interposition of another officer between himself and the President might seriously curtail the effectiveness with which the interests of the Navy were presented and maintained."[28] King later remarked: "I did not object to Adm. Leahy personally. I was—and still am—opposed to the basic idea of the President's having a single Chief of Staff. . . . President Roosevelt made the appointment after I had voiced my objection to him in person."[29] King and Leahy, nevertheless, would have a harmonious relationship in their JCS and CCS work over the next three and a half years.

While Leahy was at his small office in the State Department in late June, Marshall paid him a visit and informed him that, upon his recommendation, Roosevelt was considering the creation of the post of presidential chief of staff and that, once he had proposed Leahy for the job, King had become more agreeable to the proposition. Not until July 6 did Roosevelt mention the job to Leahy, and then only briefly. The president simply said, according to Leahy, that "he wanted me on his staff as a military and naval adviser to the Commander-in-Chief." Leahy did not see him again until July 18 when he tendered his resignation as ambassador. The president informed him that he had ordered Knox to recall Leahy to active duty in the new position of "Chief of Staff to the Commander-in-Chief of the United States Army and Navy."[30]

The only officer ever to hold that title, Leahy assumed his post on July 20, 1942. At first his office was in the Public Health Building in downtown Washington, where the Joint Chiefs of Staff and the British Staff Mission also had offices. In September, however, Roosevelt gave him an office in the east wing of the White House. Roosevelt interpreted Leahy's key functions to be in his capacity as his chief of staff, but the admiral also became the de facto chairman of the Joint Chiefs. His latter role came into being when, at his first meeting with the JCS on July 30, according to a reliable account, "he simply took the chair by default, by prior informal arrangement with Marshall and by right of seniority."[31] He proved so satisfactory that he continued to serve as both presidential chief of staff and Joint Chiefs' chairman until March 1949. Also, during World War II he alternated with Alan Brooke as chairman of the meetings of the Combined Chiefs of Staff.

One source states that Leahy "presided over meetings of the Joint Chiefs of Staff, prepared its agenda, and signed its major decisions, but he did not exert strong leadership on the committee and recognized that important decisions were often made between Roosevelt and individual members of it, especially Marshall."[32] Another authority concludes that he "probably drafted most of the messages sent to the Prime Minister [Churchill]" by Roosevelt.[33] The JCS chronicle says of his new job:

This new position was without precedent in American military history. It was, however, a natural and valuable development in a war in which the President was actively functioning as Commander in Chief, with the military leaders, incorporated in the Joint Chiefs of Staff, directly responsible to him in a military chain of command. Admiral Leahy's position as Chief of Staff to the President endowed this arrangement with a more valid military form. Exercising no command authority himself, he served as the channel for daily passage of the decisions, intents, and requirements of the Commander in Chief to his staff; he returned to that Commander the opinions and recommendations of the Joint Chiefs of Staff and other data essential to the making of informed decisions. While this by no means precluded direct consultation by the President with General Marshall, Admiral King, and General Arnold, it removed the necessity for frequent resort to such gatherings for the routine exchange of opinions, information, and direction.[34]

Because of his unique position in the White House, Leahy might have been replaced when Harry Truman became president in April 1945. Following his first meeting with the Joint Chiefs and the service secretaries, Truman met privately with Leahy. The admiral suggested that he should name an officer of his own choosing because the job involved such a close working and personal relationship. Leahy also informed him that he had spoken "very frankly" when he had disagreed with President Roosevelt, and if he were Truman's chief of staff he would continue to "say what's on my mind." Truman replied, "That's exactly what I want you to do. I want you to tell me if you think I am making a mistake. Of course, I will make the decisions, and after a decision is made, I will expect you to be loyal." Leahy responded, "You can count on me."[35] Truman would recall the next four years with Leahy happily and conclude that "he typified the Navy at its best."[36] Amazingly, though Roosevelt and Truman were quite dissimilar in personality and leadership style, both discovered in Leahy a rare person who could provide deep friendship and judicious counsel during the countless crises in directing a global war and leading a great nation into the Cold War era.

Admiral Thomas C. Hart, commander of the Asiatic Fleet, recalled that when he and Leahy were classmates at the Naval Academy if "a problem" or "a dispute" arose among their midshipmen colleagues "someone would say, 'Let's go ask Bill Leahy. He's got better sense than all the rest of us put together.' That was always true for his common sense; his wisdom was profound all through his life. Leahy was a born diplomat." Hart added that his diplomatic forte came to the forefront in World War II: "He could reason with and persuade Petain and even the British used him. That's always been Leahy: fundamentally wise, quick to pluck the right answer out of the air, without any powerful celebration, intuitive, instinctive, smart."[37] Admiral Richard Conolly called Leahy "a great administrator" and rated him and King "unsurpassed in an appreciation of the interrelationship of military strategy and world politics."[38]

Leahy contributed a stabilizing influence to sessions of the Combined Chiefs of Staff, where both his American and British colleagues respected him highly as the president's personal spokesman. British approval of Leahy extended to Churchill, who referred to him as a man "of so much influence and character."[39] In contrast to his good relations with the British, Leahy disliked and distrusted, for different reasons, the Free French and Soviet leaders. Rooted partly in his Vichy experience, Leahy's strong opinions about General Charles de Gaulle undoubtedly affected Roosevelt's increasingly hostile view of the Frenchman. Leahy also advised against blind cooperation with Stalin, especially after attending the Yalta Conference. Deeply anticommunist, Leahy was consulted often by Truman regarding policy toward the Soviet Union during the final months of World War II and the early years of the Cold War. Because of the paucity of data about his impact on White House decisions, however, Leahy's precise influence on military and diplomatic policy making under Presidents Roosevelt and Truman remains speculative.

"A forceful man with pince-nez and a scowl that masked a considerable charm," a respected correspondent-historian observes, Admiral Leahy "was not a policymaking official but an articulate, informed, prestigious man in places where policy was made."[40] Another commentator on Leahy asserts that he was "a vital link in the wartime command structure. . . .The basic integrity, unswerving loyalty to superiors, devotion to national service, and lack of political ambition or need for popular acclaim made the admiral ideally suited to the role of presidential advisor."[41] Unlike the other Joint Chiefs, Leahy did not head one of the armed services, and unlike the senior field commanders, he did not lead powerful forces in combat. But when communication and coordination between the president, the Joint Chiefs, the Combined Chiefs, and the theater commanders were effective, Leahy was often the crucial liaison between these loci of military power.

THREE

CRISIS IN COMMAND

THE SURVIVORS AND
THE REPLACEMENTS
(DECEMBER 1941–MAY 1942)

The American command phenomenon of 1941–45 probably cannot be characterized precisely. A process of natural selection seemed to be at work in the rise and decline of the high commanders. Some officers responded well to wartime challenges or adapted rapidly to changing combat situations, while others failed to react or to adjust adequately. Still others were assisted or doomed by chance, or luck. Indeed, the observation of Carl von Clausewitz, the nineteenth-century Prussian strategist, may have come closest to the truth for many commanders: "There is no human affair which stands so constantly and so generally in close connection with chance as war."[1]

The development of the senior command nucleus of the American military establishment during the Second World War was neither orderly nor consistent much of the time, but it was blessed by two fortuitous turns of events. First, within a relatively short time after the attack on Pearl Harbor, the top echelon of the high command for the duration of the war was in place. Not until the late stages of the fighting, after the leadership of the principal forces had been determined and after victory was on the horizon in both Europe and the Pacific, were there changes in the elite group in Washington that made the key selections: Roosevelt, Hopkins, Marshall, and King, and, to a lesser extent, Arnold, Leahy, Stimson, and Knox.

In the second place, the series of defeats that afflicted American forces during the initial six months of the war with Japan precipitated changes in commanders and command structures at a faster pace than would have occurred without such adversities. The established command system was shaken by a seemingly unending wave of shocks: the surprise and devastation of the first-day air raids on Oahu and Luzon bases; the astonishingly swift Japanese conquests of Southeast Asia and the West Pacific, including the American territories of Guam, Wake, and the Philippines; the unexpected vulnerability of the supposedly impregnable fortresses of Singapore and Corregidor; and the disheartening collapses of Allied defenses from Burma to Singapore to Java, the scattered remnants fleeing all the way to India and Australia that dark spring of 1942.

Nevertheless, the setbacks of the first six months of hostilities produced some positive consequences for the American high command in purging a number of senior officers who might have been satisfactory for peacetime but not for wartime leadership, in bringing to the forefront replacements with promise, and in preserving worthy survivors of the prewar high command. As a recent study of the Oahu fiasco concludes, "While Pearl Harbor was not in itself the cradle of great leaders, it did create the climate that sped the search for new men in top positions."[2] The operations of the first half year also bought time to reorganize the command structure of the American Army and Navy and to accelerate the expansion of the ground, sea, and air forces. Moreover, those early confrontations involved comparatively small American combat units and, as it turned out, were not as strategically critical to the outcome of the war as were later campaigns when huge forces were involved, the stakes were more decisive for the long run, and sound high-level leadership was essential.

The period of command crisis, which ended with the United States Navy's thwarting of enemy advances in the battles of the Coral Sea and Midway in May and June 1942, would be followed by a two-year phase of building force strengths and launching limited offensives in various theaters—a time when the search was intense to identify the officers who could lead successfully the future forces of enormous size and firepower. The final period, beginning with the Normandy and Marianas invasions of June 1944, saw the commitment of maximum American and Allied power under the command of officers who had survived the earlier stages of crisis and testing.

The command changes during the first half year of American forces in combat were both vertical and horizontal, that is, movements up and down the chain of command as well as into different positions of roughly equal responsibility. Interestingly, during that stage the ranks of senior generals and admirals were not decimated by natural or combat-related deaths. Some in high-level posts who were nearing retirement or had health problems were quietly shunted aside in favor of younger, more robust commanders. But it seemed that if a particular individual were really wanted, his age was not a negative factor. Generals Marshall, MacArthur, and Krueger, along with Admirals Leahy and King, all reached the statutory retirement age of sixty-four prior to the end of the war but were retained in important roles during and after hostilities. Likewise, health or physical problems did not necessarily mean the end of a career, some notable cases in point being General Arnold, the heart-attack-prone air chief; Lieutenant General Lesley J. McNair, the nearly deaf commander of Army Ground Forces; and Lieutenant General Joseph W. Stilwell, head of American Army forces in the China-Burma-India theater, who was nearly blind in one eye. During the first six months of fighting only one senior commander was captured, Lieutenant General Jonathan M. Wainwright, who succeeded MacArthur as commander of the troops defending the Philippines.

At least two senior men lost their early wartime slots because of political machinations or professional differences with their superiors. Admiral Thomas C. Hart, the capable Asiatic Fleet commander, became the head of the ABDA-COM naval forces but was forced out of the latter post because of the maneuverings of hostile Dutch and British leaders. Lieutenant General Hugh Drum, leader of the First Army, fell out of grace with Marshall and Stimson after criticizing the mission of a new command he was offered. Eisenhower wrote in his diary in early January 1942 that Drum "wants none of it because he doesn't like the looks of the thing."[3] The next year, with his military career at a dead end, Drum took early retirement and became a business executive.

Those who lost their commands in the aftermath of the Pearl Harbor episode included the early scapegoats, Admiral Husband E. Kimmel, commander in chief of both the United States Fleet and the Pacific Fleet, and Lieutenant General Walter C. Short, head of the Hawaiian Department, who were quickly relieved and who soon retired; and two top admirals shortly transferred to posts of less command responsibility—Harold Stark, who, as earlier mentioned, was shifted from chief of naval operations to commander of American naval forces in Europe, and Rear Admiral Claude C. Bloch, who was moved from head of the Fourteenth Naval District, in Hawaii, to the quiet backwaters of the General Board in the Navy Department. Shortly before his career ended in oblivion, Bloch, once commander in chief of the United States Fleet, expressed the sentiment of many senior commanders when in March 1942 he wrote Rear Admiral James O. Richardson, Kimmel's predecessor as Pacific Fleet commander: "I feel very sorry for both Kimmel and Short. . . . I think both you and I are very lucky because the same thing might well have happened to either or both of us."[4]

A number of officers who were thrust into authoritative posts during that first half year would be transferred later to lesser positions. Among them were Major General James E. Chaney, commander of American Army forces in the British Isles; and Vice Admiral Frank Jack Fletcher, task force leader in early attacks against the Japanese mandated islands and subsequently commander in the Battle of the Coral Sea.[5] Not all judgments on such officers were as harsh as that of Brigadier General Ira Eaker, who wrote from Britain to a headquarters officer in Washington that spring regarding Chaney: "I could not believe any man did not wish to be pushed up to a higher job, but I found one."[6] Despite Fletcher's strategic, if not tactical, victory in the Coral Sea action, King continued to regard Vice Admiral William F. Halsey as "his best carrier admiral" and "mistrusted" Fletcher, primarily for his alleged lack of aggressiveness.[7]

Nimitz retained his confidence in Fletcher, but he especially took note of the effective leadership demonstrated since December by both Halsey and Rear Admiral Raymond A. Spruance, Halsey's close friend and cruiser division commander. A number of admirals were given opportunities that spring to lead task forces and surface units in the first attempts to strike back against the Japanese. By June, however, only three—Fletcher, Halsey, and Spruance—stood out. The reasons, actual and alleged, why the others did not continue or go on to higher commands differ as widely as the circumstances of their sundry roles in the early Pacific operations.[8]

None of the American ground and sea commanders who showed unusual promise through the spring of 1942 enjoyed the spectacular success in combat achieved by two ambitious airmen: Colonel Claire L. Chennault, the already legendary leader of the American Volunteer Group, the "Flying Tigers," in the air war over Burma and China; and Lieutenant Colonel James H. Doolittle, who in April led the morale-boosting first air raid on Tokyo. Both men had been among the pioneers in American military aviation, had left the Army for commercial jobs between the world wars, and had returned to the service for World War II, becoming brigadier generals by mid-1942.

Some of the key leaders later in the war were officers closely identified with the greatest disasters and defeats of the first six months. Those whose careers were preserved despite strong criticisms of their alleged roles in the Pearl Harbor affair were George Marshall, the Army's chief of staff; Brigadier General Leonard T. Gerow, chief of the War Plans Division of the War Department; and Rear Admiral R. Kelly Turner, Gerow's counterpart in the Navy Department. Although the Clark Field disaster in the Philippines was never thoroughly investigated, there was much criticism in military circles of the leadership of Douglas MacArthur, the overall Army commander in the defense of the archipelago, and Major General Lewis H. Brereton, head of the Far East Air Force, the main air arm in the Philippines. Also identified with a major setback but justifiably less blameworthy was Joseph Stilwell, who became head of American troops in the China-Burma-India theater and chief of staff of the Chinese Army in February 1942, reporting for duty just in time to participate in the ignominious retreat of the Allied defenders from Burma into India. MacArthur came out of the Philippine defeat vowing, "I came through and I shall return," though the Joint Chiefs and Roosevelt were not certain then that he would lead the attack. Stilwell also wanted to return: "We got run out of Burma and it is humiliating as hell. I think we ought to find out what caused it, go back and retake it."[9] Fortunately both men would be spared to lead the reconquests of the areas where the Japanese had first beaten them.

Strangely, no heads rolled despite the grim situation in the Battle of the Atlantic during early 1942, which was marked by record losses of American and Allied ships. Many of the sinkings took place within sight of horrified residents along the coast from Maine to Texas. In fact, states a leading naval historian, Samuel E. Morison, the "U-boat blitz gave the Gulf Sea Frontier the melancholy distinction of having the most sinkings in May (41 ships, 219,867 gross tons) of any one area in any month during the war."[10] Yet the inability to curtail the attacks of the German submarines, even off the mouth of the Mississippi River, did not seem to bring serious criticism of the two admirals chiefly involved in deciding antisubmarine strategy at the time: Admiral Ernest King, chief of naval operations and commander in chief, United States Fleet; and Admiral Royal E. Ingersoll, formerly deputy chief of naval operations under Harold Stark and now commander in chief of the Atlantic Fleet.

Finally, there were the five officers installed in posts of great responsibility during this early, dark period, but whose stature and power would increase until they earned their places among the great captains of the Second World War: King, who by March 1942 possessed more authority than any American admiral had ever held and was exercising it aggressively; Admiral Chester Nimitz, who quickly proved his mettle that spring as both commander in chief of the Pacific Fleet and head of the vast new theater, Pacific Ocean Areas; Brigadier General Dwight Eisenhower, chief of Marshall's command center, the Operations Division, and already secretly under consideration by the Army chief of staff for much bigger roles; and Major General Carl Spaatz and Brigadier General Ira Eaker, Hap Arnold's best and brightest, who were busily preparing for the coming of the Eighth Air Force to England and the start of the American bombing offensive against Hitler's Europe.

In retrospect, Army leadership was not faulted as severely as that of the Navy for the early reverses in the Pacific, even though the Army commands bore the primary responsibility for the protection of Pearl Harbor and Clark Field and for the defense of the Philippines. No full generals saw their careers ruined in the aftermath of the early defeats, but those setbacks cost the Navy four admirals who then or formerly held four-star rank—Harold Stark, Husband Kimmel, Thomas Hart, and Claude Bloch. Interestingly, too, of the five senior officers who became widely acclaimed heroes to the public during the first half year of hostilities, four—

Douglas MacArthur, Jonathan Wainwright, Claire Chennault, and Jimmy Doolittle—were Army officers, and only one, William Halsey, was naval. This is especially ironic since American combat action so far had occurred mainly in the Pacific, which the Washington war planners had long predicted would be the Navy's main arena in case of war with the Axis powers. Surely the most notable cases of later success by a survivor and by a replacement in the high command in this beginning stage of American operations were, respectively, General Douglas MacArthur and Admiral Chester Nimitz.

FROM UNINVITED GUEST
TO HOST: MACARTHUR

Adelaide, Australia, March 1942. Upon his escape from surrounded Corregidor Island in Manila Bay and his long, perilous journey to Australia, General Douglas MacArthur announced to the crowd at the Adelaide railway station that President Roosevelt had ordered him to leave the Philippines and go to Australia where, "as he understood it," he was "to organize the American offensive against Japan, a primary object being the relief of the Philippines." He ended with his famous pledge to return and liberate those islands.[11]

The battleship *Missouri,* Tokyo Bay, September 1945. In the presence of hundreds of civil and military dignitaries of the thirteen nations that had been at war against Japan, MacArthur presided augustly over the Japanese surrender ceremony as the supreme commander for the Allied powers.

In less than four years MacArthur had proved himself as the ultimate survivor of the early Pacific defeats. In the spring of 1942 he had been a tired, vanquished general who assumed the role of uninvited guest in the eyes of Washington naval leaders when they contemplated future offensives across the Pacific. MacArthur's subsequent progression that saw him advance to the position of host at the Tokyo Bay ceremony was not anticipated by King and his admirals nor by many Army leaders.

After a spectacularly successful career of thirty-six years in the Army, beginning with top honors at West Point and climaxing with a five-year stint as Army chief of staff under Presidents Hoover and Roosevelt, MacArthur moved to Manila in late 1935 to become military adviser to the Philippine Commonwealth. He retired shortly after from the United States Army and became a field marshal in the Philippine Army. For nearly six years he and his small advisory mission of American Army personnel tried to develop adequate defenses for the archipelago but fell short because of weak funding from the American and Philippine governments.

Like many American and Philippine leaders, MacArthur was acutely aware of the worsening relations between Japan and the United States. Eager to hold a high command when the long-expected hostilities erupted, he wrote to Steve T. Early, his friend and Roosevelt's assistant, in April 1941, asking him to approach the president with the idea of recalling him to active duty as head of American Army forces in the Far East. The creation of such a command had been under consideration in the War Department for some time. Although the general received no immediate response to his request, the next month Marshall told Stimson "that in case of trouble out there [the Far East], they intended to recall General MacArthur into service again and place him in command."[12] After all, he had recently been the military head of the American Army and was reported to be as robust and sharp as ever. Besides, it would be advantageous to have the defense of the Philippines led by the officer who, after four tours of duty there, was reputed to be the American military's most knowledgeable expert on the Filipinos and their land.

In the meantime MacArthur, fretting in Manila about getting the command he wanted and hoping to force the issue, informed Early and Marshall in late May that he planned to resign soon as military adviser and retire to Texas. His message prompted Marshall to ask him to stay in the islands a while longer and to reassure the despairing MacArthur: "Your outstanding qualifications and vast experience in the Philippines make you the logical selection for the Army Commander in the Far East should the situation approach a crisis." The Army chief of staff told him that Stimson intended to recommend his appointment to Roosevelt at the appropriate time.[13]

The critical stage came in July when Japanese forces, having moved into northern French Indochina the previous summer, now marched into the southern portion of the colony and, in effect, seized control of Indochina. Nearly all Western military observers agreed that the Japanese had gained ideally located springboards for thrusts far south, into Malaya and the Netherlands East Indies, where Japan was expected to grab strategic raw materials to refurbish her stalled war machine in China. On the epochal day of July 26, 1941, after receiving further intelligence about Japan's aggressive plans in Southeast Asia, President Roosevelt suddenly froze all Japanese assets in the United States, closed the Panama Canal to Japanese shipping, federalized the Philippine Army, established a new command called United States Army Forces, Far East (USAFFE), and recalled MacArthur to active duty as its head. As chief of staff of the Army from 1930 to 1935, MacArthur had the temporary rank of four-star general but reverted to his permanent two-star rank when he left that post. Thus when Roosevelt appointed him USAFFE commander, it was in the rank of major general. The next day, however, he was promoted to lieutenant general and in December to full general again.

Following the Japanese invasion of North Luzon in late December, MacArthur moved USAFFE headquarters from Manila to Corregidor, the island fortress at the entrance to Manila Bay. From there he directed the operations of his forces as they were pushed back onto Bataan, the peninsula just north of Corregidor. Japanese bombers repeatedly attacked Corregidor, narrowly missing MacArthur several times. His remarkable courage and determination, dutifully reported back to the States by his public relations staff and some American correspondents caught on the island, gave the people of the United States their first inspiring figure of hope in the war. It would not be long before some conservative groups saw him as not only a hero but also a possible candidate in the next presidential election. Meanwhile, MacArthur was sending almost daily messages to Washington pleading for reinforcements, while mostly conservative papers were demanding at home that Roosevelt help him or rescue him. By the end of January 1942, President Roosevelt and his top military advisers, while still trying to get assistance through the enemy blockade, regarded the defense of Bataan and Corregidor as hopeless.

In early February the president, largely at Marshall's behest, concluded that MacArthur must be evacuated. Roosevelt and Marshall sent separate messages to him stating that his evacuation would be effected only by the president's "direct order" and would be undertaken only when MacArthur felt it was propitious. At first the USAFFE commander responded that he, along with his wife and young son, would remain on Corregidor and "share the fate of the garrison."[14] During the following days he cooperated fully in arranging the escapes by submarine of Philippine President Manuel L. Quezon and High Commissioner Francis B. Sayre, together with their families, but MacArthur showed no readiness to leave Corregidor. Finally, Roosevelt sent him orders on February 22 to go to Australia to command a Southwest Pacific theater, not yet established formally. The general agreed but got permission to decide the date of his departure. On the evening of March 11, MacArthur, his family, and some of his staff left Corregidor on patrol torpedo boats. Upon reaching Mindanao after numerous near encounters with enemy naval and air patrols, the MacArthur party continued on to Australia by air, then traveled by train to his new headquarters locale, Melbourne, where they arrived on March 21.

MacArthur was shocked by the paltry forces then in Australia: a few ships, mainly destroyers, of the Royal Australian

Navy; only one regular division of the Australian Army; and about 25,000 troops and 250 combat planes from the United States. The bulk of Australia's forces was then committed to the North African desert war. MacArthur was disappointed, too, that the new theater organization had not been set up. "He was so upset," observed Brigadier General Le Grande A. Diller of his staff. "Here he was in a strange country with no orders, no command."[15] On the other hand, he was delighted by the warm reception he got from Prime Minister John Curtin and his top officials, as well as from the Australian people, who all seemed enthusiastic about the arrival of so prestigious an American commander. Like Curtin, MacArthur quickly envisioned the transformation of Australia into a significant base of operations in the war against Japan that could produce a mutually beneficial alliance between the United States and Australia, besides abetting the careers and interests of both the prime minister and the general.

Back in February, as ABDACOM collapsed, Curtin had asked Roosevelt on behalf of his own government and that of New Zealand to organize a Southwest Pacific theater and to name an American as its supreme commander. When MacArthur reached Australia, the War Department issued a press release stating that he went there "in accordance with the request of the Australian Government."[16] Actually Curtin learned of his coming when Lieutenant General George H. Brett, head of American Army forces in Australia, informed him on March 17 and relayed Roosevelt's "suggestion" that he nominate MacArthur to head the new Allied theater. Curtin was pleased to do so and sent the nomination to the White House immediately. MacArthur confidently began preliminary organization of his new headquarters at Melbourne while formal authorization was still pending. The JCS, meanwhile, wrestled with a few minor tangles in Allied negotiations on the terms of MacArthur's new command directive, especially regarding his authority over national forces. Also, the Joint Chiefs had to work out the basic command and geographical lines of his new theater in relation to the Navy-proposed theater covering the huge Pacific expanses beyond the Southwest Pacific region.

On March 30, with presidential approval, the Joint Chiefs issued directives to General MacArthur and Admiral Nimitz as the commanders in chief of the new theaters, respectively, Southwest Pacific Area (SWPA) and Pacific Ocean Areas (POA). Concurrences on the final wording of the SWPA directive had to be obtained from the Australian, New Zealand, British, and Dutch (exile) governments, which took nearly three weeks. It was not until April 18 that MacArthur was able to establish officially the new SWPA command. Except for Australian General Thomas Blamey, whom he named to head Allied Land Forces, MacArthur selected American officers to command the Allied theater's field commands and to staff his GHQ. Nevertheless, he would be heavily dependent upon Australian men and materiel in his operations until early 1944.

Pentagon planners, beginning in the autumn of 1944, increasingly discussed possible future assaults on the Japanese home islands. Unless the Joint Chiefs' directives of March 1942 were superseded, Nimitz would command the invasion of Japan because the northern boundary of MacArthur's theater ran just above the Philippines. Marshall and Stimson were opposed to having MacArthur and his predominantly Army forces shunted aside during what promised to be the largest ground campaign of the Pacific war. Also, not unlike the admirals' steadfast opposition to placing the Pacific Fleet under MacArthur, War Department leaders did not want to entrust their armies and land-based air forces to the leadership of Nimitz for the invasion of Japan. Moreover, a number of right-wing Republican leaders and newspapers that had supported a MacArthur-for-President boom earlier in 1944 now widely promoted the call for a new Pacific command structure, with MacArthur to be given supreme command in the war with Japan.

Without doubt, the Southwest Pacific chief was eager to lead the invasion of Japan, and he had been critical previously of the lack of unity of command in the war against

Japan. Apparently realizing that King and his cohorts in the Navy Department would obstruct any move to make him supreme commander in the Pacific, MacArthur decided in mid-December 1944—about the time he and Nimitz both were elevated to five-star rank—to make his bid for control of all Army ground and air forces in the Pacific while still retaining his Southwest Pacific post. He wrote Marshall that he no longer favored a unified Pacific command but now believed "that the Naval forces should serve under Naval Command and that the Army should serve under Army Command. Neither service willingly fights on a major scale under the command of the other." He added, "Only in this way will there be attained that complete flexibility and efficient employment of forces that is essential to victory."[17]

Undoubtedly for different reasons than MacArthur's, Marshall, Stimson, and other War Department leaders reached conclusions similar to those of the Southwest Pacific commander regarding the matter. For a while, King and other influential admirals stubbornly defended the arrangement of March 1942, which gave Nimitz control over the assaults on Japan proper. General George Kenney, who was in Washington in March 1945, got an early indication of the president's view when, during a private session at the White House, Roosevelt remarked, "You might tell Douglas that I expect he will have a lot of work to do well north of the Philippines before long."[18] MacArthur and Roosevelt had a long, if alternately hot and cold, friendship dating back to 1916–17 when they worked in the War and Navy departments, respectively. The general also knew several important people in the White House who were sympathetic to him, including Steve Early, General Edwin Watson, and, often, William Leahy. Roosevelt and MacArthur, however, were such masters of role taking that their relationship will always be enigmatic.

To what extent Roosevelt influenced the Joint Chiefs on the issue of command restructuring for the final phase of the war with Japan is not known. The Joint Chiefs and their planners worked out what they viewed as a compromise of sorts, though many Navy leaders regarded the decision as a defeat. In a directive issued in early April 1945, the Joint Chiefs designated MacArthur as commander in chief of United States Army Forces, Pacific (AFPAC). He was given control of all American Army and Army Air Forces units and facilities in the Pacific except for the Marianas-based B-29s of the Twentieth Air Force and the Army resources in the inactive North Pacific subtheater. He was to be overall commander of future ground operations and Nimitz of naval operations. Pacific naval forces and installations were all to be under Nimitz. As before, the Joint Chiefs would function as the supreme command body for the Pacific in deciding strategy and assigning major missions and forces. MacArthur formally established AFPAC on April 6, using staff officers of his Southwest Pacific GHQ, most of whom were American Army anyway, to serve concurrently at the new headquarters.

As the war against Japan drew to a close, the question of which officer would preside at the Japanese surrender ceremony sparked displays of interservice rivalry in Washington. But President Truman's decision in favor of MacArthur to head the occupation of Japan, apparently made about August 8, also settled the question of who would accept the surrender as representative of all the Allied powers. Probably with the counsel of confidants Admiral Leahy and James F. Byrnes, both of whom admired MacArthur and favored tough stands against the Soviets, Truman chose MacArthur to oversee the occupation that the president and his top advisers already had resolved would be virtually an all-American show of policy and administration. Truman was influenced undoubtedly by MacArthur's longstanding identification with anticommunist groups in America and by the likelihood that the general, on the grounds of both personality and ideology, would run occupied Japan without permitting much input from the Soviet Union or the Japanese Communist Party. The president's decision in favor of MacArthur as supreme commander in Japan surely was affected, too, by the fact that he was the most experienced and best qualified officer available and also that, with the American Eighth Army constituting the principal occupying force, an admiral would not be suitable for the post.

When the United States government solicited the views of the Soviet, British, and Nationalist Chinese governments regarding the appointment of MacArthur as supreme commander for the Allied powers in Japan (SCAP), the Soviets proposed that a marshal of their army serve jointly with MacArthur over the surrender ceremony and preferably over the subsequent occupation. W. Averell Harriman, the United States ambassador in Moscow, conveyed the president's response to Vyacheslav M. Molotov, Soviet commissar of foreign affairs, that the United States, which had been at war with Japan for nearly four years, had no intention of sharing that authority equally with the U.S.S.R., which had not entered the war against Japan until August 8. Remaining adamant on the matter, Truman obtained approvals on August 12 from the British, Soviet, and Nationalist Chinese governments to appoint MacArthur as supreme commander in Japan.

The next day the president approved the final text of the SCAP directive, and on August 15, V-J Day, the Joint Chiefs sent it to the AFPAC commander. Although he was to execute, not initiate, policy, MacArthur was pleased by the power he was given, as the following provisions of the directive indicate:

> *5. From the moment of surrender, the authority of the Emperor and Japanese Government to rule the state will be subject to you and you will take such steps as you deem proper to effectuate the surrender terms.*
> *6. You will exercise supreme command over all land, sea and air forces which may be allocated for enforcement in Japan of the surrender terms by the Allied Powers concerned.*[19]

MacArthur promptly replied to Truman: "I am deeply grateful for the confidence you have so generously bestowed upon me. . . . I shall do everything possible to capitalize [upon] this situation along the magnificently constructive lines you have conceived for the peace of the world."[20] The period of peace and harmony between the general and President Truman was not destined to last for long, but it would be nearly six years before their differences would reach a climax over strategy and command in the Korean conflict.

Colorful and controversial throughout his long career, MacArthur forcefully displayed his many contradictory traits during World War II, making himself charismatically attractive to some contemporaries but contemptible to others. He was brilliant in planning, versatile in his knowledge, imaginative in his use of strategy, and shrewd in his exploitation of diminutive logistical resources. Those close to him found him charming, gracious, and aristocratic, but others described him as arrogant, vain, and hypersensitive to criticism. His bold moves in bypassing enemy strongholds in the Southwest Pacific campaigns earned him many accolades.

After the war British leaders were reticent in their praise of American officers generally, but Churchill, Alan Brooke, and Bernard Montgomery were enthusiastic about MacArthur, rating him as one of the foremost commanders of World War II. Brooke, chairman of the wartime British Chiefs of Staff, commented in 1957: "From everything I saw of him [MacArthur] I put him down as the greatest general of the last war. He certainly showed a far greater strategic grasp than Marshall." Five years later he wrote an American friend: "I still consider that in years to come when you look back on the war you will consider him [MacArthur] as your greatest general."[21]

Hap Arnold wrote in his diary in late 1942 that MacArthur "gives me the impression of a brilliant mind—obsessed by a plan he can't carry out—frustrated—dramatic to the extreme."[22] In early 1945 Ernest King commented, "I thought MacArthur had a high degree of professional ability, mortgaged, however, to his sensitivity and his vanity."[23] Though he may never have known of it, MacArthur undoubtedly would have ranked among his favorite plaudits

Admiral Halsey's remarks about him in a letter in late 1943 to an old Annapolis classmate: MacArthur "is a damn good soldier and he is doing a damn good job. If he wants to strut his stuff, let him strut. It does no harm and works off excess energy."[24] Turner Catledge observed after he and Arthur H. Sulzberger, both of the *New York Times,* conferred with MacArthur on Leyte in November 1944: "Sulzberger and I later agreed we had never met a more egotistical man, nor one more aware of his egotism and more able and determined to back it up with his deeds."[25]

After leading the ill-fated defense of the Philippines and then assuming command of the low-priority Southwest Pacific theater, MacArthur had managed to force the Navy's leaders to compromise on command and strategy in the Pacific, where it had been long assumed that the war would be fought mainly by naval forces. The general would be pleased that four decades later most Americans still believe he was the supreme commander in the war against Japan.

A CALM, CONFIDENT LEADER
COMES TO PEARL HARBOR: NIMITZ

The career of Ensign Chester W. Nimitz almost ended in the Philippines three and a half years after he had graduated near the top of his class at the United States Naval Academy. On a July evening in 1908, Nimitz, the twenty-three-year-old captain of the destroyer *Decatur,* ran the ship aground while trying to enter a small harbor south of Manila Bay. Displaying remarkable calmness after failing to get the destroyer off the mudbank, he "set up a cot on the deck and went to sleep," in his own words. The next morning a steamer pulled the *Decatur* free. A court martial followed, and he was found guilty of "neglect of duty." Considering his good record and the poorly charted area of the accident, the court sentenced him only to a public reprimand by Rear Admiral J. N. Hemphill, commander of United States Naval Forces, Philippines. The admiral, in turn, decided that the court's penalty was carried out sufficiently by "the promulgation of these findings and sentence."[26] Nimitz was relieved of command of the *Decatur,* and his request for battleship duty was turned down by the Navy Department. Instead, he was transferred to the underwater service where he quickly achieved success as a submarine captain and also became an authority on diesel engines. Less than two years after his court martial, he was promoted to lieutenant, senior grade, skipping the rank of lieutenant, junior grade. Thus the mercy and perspicacity of some of his early superiors, as well as Nimitz's ability to rebound professionally, combined to set on course again what was destined to become one of the most brilliant careers in American naval annals.

During America's participation in the First World War, Nimitz, by then a lieutenant commander, served as aide and later chief of staff to Captain Samuel S. Robison, who led the Submarine Force, Atlantic Fleet. In the early 1920s, after graduating from the Naval War College, he again became aide to Robison, who headed the Battle Force; Nimitz remained on his staff when Admiral Robison became commander in chief, United States Fleet. The two men, though far apart in age and rank, became close, and Robison was undoubtedly influential in Nimitz's advancement.

After commanding a submarine division and then the heavy cruiser *Augusta,* the Asiatic Fleet's flagship, Nimitz was ordered to Washington in 1935 as assistant chief of the Bureau of Navigation, the Navy Department's agency in charge of personnel matters. Three years later he was promoted to rear admiral and transferred back to sea duty, commanding successively in the Pacific Fleet a cruiser division, a battleship division, and a task force (including an aircraft carrier). In early 1939 his task force was engaged in at-sea refueling exercises, many of the techniques used therein having been invented earlier by him, and his ships also participated in amphibious training with Marine units, the amphibious assault having been long foreseen by him as essential in a war with Japan. He was thoroughly enjoying his command and was quite disappointed when he received or ders that spring to return to the Navy Department as the chief of the Bureau of Navigation. Admiral Claude C. Bloch, commander in chief of the United States Fleet, wrote him when he learned of his appointment: "You have a big job on your hands in the Bureau of Navigation. . . . Your ingenuity and cleverness both are going to be taxed to the utmost."[27]

For the next two and a half years Nimitz was intensely busy with the many responsibilities and burdens related to the training, education, and assignment of naval personnel. Under him the Bureau of Navigation became known for the long hours exacted of its members. It was a period of rapid expansion for the Navy, and Nimitz often found himself pushed to the point of exhaustion. Also, he discovered that much about the job was less than inspiring, as he later confided to William Halsey: "One of the crosses I had to bear as Chief of Naval Personnel was the washing of much of the Navy's dirty linen. I was made the repository of many unwholesome secrets and had the unpleasant duty of investigating many charges and allegations made by one officer against another."[28] On the other hand, the unwelcome tour of duty gave him key roles in the buildup of naval forces before the outbreak of hostilities and in working with the main leaders of the naval establishment, including not only senior admirals like Harold Stark, Husband Kimmel, Thomas Hart, Ernest King, James Richardson, and Claude Bloch but also President Roosevelt and Secretary Frank Knox.

During his stay in Washington, Nimitz had an opportunity to command the Pacific Fleet in January 1941. His own version, given in the third person but substantiated in other sources, is that "when Admiral Richardson, who was the predecessor to Kimmel, had belly-ached about the fact that the fleet was based on the West Coast, the President had decided that Richardson must be detached. At that point Secretary Knox had proposed Nimitz as the successor to Richardson. Nimitz said that he was too junior, however, and recommended some other officer. Then it was that they proposed Admiral Kimmel."[29] And thus Nimitz was spared the possible scapegoat role that would be Kimmel's before the year ended.

During the week following the disaster at Pearl Harbor, Nimitz was confronted by crises related to the greatly accelerated mobilization of the armed services as well as by the sad tasks associated with the burial of the dead and the care of the wounded of the Pacific Fleet and the assignment of their replacements. Meanwhile, Knox returned from his trip to Oahu and reported to Roosevelt on the evening of December 15, describing the devastation of the Pacific Fleet and offering recommendations for a prompt investigation, the relief of Kimmel, and the restructuring of the post of commander in chief, United States Fleet. They quickly agreed on King for the last-named slot, and in a White House session the next morning they decided on Nimitz as the new head of the Pacific Fleet. (Kimmel had commanded the Pacific and United States fleets concurrently.) When Knox went back to his office on the sixteenth, he summoned Nimitz and told the surprised admiral, "You're going to take command of the Pacific Fleet, and I think you will be gone for a long time." Nimitz was taken aback since, according to his biographer, "the year before he had begged off from the command for lack of seniority. That reason still applied, and now he would have the additional embarrassment of relieving an old friend." But he assented because "in time of war one does not question an order."[30]

That evening when Nimitz went to his apartment on Q Street in Washington, he broke the news to his wife, intending to announce it at dinner to his three daughters and his visiting daughter-in-law (his son was a submariner at sea). He was unusually solemn at the table, but as he began to tell the young women he had some important news, two of them exclaimed in unison, "You are going to Pearl Harbor!" Everyone laughed, dispelling the heavy atmosphere. At the end of the meal he jotted on a pad a statement for the press since the White House announcement of his appointment would be made the next day: "It is a great responsibility, and I will do my utmost to meet it." When he passed the pad around the table to solicit opinions, one daughter "tore off the sheet. 'I'm sure this is history,' she said, sticking it in her pocket, 'so make another copy.' " Nimitz then had to write copies of his statement as mementos for the other girls. "Then at last," says E. B. Potter, the admiral's longtime friend and biographer, "the future Commander in Chief, U.S. Pacific Fleet and Pacific Ocean Areas, was permitted to write out a copy of the statement for himself and the public."[31]

When Nimitz arrived by air at Pearl Harbor on Christmas morning, he was met by a group of somber officers, including Vice Admiral William S. Pye, acting commander of the Pacific Fleet. As he left the Catalina patrol bomber, the destruction in the main anchorage area was shocking, as were also the strong smells of "a miasma of black oil, charred wood, blistered paint, and burned and rotting bodies." After breakfast Admiral Kimmel, now wearing two instead of four stars, joined Nimitz and Pye; not surprisingly, he was still sorely depressed by the tragedy that had struck his fleet. "You have my sympathy," Nimitz remarked as he shook his hand, adding, "The same thing could have happened to anybody."[32]

On December 31, Nimitz assumed command of the Pacific Fleet in a short ceremony on the deck of the submarine *Grayling* alongside the wharf of the submarine base at Pearl. He had been in charge of the construction of that base two decades ago. Later in the day he addressed a gloomy assembly of Kimmel's and Pye's staff officers, pleasantly surprising them with the news that he had confidence in them and wanted them to stay with him. The man who probably least expected to be retained by Nimitz was Lieutenant Commander Edwin T. Layton, Kimmel's intelligence officer. He would become the only Pacific Fleet headquarters officer to keep his position throughout the war, fully repaying his new commander for his trust. Layton would become "fired up," as he expressed it, by Nimitz's "enthusiasm and determination to restore the reputation of the fleet."[33] Another naval officer at Pearl Harbor in early 1942 recalled, "The aura of confidence that radiated from Admiral Nimitz renewed everyone's morale."[34]

Three months after Nimitz took command of the Pacific Fleet, the Joint Chiefs gave him the additional responsibility of heading the huge Pacific Ocean Areas (POA) theater, which comprised all the Pacific except MacArthur's Southwest Pacific Area. So well had Nimitz performed in his short span at Pearl Harbor that the JCS did not seriously consider anyone else for the POA position. In addition, he retained command of one of his three subtheaters, the Central Pacific Area, while the North and South Pacific areas were commanded by admirals subordinate to him but selected by Ernest King. The South Pacific subtheater was expanded westward that summer by the Joint Chiefs so that it encompassed Guadalcanal and Tulagi in the southern Solomon Islands— sites of assaults by Marine and Navy forces in August that would have been commanded by General MacArthur otherwise. In large measure due to King's persistent demands, the Joint and Combined Chiefs decided in early 1943, despite MacArthur's vehement objections, to inaugurate that autumn a Central Pacific offensive and to give it logistical priority over the Southwest Pacific axis of advance toward Japan. Thereafter Nimitz's responsibilities, as well as his sea, air, and ground forces, grew enormously. By 1945, according to a noted authority, Nimitz "commanded thousands of ships and aircraft and millions of men, amounting to more military power than had been wielded by all the commanders in all previous wars."[35]

There was widespread approval in the Navy when Nimitz was named as one of the seven officers elevated to five-star rank in December 1944 (the others being Leahy, Marshall, King, Arnold, MacArthur, and Eisenhower). As mentioned previously, the Joint Chiefs of Staff designated him to lead naval operations in the invasion of Japan that was projected for the fall of 1945, and when the Japanese capitulation occurred sooner than expected, he was given the honor of signing the instrument of surrender as the representative of the United States in the ceremony aboard the battleship

Missouri. In view of his fondness for the "silent service" and of the tremendous destruction of Japanese naval and merchant ships wrought by his submarines, it was appropriate that when Admiral Ray Spruance succeeded him as commander in chief of POA and the Pacific Fleet in late November 1945, the change-of-command ceremony took place on the deck of a submarine at Pearl Harbor. Nimitz, in turn, replaced King as chief of naval operations in mid-December. The appointment, finally decided by Truman, was not as simple as many anticipated, however, because for a while, states a naval historian, Nimitz's selection as CNO "was opposed by Secretary of the Navy James V. Forrestal, whose relations with King had been poisonous and who may have viewed Nimitz as a no more pliable figure," particularly since "King pressed Nimitz's claim to the billet."[36]

In retrospect, Nimitz ranks with Field Marshal William Slim of the British Army as the senior commander whose leadership in World War II has come closest to winning universal praise from professional contemporaries and from military historians. Spruance, not known for fulsome remarks, said of Nimitz: "His personality, character and ability are those that any young man could emulate and make no mistake."[37] Admiral Richard L. Conolly, a veteran task force leader in World War II, was especially impressed by Nimitz's willingness "to take upon himself full responsibility" for his command's mistakes and setbacks: "If anything went wrong, he leaned over backward to face up to it with Cominch [King], and he didn't want Cominch criticizing his commanders."[38] In a tribute following the death of Nimitz in 1966, E. B. Potter wrote:

Nimitz's success in war and in dealing with men was the product of his extraordinary balance. He wielded authority with a sure hand but without austerity or arrogance. His perfect integrity was untinged with harshness. He demanded the best from those who served under him but never failed to give credit where credit was due. He was courteous and considerate without

*leaving any doubt who was running the show. He was
serene and unruffled and at the same time vigorous
and hardworking. He took his responsibilities with
deadly seriousness, yet never lost his sense of humor.
He grew with his responsibilities, but even when he
commanded 2,500,000 men, he retained his simplicity
and common touch.*

*He surrounded himself with the ablest men he could
find and sought their advice, but he made his own
decisions. He was a keen strategist who never forgot
that he was dealing with human beings, on both sides
of the conflict. He was aggressive in war without hate,
audacious while never failing to weigh the risks.*[39]

Remarkably, this eulogy portrays Nimitz in much the same
manner as did many of his peers in World War II, and some
of those officers were exceedingly frank, tough-minded individuals. He managed to establish a close, effective working
relationship with his cantankerous, often distrustful superior,
Admiral King. Nimitz, along with Halsey, got along with the
difficult, sensitive Southwest Pacific commander, General
MacArthur, more harmoniously than did most other senior
naval officers. He developed, moreover, good coordination
with Vice Admiral John H. Towers and other naval aviators
at the flag level despite their often adverse attitudes toward
nonaviators like Nimitz and Spruance. And he displayed
great patience and wisdom in overseeing such strong-willed,
fiery subordinates as Admirals William "Bull" Halsey and
R. Kelly "Terrible" Turner and Marine General Holland M.
"Howling Mad" Smith, whose antics frequently justified their
press nicknames. Perhaps no other wartime leader besides
Nimitz could have worked with all these dynamic commanders and earned the affection and respect of all of them.

Many honors were bestowed on Nimitz for his leadership
of the principal theater in the war against Japan, but none
probably impressed him as much as his nomination for the
post of chief of naval operations by that most caustic and
severe judge of officers, Ernest King. Indeed, he would have

been pleased with the unadorned, professional way King put it to President Truman in his letter of resignation as CNO in November 1945: "May I commend to your consideration as my successor the officer who has so successfully exercised high command in the Pacific throughout the war and is otherwise eminently qualified, Fleet Admiral Chester W. Nimitz."[40]

FOUR

TROUBLED BEGINNINGS IN BRITAIN AND AFRICA

THE COMMAND SEARCH
(EUROPE, MAY 1942–MAY 1943)

During the first eighteen months after America entered the war against Germany and Italy, the need for senior American commanders grew mainly because of efforts to build up forces in the British Isles for a future invasion of West Europe, to start a round-the-clock strategic bombing offensive, and to turn the tide in ground operations through assaults in Northwest Africa, Sicily, and Italy. If the United States Navy's high command had suffered severely during the first phase of the Pacific war, it would be American Army and Army Air Forces generals who, together with their British counterparts, would be sorely tested in the early stage of United States operations in the European and Mediterranean theaters.

At the end of the secret ABC (American-British Conversations) military meetings in Washington in early 1941, the Anglo-American participants, with Roosevelt's and Churchill's concurrence, agreed to set up an American Army mission in London ostensibly to "observe" but really to work with British officers on coordinated military planning. George

Marshall picked Major General James Chaney, of the Army Air Corps, to head this group, which arrived in England that May. Chaney got along fairly well with the British, and he was retained in command when a larger organization was established in January 1942, U.S. Army Forces in the British Isles. As American units, especially of the Eighth Air Force's Bomber Command, arrived in growing numbers, the War Department redesignated Chaney's command on June 8 as the European theater of operations, U.S. Army (ETOUSA). Three days later, however, Marshall abruptly relieved him of command, though the Army chief of staff's displeasure with him had been growing for some time. He had heard much criticism of Chaney's uninspired leadership and his failure to keep the War Department posted on his command's activities. Chaney allegedly would not cooperate with Brigadier General Ira Eaker and had on his staff some key officers who were "unalterably opposed" to the plans of Major General Carl Spaatz and Eaker for expanding Army Air Forces installations and programs in the United Kingdom.[1] Marshall picked Eisenhower as his successor and recalled Chaney to less critical duties stateside. While Eisenhower's star rose rapidly, Chaney's fell fast. He ended the war as garrison commander on Iwo Jima once the Marines had secured the island.

After Eisenhower took command of Torch and moved to Algiers to direct the ensuing campaign for Tunisia, Marshall chose Lieutenant General Frank M. Andrews to command ETOUSA, with headquarters in London. When Andrews was killed in a plane crash in Iceland in May 1943, Lieutenant General Jacob L. Devers replaced him. In turn, when Eisenhower came back to London in January 1944 as Overlord commander, Marshall transferred Devers to North Africa and gave Eisenhower command of ETOUSA also. With the priority on the mounting of Overlord, Eisenhower delegated most of his ETOUSA duties. One of the principal functions of ETOUSA had been the administration of the buildup, supply, and training of American Army ground and air forces in the British Isles in preparation for Pointblank, the strategic bombing offensive, and Overlord, the cross-channel attack. Although never getting much credit publicly, Andrews and Devers had performed efficiently in heading ETOUSA during the crucial period before Eisenhower's return.

The first ground actions pitting Americans against Germans in World War II resulted from the often heated deliberations of Roosevelt, Churchill, and their chiefs from January to July 1942 when Roosevelt finally decided in favor of Operation Torch, the invasion of French Morocco and Algeria. The Joint Chiefs vehemently but futilely opposed the president and the prime minister on this issue. "The President's principal objectives for the first American offensive were political—to arouse American public interest in the war against Germany and to indicate to America's allies, particularly the Soviet Union, that the United States was committed to unlimited participation in the European war," states an authority on Torch strategy.[2] The Joint Chiefs desperately searched for a viable alternative that was not so flagrantly tangential to their preference for a massive invasion of West Europe. Marshall even advocated the high-risk Sledgehammer plan for a brief time; it called for a limited-objective cross-channel assault in late 1942 that might have been disastrous but if successful would have averted the peripheral move into Northwest Africa that most American strategists opposed.

The decision to launch Torch was made on July 30, 1942, only two months before the operation would be undertaken. Even with time at a premium, progress was incredibly slow for a while thereafter. The Combined Chiefs did not appoint Eisenhower and Brigadier General Mark W. Clark as commander in chief and deputy commander, respectively, for the Torch invasion until August 11. The new headquarters was not officially activated until September 12, according to the U.S. Army history, "when in General Order 1, the command announced its own birth, gave itself a birth certificate, and officially took the name of Allied Force Headquarters (AFHQ)."[3]

The command arrangement for Torch was a complicated Anglo-American mixture, but the wily British chiefs gained the edge, getting their officers in the top sea, air, and ground field commands. Rear Admiral H. Kent Hewitt, Amphibious Force commander, U.S. Atlantic Fleet, headed one of the three Torch naval task forces, but the other two were led by Royal Navy officers and the overall commander of Torch naval forces was a British admiral. The initial Torch air organization was cumbersome: Royal Air Force units comprised the Eastern Air Command, headed by a British air marshal, while American Army Air Forces squadrons made up the Western Air Command, led by Brigadier General Jimmy Doolittle, who also commanded the U.S. Twelfth Air Force. At the Casablanca Conference of Roosevelt, Churchill, and their military chiefs in January 1943, a superior air position was established—air commander in chief, Mediterranean—and a British officer was given the job, which involved working closely with Eisenhower and his AFHQ planners at Algiers. In the Allied advance into Tunisia, the principal ground forces were British Lieutenant General Kenneth A. N. Anderson's First Army and British General Bernard L. Montgomery's Eighth Army. The largest American Army unit was Major General Lloyd R. Fredendall's II Corps, which was attached to the British First Army. At Casablanca it was decided to create the Eighteenth Army Group and to appoint Field Marshal Harold Alexander as its commander. Thus Fredendall was placed not only under a British army commander but also under a British army group commander. As for the Torch commander in chief, Eisenhower was effectively divorced from control of operations by the Casablanca machinations and found himself even outranked by the widely esteemed, experienced Alexander and the bright but arrogant Montgomery.

It was not the best of command situations for the Americans in Northwest Africa. Eisenhower, who seemed "jittery" and "under stress" at the Casablanca Conference, found no consolation in learning that Roosevelt had turned down Marshall's suggestion to promote Eisenhower to four-star rank. According to Hopkins, Roosevelt told Marshall between the Casablanca sessions "that Eisenhower's army is mired in the mud, . . . that he would not promote Eisenhower until there was some damn good reason for doing it, . . . [and] that while Eisenhower had done a good job, he hasn't knocked the Germans out of Tunisia."[4]

Eisenhower had caught much public criticism for the deal he and Clark worked out with Admiral Jean Darlan whereby the pro-Vichy naval officer had become head of French forces in Northwest Africa. In London and Washington military circles Eisenhower had been criticized also for not driving his forces into Tunisia before the German defenses were readied. He was to catch much flak from the British and American press shortly for the poor performance of the American troops in their first major encounter with the German Army. In late February, Field Marshal Erwin Rommel's Africa Korps surprised and defeated Fredendall's corps in the battle of Kasserine Pass in western Tunisia. The encounter was a shocking revelation of the inexperience of the American soldiers and the inadequate leadership of Fredendall and some of his subordinate commanders, though actually the Americans' failure was precipitated by poor performances and communications of French forces on their left flank. American casualties in this baptism under fire were heavy: about 300 killed, 3,000 wounded, and 3,000 missing in action—total casualties of over 20 percent of the corps' strength. American losses in weapons, equipment, and supplies were severe, too.

Although the Kasserine Pass action was a limited tactical success rather than a major strategic triumph for Rommel, it led to a number of command changes in the II Corps, ranging from small-unit levels to the corps commander himself. In the wake of the battle Eisenhower flew to the front and also dispatched several trusted officers on separate visits to the corps sector to determine what had gone wrong. His informal investigators included Major General Ernest N. Harmon, the aggressive head of the Second Armored Division, which had not been engaged in the battle; Brigadier

General Lucian K. Truscott, the gifted, versatile AFHQ deputy chief of staff who was shortly to assume command of the Third Infantry Division; and Brigadier General Omar Bradley, Eisenhower's old friend who had recently joined the AFHQ staff after heading a division in the States. Each of Ike's subordinates became convinced of the need to replace General Fredendall after their queries at the front produced widespread criticisms of his ineffective command procedures and overbearing manner that had bred distrust, friction, and lack of cooperation even before the Kasserine Pass engagement. Bradley's conclusion was typical: "It became apparent in my first week on the front that Fredendall had lost the confidence of his division commanders."[5] On the basis of his own observations and those of the officers he sent to the II Corps after the battle, Eisenhower decided to replace Fredendall. Lieutenant General James M. Gavin recalled, however, that at the time "many American officers thought he had been sacrificed to the whims of the senior British general, General Alexander."[6]

Eisenhower offered the corps command to Ernest Harmon, but the latter was persuasive in arguing that since he had strongly urged Fredendall's relief he should be disqualified as a candidate. He suggested Major General George S. Patton, Jr., for the post. Thereupon Eisenhower, with the approval of Marshall, ordered Patton to leave his task force command in Morocco and to take charge of the demoralized II Corps in Tunisia. Patton assumed his new command on March 6 and within days began to transform the outfit, the colorful general "radiating glamor, action, and determination," quickly producing "an aggressive spirit" and "a surge of confidence" in the ranks, demanding more rigorous training programs, and leading the corps on successful counterattacks.[7]

After six weeks on the Tunisian front Patton returned to Morocco to train and lead the American troops scheduled to participate in the summer invasion of Sicily. On April 15, Bradley, who had been serving as Patton's deputy, succeeded to command of the II Corps, which went on to distinguish itself under his leadership in the drive to Bizerte and later in Sicily. The road from Kasserine to Bizerte proved to be an important testing ground for three successive commanders of the II Corps, one who failed and two who began meteoric rises to fame.

The strategic decisions at Casablanca included authorization of the Combined Bomber Offensive, or Operation Pointblank. Its grandiose aim was for the Royal Air Force and U.S. Eighth Air Force heavy bombers stationed in the United Kingdom to bring about "the progressive destruction and dislocation of the German military, industrial, and economic system, and the undermining of the morale of the German people where their capacity for armed resistance is fatally weakened."[8] Carl Spaatz, the commander of the Eighth Air Force since it began operations from bases in England in the summer of 1942, had been summoned by Eisenhower to head the new Northwest African Air Forces in early 1943. Ira Eaker, who had led the VIII Bomber Command under Spaatz, succeeded him in command of the Eighth Air Force and thus was charged with the responsibility of getting the American portion of the Pointblank program underway.

Since the Eighth's first heavy-bomber raid, a twelve-plane strike in August 1942, many of the American B-17 and B-24 heavy bombers at bases in the United Kingdom had been transferred south to support Torch. During the spring of 1943, Eaker faced continuing shortages of bombers, pilots, crews, and parts because of the demands of the Tunisian campaign. His bombing missions against the Continent, usually of thirty or fewer planes, were far below the expectations of the Combined Chiefs. He soon felt increasing pressure from them and also from Hap Arnold, never known for his patience, to accelerate his Pointblank attacks. It would not be until August, however, that large-scale American raids on Germany would begin, and Eaker, an able but overburdened leader confronted by almost insurmountable logistical difficulties, bore the brunt of mounting criticisms of the disappointingly modest American strategic air war over Europe.

In the meantime, Jimmy Doolittle was drawing many adverse comments in high Anglo-American military circles because of his antagonistic, uncooperative attitude toward British air leaders in Northwest Africa. On the other hand, Spaatz grew in favor with Eisenhower, Arnold, and the British high command because of his enlightened, tactful leadership during the final operations in Northwest Africa that culminated in the German-Italian forces' capitulation in Tunisia in May. The careers of the three longtime friends and military aviation pioneers—Spaatz, Eaker, and Doolittle—seemed by the end of the spring of 1943 to be headed in different directions.

Surprisingly, Bradley, who was close to Eisenhower and who led the largest American ground force for the longest period of offensive combat in the Northwest African campaign, was not selected to command either of the first two American armies to go into action against the European Axis. Among the compromises and deals struck by the Americans and the British at the Casablanca Conference was the Joint Chiefs' acceptance of the British Chiefs' proposal for an assault on Sicily that summer in return for stepped-up American offensive operations in the war against Japan. The Combined Chiefs chose Eisenhower to command Operation Husky, the invasion of Sicily, but left Harold Alexander in the army-group post and thus in control of ground operations, which were to be conducted by the U.S. Seventh Army, headed by Patton, and the British Eighth Army, which continued to be commanded by Montgomery. Meanwhile, the Combined Chiefs, to the delight of Churchill, had begun planning a possible invasion of Italy following the conquest of Sicily. They anticipated the deployment of one British and one American army in the Italian campaign. Marshall and Eisenhower agreed in January 1943 to establish a new army for that mission, the Fifth, and Major General Mark Clark, the Torch deputy commander, was their enthusiastic choice for the army command. Clark began organizing and training the Fifth Army near Oran, Algeria, that month, thus missing out on combat commands in Tunisia and Sicily.

So far the American command search had identified some men who would excel in high-level, large-force responsibilities, though few such slots had opened yet in the European-Mediterranean war. Some talented officers to be inducted into the high command in the conflict against Germany and Italy had not yet emerged. Bradley, the II Corps commander, explained humbly how he obtained the army and army-group commands that he held later but had not anticipated in the spring of 1943: "I would say luck plays an awfully large part in your success. You have to be able to perform when the opportunity occurs; however, the opportunity doesn't occur for everyone. I was very lucky, being at the right place at the right time to get a good job, and having a lot of good people to help me do it."[9]

Although the British military leadership was paramount in Anglo-American operations to May 1943, Eisenhower and Spaatz had already established their reputations as the foremost Americans in theater-level administration and airpower strategy, respectively. Despite a host of problems and controversies that lay ahead, these two officers, later joined by Bradley, would be the key triad of the American high command in the war in Europe when Germany surrendered two years hence.

AT EASE WITH MARSHALL
AND CHURCHILL: EISENHOWER

Most American officers who had headed sizable units in combat in World War I had retired or died by 1941. Only a small minority of the high command of the United States during the Second World War had extensive experience in troop command, and even fewer had participated in combat, much less led large forces in battle. Surprisingly, the majority who had little or none of these experiences included not only General Marshall, the chief of staff of the largest army the United States has ever fielded, but also General Eisenhower, the supreme commander of the Allied forces that undertook the largest amphibious invasion in history and the ensuing offensives of unprecedented firepower that devastated the German armies from Normandy to the Elbe River. In American military circles, where they are usually ranked among the great commanders of modern times, it is seldom noted that Marshall and Eisenhower had in common the fact that neither man had led soldiers on a battlefield or had been the target of enemy fire. By the time Germany and Japan capitulated, nevertheless, it was obvious to most of their colleagues that their staff-weighted careers and shortage of troop commands had not diminished their wartime leadership one iota.

Destined for distinction as a military manager instead of as a warrior, Dwight Eisenhower graduated from the United States Military Academy in the 164-man class of 1915 that included Bradley and 57 other cadets who would attain the rank of brigadier general or higher. Ike was a popular cadet, fond of pranks and good in football at West Point, but in professional advancement he soon fell behind some of his former classmates who served in France in World War I while he was left in the States training armored troops. In the years between the world wars he drew mostly staff, instead of command, assignments and at first often got the additional duty of football coach of the unit or post. He seemed to be headed toward a less than distinguished career when, as executive officer of an infantry brigade in Panama, 1922–24, he caught the eye of the unit commander, Brigadier General Fox Conner. Eisenhower learned much about the nature of command and "knowledge of men and their conduct" from Conner, who was a fast friend of Pershing and was known as one of the "brains" of the Army. "Life with General Conner," Eisenhower observed later, "was a sort of graduate school in military affairs and the humanities. . . . It took years before I fully realized the value of what he had led me through. . . . In a lifetime of association with great and good men, he is the one more or less invisible figure to whom I owe an incalculable debt."[10]

Eisenhower developed other relations in the interwar

period that proved crucial to his professional progress. He had first met Conner at Camp Meade, Maryland, through a mutual friend, Major George Patton. The paths of Eisenhower, Patton, Omar Bradley, Mark Clark and other officers on the rise would cross numerous times in the years before Pearl Harbor. In the late 1920s Eisenhower served under General Pershing for a year and a half, assisting the latter's staff of the American Battle Monuments Commission in preparing a World War I battlefield guide. That duty gave him a chance to become acquainted also with Colonel George Marshall. In early 1933, General MacArthur, then Army chief of staff, added Major Eisenhower to his staff as a "personal military assistant" and "amanuensis to draft statements, reports, and letters for his signature."[11] MacArthur was so impressed by Eisenhower's work and versatile skills that he took him along as his mission chief of staff when he moved to Manila in the autumn of 1935 as the military adviser to the Philippine government. Ike was a forty-nine-year-old lieutenant colonel when he was transferred to the United States in December 1939 to command an infantry battalion at Fort Lewis, Washington. Regarding later talk of enmity between him and MacArthur, Ike said, "The hostility between us has been exaggerated. After all, there must be a strong tie for two men to work so closely for seven years."[12]

Working assiduously at his various assignments at Fort Lewis from 1940 to 1941, he earned a promotion to colonel and advancements in position to chief of staff of the Third Infantry Division and then of the IX Corps. In June 1941, he was elevated to chief of staff of the Third Army, which was commanded by General Walter Krueger, with headquarters at San Antonio, Texas. In August and September, the Second and Third armies, totaling over 420,000 troops, were engaged in war maneuvers in Louisiana, during which Eisenhower's superb planning and staff work won accolades from a number of superiors, including Generals Krueger, Marshall, Lesley McNair, Mark Clark, and Ben Lear, who were observing or participating in the exercises.

Back in San Antonio five days after the Pearl Harbor

attack, Ike received a call from the War Department stating that Chief of Staff Marshall wanted him there immediately. Some sources say that Clark, the operations chief in the War Department and soon to become deputy commander of Army Ground Forces, was of paramount influence in getting Marshall to bring Eisenhower into the War Plans Division, then headed by Major General Leonard Gerow. On the other hand, Eisenhower's main biographer maintains that "MacArthur said Eisenhower's chief strength was his ability to look at problems from the point of view of the high command," while "Marshall picked Eisenhower partly because of his long service with MacArthur, partly because he was known in the Army as a man who would assume responsibility. Marshall's desire for independent men fitted in with the way he wanted War Plans Division (WPD) to operate."[13]

Eisenhower, now a brigadier general, found himself in daily contact with the Army chief of staff, and he was given important duties in the top-level planning for the war against Japan at first and soon for the conflict against the European Axis, too. Marshall and Gerow came to admire Eisenhower's unusual perceptiveness regarding global strategic concepts and priorities. When Gerow departed to take a divisional command in February 1942, Marshall, on Gerow's recommendation, named Ike to succeed him as both division chief and assistant chief of staff. In the reorganization of the War Department the next month the division was redesignated the Operations Division and was transformed by Marshall into his "brain center" for directing American army ground and air forces on a worldwide basis.

Promoted to major general that spring, Eisenhower frequently accompanied Marshall to the White House for sessions with the president on issues of strategy, logistics, and high command. Both generals managed to retain Roosevelt's good will despite arguing steadfastly against his idea for invading Northwest Africa and other militarily unwise schemes that they suspected originated with his clever friend Churchill. Marshall and Arnold, both fervent advocates of a cross-channel invasion as soon as practicable, were pleased with Eisenhower's strong dedication to Operation Bolero, the buildup of men and materiel in Britain, and Operation Roundup, an assault on the West European coast contemplated for the spring of 1943 (later replaced by Overlord). In the amazingly short span of twenty-eight months Eisenhower had moved fast, rising from lieutenant colonel to two-star general, attracting powerful friends in the nation's capital, and making his voice heard in the high-level direction of the war.

Uneasy over reports of James Chaney's inadequate leadership, Marshall sent Arnold, Eisenhower, and Clark to check on that situation and to discuss assorted common problems with the British high command. Returning to Washington in early June after about ten days in Britain, all three officers had been impressed by most of the British chiefs but not by Chaney. Eisenhower recommended to Marshall that Major General Joseph T. McNarney, deputy chief of staff of the Army and an Army Air Forces officer, replace Chaney and that Clark be given command of the first corps to be shipped to the United Kingdom. Arnold and Clark, on the other hand, proposed Eisenhower as the successor to Chaney. Marshall later quipped to Clark, "It looks to me as if you boys got together."[14] On June 11, the Army chief of staff appointed Eisenhower as commander of the European theater of operations, U.S. Army (ETOUSA); he would assume the post on the twenty-fourth when he arrived back in England. Marshall also named Clark as head of the II Corps, which was to be stationed in Britain for the time being, but he retained McNarney as his deputy in Washington. In an unusually cooperative mood, Admiral King told Eisenhower that he would instruct all American naval forces in the British Isles to recognize the general as the top United States officer there, thus making ETOUSA a de facto joint command. Long impatient to get the American effort underway against Germany, Eisenhower wrote in his diary on the night of his appointment: "Now we really go to work" pushing the Bolero program.[15]

Within seven weeks, however, Eisenhower was chosen to lead Torch, an operation that would severely drain Bolero resources but would provide a more challenging opportunity. Even before the decision to launch Torch had been finalized, the Combined Chiefs had agreed to King's proposal in July to charge Eisenhower with the planning of the Northwest African invasion. Considering the antagonism many Frenchmen felt toward the British, Churchill and the British chiefs acknowledged that the landings might be better received by French forces in Morocco and Algeria if an American were the Torch commander. They also favored an American supreme commander who would be the overall head of both Torch and the future Roundup assault. Churchill told Roosevelt that Marshall was the British preference for that post, with Eisenhower as his deputy and the actual field commander of Torch. Roosevelt preferred to postpone a decision about command arrangements for Roundup, though he and the American chiefs approved Eisenhower as head of the Northwest African invasion. It took another two weeks of Combined Chiefs' discussions to resolve Anglo-American differences over strategic plans before the directive for Eisenhower was issued and he formally assumed command of Torch (while also retaining the ETOUSA position for several months).

The two chief nominees for the Torch command had both opposed the operation earlier, but, in proper soldierly fashion, Marshall and Eisenhower buried their criticisms once the decision was made to invade Northwest Africa, and they strove zealously to make Torch a success. But, as Eisenhower confided in his diary in early September, he and Clark, the deputy commander, still had dark misgivings about Torch: "Our own conviction is that we are undertaking something of a quite desperate nature and which depends only in minor degree upon the professional preparations we can make or upon the wisdom of our own military decisions."[16]

In early February 1943, only a few weeks before the battle of Kasserine Pass, Eisenhower was promoted to four-star general and was designated commander of the North

African theater of operations, U.S. Army (NATOUSA), while continuing as head of Allied forces, Northwest Africa. At the same time Lieutenant General Frank Andrews succeeded him in charge of ETOUSA. For one month, beginning in early December 1943, Eisenhower also served as commander in chief of Allied forces in the new Mediterranean theater of operations (MTO). For the first time, states the official American Army chronicle, the Combined Chiefs "brought the whole offensive in the Mediterranean under a single command."[17] But after his short term British generals held the MTO command for the remainder of the war.

During the fourteen months from the Torch landings in November 1942 until his move back to London in January 1944, Eisenhower served as supreme commander over the Allied ground, sea, and air forces that conquered French Morocco, Algeria, Tunisia, Sicily, and southern Italy. He demonstrated political skills in sensitive negotiations with French leaders in Northwest Africa and later with officials of the Italian government in securing that nation's surrender. Moreover, says a noted historian, "in the process he had welded together a team of British and American officers unequaled in the annals of warfare for its cooperation."[18] Of course, Ike ran into increasing public scrutiny the higher he rose and the more sensitive his decisions. At a dark time during Torch, Arnold wrote him reassuringly: "You are doing a really excellent job. . . . By this time you no doubt realize . . . that . . . as soon as your head gets up above the pack, everybody takes a pot shot at you."[19] It was good counsel for Eisenhower to take with him to the Overlord job.

At the Quebec Conference of August 1943, Roosevelt, Churchill, and the Combined Chiefs of Staff agreed that the Overlord supreme command should go to an American. British concurrence was based, in large measure, on their realistic expectation that their nation's limits in manpower and industrial mobilization would soon be reached and that henceforth the American contributions in men and materiel in the war against Germany would grow to more than twice those of the United Kingdom. Once the Quebec conferees decided an American should lead Overlord, the final choice of the officer would be made, of course, by the president. Since July 1942 when Marshall had first been mentioned for leadership of the cross-channel assault, the widely esteemed Army chief of staff had been generally regarded among his professional colleagues as the principal candidate, with Alan Brooke and Eisenhower the only other officers seriously mentioned. The Quadrant Agreement at the Quebec Conference eliminated Brooke from contention, leaving the two American generals as the only candidates prominently mentioned in top military circles and in the press. No one, however, was quite certain of how the matter was viewed by Roosevelt, who could sometimes be casual and even capricious in his personnel decisions.

Aboard the battleship *Iowa* en route to the First Cairo Conference in November, Roosevelt told the Joint Chiefs that he hoped to convince the British to agree to a unification of the European and Mediterranean commands and to the appointment of Marshall as the supreme commander of the new theater. Whether that meant also the Overlord post for Marshall was not clear. Going ashore at Oran, Algeria, and traveling by automobile with Eisenhower on a battlefield tour to Tunis, the president seemed to suggest to the Northwest African commander that he was leaning toward Marshall for the Overlord post. Also, Admiral Ernest King remarked to Ike that he thought Roosevelt would send Marshall to Europe shortly and bring back Eisenhower as chief of staff. The comment was remarkably similar to one made by Churchill to Eisenhower at Malta a few days earlier. Eisenhower felt that such words constituted "almost official notice that I would soon be giving up field command to return to Washington."[20]

During the First Cairo Conference in late November and the ensuing Teheran Conference, the president pushed the idea of an overall Anglo-American command in the war with Germany in sessions limited to American and British conferees. But Churchill and his chiefs were adamantly opposed, arguing that the British had the main forces in the Mediterranean and ought to get the supreme command there. If an American were to head a unified European-Mediterranean theater, they feared that he would draw units from the Mediterranean for Overlord despite British objections. At a meeting of the Big Three heads of state during the Teheran Conference, Marshal Joseph Stalin raised the question of who was to command Overlord, but Roosevelt could only respond that the selection had not been made yet. Churchill replied that the decision "would be forthcoming within a fortnight," but his basis for this assurance to Stalin is not known.[21] By the time the American and British leaders returned to Cairo from Teheran in early December, Roosevelt had dropped the unified-theater scheme.

Apparently Roosevelt made up his mind shortly after arriving for the Second Cairo Conference that he would retain Marshall in Washington and give the Overlord command to Eisenhower. A major consideration in his thinking, maintains a leading scholar on the subject, was that "Marshall would have been senior in rank and experience—not to mention ability—to almost all his superiors" on the Combined Chiefs of Staff, from whom the Overlord commander would take his orders. "Most of all, Roosevelt realized, putting Marshall on OVERLORD would mean losing his services as the advocate of the American case in CCS sessions."[22] As for the positive considerations in favor of Eisenhower, they were many, one of the most important being his experience as a winning Anglo-American team leader: "Overlord, like Torch, was going to be a joint operation, and Eisenhower had proved that he could create and run an integrated staff and successfully command combined British-American operations. No other general had done so."[23]

The president informed Marshall of his decision at Cairo on the 4th of December, and, as typical of the Army chief of staff, he showed no disappointment. Three days later, en route to the United States, Roosevelt flew to Tunis where Eisenhower was waiting when his plane landed. The general was puzzled because he had received "a somewhat garbled radiogram" from Marshall about Ike's "forthcoming change in assignment," the Army chief of staff having assumed that Ike had gotten word of his new command. "But, lacking such information," Ike commented later, "I was unable to deduce his meaning with certainty. The President arrived in midafternoon and was scarcely seated in the automobile when he cleared up the matter with one short sentence. He said, 'Well, Ike, you are going to command Overlord.'" The general barely had time to respond, "I hope you will not be disappointed," before the conversation turned to other matters.[24]

Eisenhower's leadership of Allied operations in France, the Low Countries, and West Germany from June 1944 to May 1945 involved him in a number of controversies over strategic alternatives, command jurisdictions, and logistical priorities. At times his critics ranged from his good friends Bradley and Patton, who thought he was too cautious and pro-British, to the hypersensitive, condescending Field Marshals Brooke and Montgomery, who had a low regard of him as a soldier and a strategist. His decision to advance into Germany on a broad front, with all his British, Canadian, American, and French armies roughly abreast, rather than to send Montgomery's army group in a narrow thrust across the Northwest German plains was scathingly criticized then and later by mostly British political and military leaders, journalists, and historians as needlessly allowing the Soviet Army to seize Berlin. In January 1945, only a month after his promotion to five-star general, Eisenhower came close to bringing an instance of Montgomery's insolence in differing with him over this and other issues before the Combined Chiefs. Possessing a fiery temper though usually long suffering, Eisenhower recovered his demeanor and managed to keep his relationship with Monty workable, if not cordial.

Eisenhower's uncanny ability to retain the trust and cooperation of the many volatile Allied leaders with whom he had to deal and who often disagreed with his decisions was one of the traits that made him probably the best possible choice for supreme commander of the huge Allied Expeditionary Force, Northwest Europe. Even Montgomery later admitted that Ike "has the power of drawing the hearts of men towards him as a magnet attracts the bits of metal."[25] Forrest C. Pogue, a combat historian with the First Army in the European campaigns and later official chronicler of Eisenhower's supreme command of 1944–45, emphasizes the general's "ability to get people of different nationalities and viewpoints to work together," but adds that "his willingness to go an extra mile with the Allies drew from some U.S. officers the gibe that 'Ike is the best commander the British have.' "[26]

General Freddy de Guingand, Montgomery's chief of staff, did his best to act as a harmonious liaison between his temperamental superior and the theater commander, and somehow he managed to like and admire both commanders. Monty would not have concurred, but de Guingand found "Eisenhower was always accessible and would talk frankly and openly about anything. More and more was I impressed with the greatness of this man. He was utterly fair in his dealings, and I envied the clarity of his mind, and his power of accepting responsibility." General de Guingand continued, "He was always natural, cool and charming, and possessed the secret of making one feel he really wanted to see you, and had plenty of time to talk. . . . A lovable, big minded and scrupulously honest soldier—a truly great American."[27] Major General Lucius D. Clay, later head of the American occupation zone in Germany, observed that Ike "had a very retentive memory and a very active mind." Clay noted, however, that his "infectious smiling" face was deceptive because "if you ever looked at General Eisenhower's face when he is serious, you know that this is nobody to fool with." Though he sometimes "breaks into a smile," Clay said usually Eisenhower's was a "pretty stern, rugged-looking countenance."[28] Assistant Secretary of War John J. McCloy commented: "I had the feeling that Eisenhower did see more clearly than the British commanders did . . . the significance of modern warfare. . . . He was prepared to make prompt and difficult decisions. . . . He was a thoroughly competent general, quite beyond the qualities he had for composing differences and commanding a combined force. He also had insight into the course that modern war was apt to take."[29]

Of incalculable importance to Eisenhower's command effectiveness during the drive from Normandy into Germany was the staunch support he received from Roosevelt, Stimson, and particularly Marshall. In the aftermath of the Battle of the Bulge in the winter of 1944–45, the Army chief of staff laid his own career on the line for him as an authority points out: "The pressure on Eisenhower to give in to Churchill and make Alexander the single ground commander in Europe was enormous; Marshall, realizing this, did everything in his power to help the Supreme Commander, even to the point of saying he would resign if the organization [Allied Expeditionary Force] did not remain as Eisenhower wanted it."[30]

After successfully holding what has been called "the most coveted command in the history of warfare" and watching his enormous ground and air forces devastate the German defense in the West, Eisenhower considered several grandiloquent drafts by his staff of a message to the Combined Chiefs of Staff—and to the world—announcing the end of hostilities. Finally rejecting all the drafts, he dictated it himself: "The mission of this Allied force was fulfilled at 0241 local time, May 7, 1945."[31] The message's simplicity and modesty reflected much of what everyone found so likable about Ike.

His talents in communicating, inspiring, and winning cooperation and trust were demonstrated repeatedly in his postwar roles as head of the American occupation forces in Germany until the autumn of 1945; successor to Marshall as Army chief of staff, 1945–48; president of Columbia University, 1948–51; supreme commander of NATO forces, 1951–52; and president of the United States, 1953–61. With each succeeding decade of scholarship about him, Eisenhower's stature as a shrewd "mover of men" increases; and his famous smile, once thought to be a reflection of shallowness, appears more complex and purposeful. In his two most important roles, as World War II commander and as president, he now appears to be a leader possessing more gifts than earlier judged. As a recent Eisenhower scholar expressed it succinctly, "The general-president knew what he was doing."[32]

COMMITTED TO
STRATEGIC AIR POWER: SPAATZ

One of the handful of pioneers of military aviation in the United States, Carl A. "Tooey" Spaatz was well known in the Army Air Corps by the late 1930s as a distinguished pilot, a close friend of Hap Arnold, and a zealous believer in strategic air warfare. Within a year after his graduation from West Point in 1914, he reset his career's course by transferring from the infantry to the Signal Corps' fledgling air program. When America entered the First World War, Colonel Billy Mitchell, who led the air arm of the American Expeditionary Forces in France, chose him to run the aviation school at Issoudun, which by the end of the war was one of the largest air training facilities in the world. During a leave in 1918, Spaatz managed to get a temporary assignment as a combat pilot, shot down three German planes, and earned the Distinguished Service Cross.

Two years after the war he won the first transcontinental air race in the United States, and during the ensuing decade and a half he went on to other flying exploits, demonstrating rare skill and courage as a pilot. With a crew that included Captain Ira Eaker and Lieutenant Elwood R. "Pete" Quesada, who would become renowned airmen in World War II, Major Spaatz set a world's record in 1929 for staying aloft—nearly 151 hours—that was accomplished by primitive, very risky air-to-air refuelings of an old Fokker C-2 transport. The feat gained him and his crew Distinguished Flying Crosses, but it almost cost him his life when the refueling hose broke loose and drenched him with aviation gasoline. Displaying the nerveless, gambling instinct that characterized him later as a master of both aerial fighting and poker playing, Spaatz removed all his clothes, had the crew cover him with lubricating oil, and continued the re-fueling. According to Eaker, who was piloting the C-2, Spaatz calmly ordered him: "You take command. Under no condition abandon this flight." Due to the fire danger, Spaatz had instructed the crew to wear parachutes throughout refueling operations. Eaker recalled looking back from the cockpit after the broken-hose episode and thinking: "Spaatz was the only nude I ever saw in a parachute."[33]

In spite of his daring performances in the air and probably due, in part, to his bold, blunt testimony in behalf of Billy Mitchell at his famous court martial in 1925, Spaatz spent sixteen years in grade as a major, finally getting promoted to lieutenant colonel in September 1939, as the German panzers raced across Poland. That autumn Hap Arnold brought him into Army Air Corps headquarters in Washington as chief of the Plans Division. Along with Major George C. Kenney, another favorite of Arnold, Spaatz served as an observer with the Royal Air Force during the aerial Battle of Britain in the summer and fall of 1940. When Arnold called him back to Washington that October, he was made assistant to the chief of the Air Corps and promoted to brigadier general. At various times during the next year and a half Spaatz also held the posts of chief of the Air Staff and head of the Materiel Division, the GHQ Air Force, and the Combat Command.

Arnold's confidence in the leadership abilities of his good friend grew as Spaatz proved outstanding in each of these assignments, so it was not unexpected when the Air Corps chief chose him to take charge of the Eighth Air Force in May 1942, Eaker having gone to the United Kingdom several months earlier to head the VIII Bomber Command. Shortly after Eisenhower took over ETOUSA that June, he appointed Spaatz to the additional position of theater air officer at his new headquarters. The official history of the Army Air Forces notes that "the step marked the beginning of a close personal relationship between Generals Eisenhower and Spaatz."[34] Later that year Eaker observed that Spaatz "was one of the earliest and probably the first American to point out the basic errors in air strategy which the Germans were making." Eaker, who was an ardent admirer of Spaatz, remarked further, "His selection to head the Air Forces in this theater is probably the result of two things: his personal desire to direct the air effort from this theater . . . and the high regard in which the Chief of the Army Air Forces holds him because of his capacity for air leadership."[35] An authority on the air leaders of World War II says of Arnold's relationship with Spaatz: "Above all, Spaatz was the friend whose judgment he valued more than any other. Spaatz was to be his number-one airman, his first among equals. No association within the air arm was more closely knit."[36]

Not long after the Torch landings in Northwest Africa in November 1942, friction developed between Jimmy Doolittle and some of the senior British air officers involved in the operations. Eisenhower, who had known Spaatz at West Point but not well, took Arnold's advice and summoned him from England to Algeria as his deputy commander for air. Eisenhower was quite upset with Doolittle and would have sent him home if Spaatz had not persuaded him to retain Doolittle. In February 1943, Spaatz became commander of the new Northwest African Air Forces in an air organizational reshuffling by the Combined Chiefs of Staff. Shortly after he also gained command of the American Twelfth Air Force, with Doolittle transferred from that post to command of the Northwest African Strategic Air Force. Meanwhile, Arnold appointed Eaker to take over the Eighth Air Force in England. With the final triumph in Tunisia in May, Eisenhower praised Spaatz for his "remarkable" leadership in organizing the air war in Northwest Africa and particularly stressed the airman's ability in a sphere of high priority to the Torch supreme commander: "Beyond all this, you have been of great assistance in proving that Allied forces can work as a unified and effective team; a lesson that will grow more and more important as we enter future phases of the war."[37]

Taciturn and unpretentious, Spaatz did not try to be a popular leader, but, nevertheless, he was able to gain wide spread respect and liking among British as well as American air officers because of his instincts for strategic air warfare, his judicious selection of subordinate commanders and staff leaders, and his success in getting results on the ground and in the air. He once jokingly yet revealingly commented to another air general: "I owe my success to two things: I drink good whiskey and get other people to do my work. I give a man a job. I never tell him how to do it. He's supposed to know how to do it."[38] Spaatz's quick, intuitive judgments on strategy and personnel in the air war against Germany became legendary. He seldom used his desk, conducted few staff meetings, and was notorious for rendering important decisions in the midst of a game of poker or billiards. When Eisenhower informed Marshall that he wanted Spaatz to head the newly established United States Strategic Air Forces, Europe, in December 1943, the Army chief of staff reputedly remarked, "You think a lot of Spaatz, don't you?" Eisenhower, who by then regarded Spaatz almost as highly as Arnold did, supposedly responded: "Yes. He's the best air commander I know. I spent two months trying to figure out how he does it and I still don't know, but he's right 90 per cent of the time!"[39] Spaatz later remarked that he and Ike developed a "mutual confidence that made it unnecessary to have long detailed explanations for courses of action."[40]

At Cairo in November 1943, Arnold proposed the establishment of the post of supreme commander for Pointblank, the strategic bombing offensive having functioned previously through the not-always-satisfactory coordination of Eaker's Eighth Air Force and Air Marshal Arthur T. "Bert" Harris' Royal Air Force Bomber Command. Arnold's idea was buried, primarily because of the strong opposition of Air Chief Marshals Charles Portal and Arthur Tedder, respectively, chief of the British Air Staff and commander of the Mediterranean Allied Air Forces. Directives from the Combined Chiefs of Staff regarding the strategic air war previously had been sent to Eaker and Harris through Portal, the executive agent of the CCS in such matters. Portal would be continued by the Combined Chiefs in that role for the duration of the European hostilities. Thwarted in this scheme, which he had hoped would lead to Spaatz's elevation to the Pointblank leadership, Arnold next determined to establish a supreme command over all American strategic bombing efforts in the Mediterranean and European theaters. At Tunis on December 8 and 12, Arnold discussed with Eisenhower and Major General Beetle Smith, his chief of staff, who should be given command of United States Strategic Air Forces, Europe. Both Eisenhower and Smith, Arnold reported in his diary, "agree Spaatz was man for job. Wouldn't take anyone else, not even Tedder" (who became Ike's deputy commander for Overlord).[41]

It turned out, however, that both Arnold and Eisenhower also favored bringing Doolittle to England, as head of the Eighth Air Force. At first uncomfortable with Doolittle, Ike had been won over by his daring leadership in Northwest Africa as well as by Spaatz's strong endorsement. In the meantime, Eaker had been subjected to growing criticism from Arnold for his failure to improve the Eighth Air Force's record in destroying Pointblank targets and for its heavy losses on bombing missions. Moreover, Eaker's support of Charles Portal had irritated the Army Air Forces chief. On December 18, 1943, Eaker was suddenly notified that he would become commander of the Mediterranean Allied Air Forces and Doolittle would assume command of the Eighth Air Force. Eaker took on his new job obediently if reluctantly and performed well in the Mediterranean, but he never fully forgave Arnold for replacing him as leader of the Eighth just when it was beginning to get the reinforcements essential to carry out its missions. In early January, Eaker wrote of his "personal disappointment" at "my undoing" to Assistant Secretary of War Robert A. Lovett, but emphasized that "General Spaatz has had no part in rooting me out here. He is a warm personal friend who never threw a curve in his life."[42]

Spaatz moved to London in January and set up the headquarters of United States Strategic Air Forces, Europe. Thereafter he provided aggressive direction for the strategic operations of the Eighth Air Force and Major General Nathan F. Twining's Fifteenth Air Force, the latter staging from bases in southern Italy. During the final week of February, Spaatz sent about 4,000 bombers of those air forces that dropped 10,000 tons of bombs in an unprecedented series of raids on the German aircraft industry. He and Marshal Arthur Harris stood together, though for different reasons, in opposing extensive use of their strategic bombers to prepare for and to cover the Overlord invasion. After much acrimonious debate over target priorities between the Anglo-American ground and air commanders in England, the Combined Chiefs authorized Eisenhower to take temporary control, beginning in mid-April, of the American and British strategic bombers to support the pre- and post-assault operations of Overlord. Eisenhower did not share Spaatz's optimism that strategic bombing, especially of German fuel resources, might render the great cross-channel invasion unnecessary. Much to Spaatz's chagrin, Ike ruled in favor of employing the heavy bombers mainly against the railway network in northern France and the Low Countries in the last weeks before Overlord. That autumn Spaatz and Harris were happily directing strikes again on strategic targets deep in Germany, with the American air groups so numerous by then that Spaatz was able to mount 1,000-bomber raids frequently and even some 2,000-bomber attacks.

The staunch fight conducted by Spaatz in early 1944 for the "Oil Plan" and against the "Rail Plan" of strategic bombardment did not lead to his alienation from Eisenhower. Indeed, their mutual admiration increased somehow under the pressures of the invasion of West Europe. In February 1945, Eisenhower prepared, apparently for Marshall, an annotated list of the top thirty-eight American commanders in the war against Germany. Ranking them according to the "value of services each officer has rendered in this war," he placed Spaatz and Bradley in a tie for first. His brief comment on Spaatz was "experienced and able air commander; loyal and cooperative; modest and selfless. Always reliable."[43] As Brigadier General E. P. Curtis, Spaatz's chief of staff, pointed out, "The very close personal and professional relationship that existed between General Spaatz and General Eisenhower all the time was of the utmost importance in the operations of both the strategic and tactical air forces."[44]

With the end of the war in Europe, the massive and complex shift of forces to the Pacific began. Arnold sent Doolittle to set up a B-29–equipped Eighth Air Force to enter the war with Japan that summer, and he chose Nathan Twining to head the Twentieth Air Force, the two forces possessing all 700 B-29 Superfortresses of the Army Air Forces. Not surprisingly, he selected his closest friend and the senior American air leader of the war against Germany, Tooey Spaatz, to assume command of the newly created United States Army Strategic Air Forces, Pacific. Spaatz, who had been elevated to four-star general in March, was given broad control over the administration and strategic operations of the Eighth and Twentieth air forces. His directive called for him to report to the Joint Chiefs of Staff through Arnold as executive agent, thus bypassing the main theater commanders, Nimitz and MacArthur. Spaatz assumed his new command on July 29, 1945, on Guam, but the sudden capitulation of Japan seventeen days later provided little time to show how the new air organization would work and how Spaatz would get along with his new chief of staff, the fiery Major General Curtis E. LeMay, who had long led the B-29 bombing operations.

Spaatz was the choice of both Arnold and Eisenhower, Marshall's successor as Army chief of staff, to become the next commanding general of the Army Air Forces, and President Truman made the popular appointment, effective when Arnold retired in early 1946. With the creation of the independent United States Air Force under the National Security Act of 1947, Truman chose Spaatz as its first chief of staff.

Of the several perceptive evaluations of Spaatz in print, one of the most provocative is by a noted military historian who compares this strategic air leader of World War II to two other commanders of that era. He believes that Spaatz and General George Kenney, the Southwest Pacific air chief from 1942 to 1945, "showed the least tendency to get hung up on tactical method and dogma, to seek for success by alternatives within the general framework of air power, and not let too many chips ride on one number." He observes, too, that Spaatz, "in spite of a certain amount of stylized bluster and pugnacity," was, like MacArthur, "a first-class mind unchallenged in his environment by frequent contact with other first-class minds."[45] Perhaps of all American military aviators, it is most appropriate that Spaatz is buried at the institution he helped to found and whose ideals he epitomized, the United States Air Force Academy.

FIVE

INTERSERVICE DIFFICULTIES IN THE WAR AGAINST JAPAN

COMMANDERS FOR THE EARLY COUNTEROFFENSIVES (PACIFIC, MAY 1942–MAY 1943)

There were more differences than similarities between the war against the European Axis and the conflict with Japan during the period from May 1942 to May 1943. In fact, their only significant factor in common was that the principal axis of advance of the Allies had been decided but not yet made operational—the Normandy invasion and the Central Pacific drive. There were four chief differences that would affect high-command considerations: (1) American Navy and Marine forces were larger and more decisive in the Pacific war. (2) Vast distances, along with inhospitable climate and terrain, posed more severe geographical challenges for commanders and troops in the war with Japan. (3) American influence was paramount in determining policy and strategy in the Pacific war, while British input was still stronger in deciding the Anglo-American direction of the war against Germany and Italy. (4) The Allied efforts to achieve coordination and cooperation were more effective in the European and Mediterranean theaters than in the Pacific and China-Burma-India (CBI) theaters.

Within the huge Pacific Ocean Areas (POA) theater that Nimitz led, the first counteroffensive was undertaken in Vice Admiral Robert L. Ghormley's South Pacific Area subtheater when Guadalcanal in the Solomon Islands was invaded in early August 1942. Admiral Ernest King, who had picked Ghormley for the South Pacific command, pushed determinedly for this assault despite much concern in the War and Navy departments over the sparseness of the ground, air, and sea forces that could be deployed. When Ghormley stopped at the Navy Department en route to his new assignment, King warned him the South Pacific command would be "most difficult" because "I do not have the tools to give you to carry out that task as it should be."[1] The landing on Guadalcanal by Major General A. Archer Vandegrift's First Marine Division began a ferocious struggle for the island that lasted until February 1943 and that precipitated daily ground and air engagements, as well as six naval battles in the surrounding waters. The long and bloody fight for Guadalcanal was also characterized by the rise of a number of officers who demonstrated high-command potential.

In the ground operations on the island the Marines were given outstanding leadership by Major General Vandegrift at the top. To his colleagues it was not surprising that he soon became head of the I Marine Amphibious Corps and then commandant of the Marine Corps. An impressive number of Marine officers at regimental and battalion levels on Guadalcanal later became generals.[2] Two Army officers who served in the final months of the hard-fought campaign went on to achieve distinction in the war against Germany: Major General Alexander M. Patch, who led a division and then a corps on Guadalcanal, commanded Operation Dragoon, the Riviera invasion in 1944, and led the Seventh Army in its push into South Germany; and Major General J. Lawton Collins, who commanded a division on Guadalcanal and subsequently in the Central Solomons, became a top corps leader in the advance through France and Germany from 1944 to 1945, and later rose to Army chief of staff.

Two days after the Marines landed on Guadalcanal the naval actions began with the disastrous battle of Savo Island, wherein four American and Australian heavy cruisers were sunk in less than an hour, with no enemy ships lost. "Some of the commanding officers concerned were broken by the defeat," observes a noted naval historian, but the two senior naval officers in the immediate area—Rear Admiral Kelly Turner, who led the naval amphibious force, and Rear Admiral V. A. C. Crutchley, an Australian in charge of the covering force—somehow escaped serious tarnishing and gained larger naval roles later.[3] Even when the Allied naval forces were more successful, however, flag officers in the savage engagements off Guadalcanal often were in great danger. Frank Jack Fletcher, the senior admiral in the Coral Sea and Midway battles and in the Solomons task force, was wounded when his flagship, the carrier *Saratoga,* was torpedoed in late August. Rear Admirals Daniel J. Callaghan and Norman Scott were killed aboard their ships in a fierce battle off Guadalcanal in mid-November. Among the surface-unit commanders who survived, a half dozen or so were marked for posts of larger responsibilities after excelling in the naval operations in the Solomons through the spring of 1943.[4]

Air officers who showed their mettle during this period in the Solomons and were given higher commands subsequently included Vice Admiral John S. "Slew" McCain, who first commanded Navy land-based aircraft in the South Pacific, then became deputy chief of naval operations for air, and later headed the Fast Carrier Force of the Third Fleet; and Rear Admiral Marc A. "Pete" Mitscher, who was commander of Fleet Air, South Pacific, and Air Solomons from late 1942 to mid-1943 and then won renown as the leader of the Fifth Fleet's Fast Carrier Force. The air leader most responsible for winning control of the skies over Guadalcanal was Major General Roy S. Geiger, who headed the First Marine Air Wing and, for a crucial time, the Air Solomons command. He went on to command the I and III Marine

Amphibious Corps and the Tenth Army. Notable also was Major General Millard F. "Miff" Harmon, who was in charge of U.S. Army Forces, South Pacific, 1942–44, and then commanded U.S. Army Air Forces, POA, as well as serving as deputy commander of the Twentieth Air Force, until his death in a plane crash in early 1945.[5]

The Guadalcanal campaign may have been handicapped at times by shortages of weapons and supplies but surely not by a lack of able senior officers. Several high-ranking officers turned in less than outstanding performances, yet only one had to be relieved of his command. Unfortunately he was the South Pacific Area commander, Robert Ghormley—an immensely likable admiral who, in an earlier assignment in Britain, had displayed unusual skills in diplomacy. Seeking a more aggressive leader when the Guadalcanal struggle reached its crisis in October 1942, King and Nimitz agreed on Vice Admiral William "Bull" Halsey as Ghormley's replacement. The decision was particularly sad for Nimitz, who had been a good friend of Ghormley since their days together at the Naval Academy. After a visit to Guadalcanal and to Ghormley's headquarters at Noumea, New Caledonia, Nimitz, like other senior officers around Ghormley, found him depressed and overly cautious about the seemingly stalemated Solomons situation. A Marine officer on Ghormley's staff put it simply: "He was a tired man. . . . Halsey was a much stronger character."[6]

Occurring at approximately the same time as the struggle for Guadalcanal was the disappointingly lengthy and even costlier campaign waged by General MacArthur's SWPA forces to recapture Papua, the southeast territory of New Guinea. Japanese troops invaded Papua in July 1942, several weeks before the American assault on Guadalcanal. The New Guinea Force, made up of Australians, stopped the enemy advance twenty miles from Port Moresby and then launched a counteroffensive that drove the Japanese back to the northern coast where they had first landed. That fall and winter the New Guinea Force was strengthened by units of Major General Robert L. Eichelberger's U.S. I Corps, but the Japanese were strongly entrenched around Buna on the north Papuan shore. As the heavy but indecisive fighting dragged on, MacArthur grew impatient and pressured Thomas Blamey into relieving two successive leaders of the New Guinea Force, and in late September he ordered Blamey himself to assume the field command. Even more severe on American officers, MacArthur relieved Major General Edwin F. Harding, the senior American commander on the Buna front, and dispatched Eichelberger to head U.S. forces in that sector. He told him ominously: "Time is of the essence. I want just one of two messages from you: that you have taken Buna or that your body lies there."[7] But the tenacious Japanese defenders delayed the Australian-American conquest of Papua until late January 1943, by which time MacArthur was displeased with nearly all senior officers associated with the campaign. Eichelberger, who had hoped his success at Buna would bring him the theater's first American army-level command, would not get appointed to head an army until mid-1944.

Lieutenant General Walter Krueger, former head of the Third Army, became commanding general of the Sixth Army in February 1943 when the War Department authorized that unit's formation and shipment to Australia as the Southwest Pacific Area's initial American army. Because of his negative views of Blamey and his Australian generals and because his theater directive forbade him to command national armies directly, MacArthur created a tactical organization of supposedly task-force functions that he called Alamo Force but consisted almost wholly of the Sixth Army's headquarters staff and field units. Under this scheme General Krueger, as Alamo Force commander, bypassed Blamey and reported to MacArthur, in effect, nullifying the Australian's role as Allied Land Forces chief. In the planning for Operation Cartwheel, which was to be a coordinated series of assaults by MacArthur's and Halsey's forces in the New Guinea, New Britain, and Solomons region to begin in June 1943, MacArthur gave the premier amphibious-assault tasks to the Alamo Force as the spearhead of his Southwest Pacific offensive, leaving the New Guinea Force, now entirely Australian again, to undertake the slow overland pushes across New Guinea's jungles and mountains. The Alamo subterfuge would prove to be the first in a series of allegedly biased decisions by MacArthur that would lead to a souring of relations with the Australian high command by the end of the war.

MacArthur's quest for aggressive field commanders not only brought ground-command changes in the Papuan campaign but also produced some turnovers for a while in his top naval and air officers. Vice Admiral Herbert Leary, the first commander of Allied Naval Forces in the Southwest Pacific theater, found himself in trouble with MacArthur for communicating directly with Nimitz and King, as well as for refusing to provide support for ground operations along the Papuan coast because of the risk to his ships in the uncharted waters. After numerous complaints by MacArthur, King sent him Rear Admiral Arthur S. Carpender in September 1942 to succeed Leary. It was not long, however, before the general experienced similar troubles with him, too, as well as a sharp clash with Nimitz's headquarters over control of submarines in the Southwest Pacific. When the Seventh Fleet was established in March 1943, Carpender was given that additional post, but his friction with MacArthur continued until he was replaced that November by Vice Admiral Thomas C. Kinkaid. Both Kinkaid and his dynamic VII Amphibious Force commander, Rear Admiral Daniel E. Barbey, would win MacArthur's respect and friendship. During the period up to the summer of 1943, however, the only admiral who could make that claim was—surprising to some contemporaries—the volatile, outspoken South Pacific commander, Bill Halsey. He and MacArthur had their first conference at Brisbane in April 1943; they coordinated their plans for the Cartwheel offensives that summer and began a lifelong relationship of mutual admiration. Later MacArthur remarked, "I liked him from the moment we met, and my respect and admiration increased with time." Halsey, in turn, commented, "I have seldom seen a man who makes a quicker, stronger, more favorable impression."[8]

MacArthur experienced professional and personal difficulties with the first Allied Air Forces commander in the Southwest Pacific Area. "From the first it became evident that he and General Brett could not get along," said Arnold, who believed Brett "should have done the 'getting along,' as he was the junior."[9] In early August 1942, Major General George C. Kenney succeeded Brett; he quickly sent home five American generals of the theater air command as "deadwood," began a greatly accelerated program of bombing and reconnaissance missions, and eventually became a member of MacArthur's close circle of confidants. When the Fifth Air Force was created in September, Kenney assumed that command, too. Brigadier General Ennis C. Whitehead, Kenney's deputy and a gifted air leader in his own right, headed the advance echelon of the Fifth Air Force in New Guinea and later succeeded to that command when Kenney became head of Far East Air Forces. Kenney and Whitehead teamed up to give MacArthur an especially satisfying triumph in March 1943 when their bombers nearly decimated a Japanese convoy in the Bismarck Sea that was transporting an infantry division to New Guinea.

The tiny but strategically located islands of Attu and Kiska in the Aleutians had been seized by the Japanese in June 1942. As plans were laid to retake the islands, the senior American officers in the North Pacific clashed, frequently because of interservice rivalries, and, says an authority, "showed no disposition to subordinate their individual convictions for the common good."[10] Rear Admiral Robert A. Theobald, who was in trouble with King for alleged miscues during the Midway battle, headed the North Pacific Area, a subtheater of Nimitz's POA command. But most forces in the region were in Major General Simon B. Buckner's Alaskan Defense Command, which, in the Army command setup, was under Lieutenant General John DeWitt's Western Defense Command, based on the West Coast. Complicating the situation further was the presence in Alaska of Brigadier General William O. Butler's Eleventh Air Force. For a time command relations between the three men were so poor that King and Marshall considered transferring them in one fell swoop to different parts of the globe. Conditions improved in January 1943 when Thomas Kinkaid succeeded Theobald as head of the North Pacific Area. Interservice cooperation was adequate, if not extraordinary, when American ground, sea, and air forces secured Attu in May after "the second most costly infantry battle of the Pacific war (in ratio to the size of the forces engaged)," the Japanese on Kiska thereafter withdrawing without a fight.[11] For the remainder of the war the North Pacific Area was comparatively inactive. When Admiral Fletcher arrived that autumn to relieve him, Kinkaid seemed unusually enthusiastic about the command change. Whether it was because he was going to command Southwest Pacific naval forces or because he was leaving the North Pacific is not known.[12]

American interservice relations in the Pacific generally had not fared well through the spring of 1943. Not without justification, talk was mounting in the Pentagon and on Capitol Hill about the need for reforming the nation's defense organization and perhaps unifying the armed services in the postwar era. In the defense of the Philippines, General MacArthur and Lewis Brereton and Admiral Thomas Hart, together with their staffs, had allowed communications to break down between them, mostly because of narrow service interests and personal animosities—a situation not unlike that on Oahu in the autumn of 1941 with the lack of cooperation and coordination between Admiral Husband Kimmel's and General Walter Short's headquarters. The Marines on Guadalcanal were left on their own logistically for a critical period at first, for which they castigated the timidity of the naval leaders about keeping their ships in the area. General Archer Vandegrift and Admiral Kelly Turner, states the official Marine chronicle, "often disagreed on the conduct of activities ashore," the latter brazenly claiming his authority as naval amphibious force commander extended to activities of the First Marine Division on the island.[13] And as just mentioned, the North Pacific Area was beset by interservice command squabbles.

The Joint Chiefs' first major directive on the Pacific, in March 1942, had been a compromise that provided theater commands for Nimitz and MacArthur, with unity of command sacrificed because the Navy objected to MacArthur and the Army to Nimitz having supreme authority. Relegating Blamey and the few other senior Australian officers in his command set up to secondary roles, MacArthur established his theater headquarters in Brisbane along conventional American Army administrative lines and filled all the key posts with Army officers unquestionably loyal to him, most having served under him on Corregidor. At Pearl Harbor, in turn, Nimitz's headquarters was dominated by naval officers, so much so that not only the senior Army officers in his command organization but also the top Marines there had little sense of belonging to the inner circle of admirals who, under Nimitz, directed the war in the POA theater. In fact, to the Army's consternation, Nimitz continued to wear three hats: as theater, subtheater, and fleet commander, he headed the Pacific Ocean Areas, the Central Pacific Area, and the Pacific Fleet.

In the fall of 1942, Arnold returned to Washington from a trip to the Pacific and proposed that an Army officer be made supreme commander over all the Pacific, his preferences being MacArthur, Joseph McNarney, or Lesley McNair. Marshall set two of his wisest staff leaders to work on the idea: Brigadier General Albert C. Wedemeyer concluded that the position should go to an airman, preferably Arnold or McNarney, while Brigadier General St. Clair Streett, an Army Air Forces officer, maintained that the prerequisite to achieving unity of command in the Pacific was to remove MacArthur and suggested that the general should be sent to Moscow as ambassador. Nothing came of these ponderings in the War Department, though Marshall did oppose efforts by King, beginning in December 1942, to revise the Pacific directive to give supreme command to Nimitz. Stimson noted in his diary that MacArthur was "a constant bone of contention" between the War and Navy departments. "The Navy's astonishing bitterness against him seemed childish," the secretary of war added.[14]

Guadalcanal and Papua had been victorious campaigns, but their unexpected length and heavy casualties gave Navy leaders the opportunity to press anew for a more direct route toward Japan, through the Central Pacific with the Pacific Fleet and the Marines leading the way. At the Casablanca Conference in January 1943, King was successful in getting Roosevelt, Churchill, and the Combined Chiefs to agree tentatively to the opening of a Central Pacific axis of advance following the attainment of the main goal of MacArthur's and Halsey's Cartwheel operations beginning that summer, the capture of the Japanese stronghold of Rabaul. King soon set his planners to work on future assaults on the Gilbert, Marshall, and Caroline islands. In early May, the Joint Chiefs approved the first long-range plan for the defeat of Japan; it provided for the Central Pacific offensive but without terminating the drives up through New Guinea and the Solomons. Later that month the Combined Chiefs approved the strategic plan at the Trident Conference in Washington. MacArthur objected vociferously but futilely to the launching of a second axis of advance, but the Joint Chiefs and their planners thought otherwise and issued a directive to Nimitz in July for the seizure of the Gilberts that fall. Henceforth the Central Pacific would enjoy a much higher priority than the Southwest Pacific in Washington decisions on allocating men and materiel resources.

In the China-Burma-India theater, international, interservice, and personal rivalries were involved from the beginning. Lieutenant General Joseph W. "Vinegar Joe" Stilwell was sent there in early 1942 under orders to try "to increase the effectiveness of U.S. aid to China and to improve the combat efficiency of the Chinese Army."[15] He was burdened, however, with four positions, each of great responsibility (with several more posts added later): chief of staff to Generalissimo Chiang Kai-shek, United States lend-lease representative to China, commander of American forces in the CBI theater, and United States delegate on the Allied military council of the China theater.

Stilwell ran into problems after the retreat from Burma that spring when he began trying to recruit and train Chinese forces and to develop plans for the reconquest of Burma. Nationalist Chinese political and military leaders, who, as frankly described by an authority, tended to be "corrupt, demoralized, inefficient, and oppressive," resisted the American general's efforts to reform the Chinese ground forces. He also encountered difficulties in meshing his plans with those of the British forces in India, led by General Archibald P. Wavell. One of Stilwell's generals, while visiting British headquarters at New Delhi, reported to Marshall that the British were "only half-hearted in their efforts to defend Burma," being more concerned about India's security, and that "a strong China was not in accordance with British policy."[16]

As an American theater chief, Stilwell faced problems also in resolving differences between Major General Claire Chennault, head of the Fourteenth Air Force in China (formerly the China Air Task Force and even earlier the American Volunteer Group, or Flying Tigers), and Major General Clayton L. Bissel, who led the Tenth Air Force in India. In addition, Chennault was seriously challenging Stilwell's authority and plans by the spring of 1943. The famed Flying Tigers leader had impressed both Chiang and Roosevelt with his bold claims that air power under his leadership could drive the enemy from China. He argued that the priority on American aid to China should go to his air force rather than to the Stilwell-sponsored programs of reforming and reequipping the Chinese Army. At the Trident Conference in May 1943, both Stilwell and Chennault presented their cases. Although he had the backing of Marshall and Arnold, Stilwell lost because Roosevelt supported Chennault (and Chiang) regarding priorities on supplies to China. Roosevelt also turned down Stilwell's proposal to withhold further lend-lease and credits to Chiang's government unless it enacted military reforms. Shortly Stilwell would find that his long-planned offensive in Burma would have to be delayed until the end of the year because of logistical shortages.

The turn of the tide in the war in China and Burma was nowhere in sight at the end of the spring of 1943. The absence of Allied teamwork at the top levels had been translated at the battlefield levels into lack of aggressive leaders, strong forces, and adequate logistics. The CBI theater had become a chaotic struggle with at least four Allied leaders—Chiang, Stilwell, Chennault, and Wavell—maneuvering against each other with almost as much belligerency as their forces altogether mounted against the Japanese invaders.

In conclusion, the period from May 1942 to May 1943 in the war against Japan was marked by six significant developments: (1) the stopping of the Japanese offensive in the Pacific; (2) the launching of the first major Allied counteroffensives, in Papua and Guadalcanal; (3) the emergence of serious American interservice problems in the Pacific theaters; (4) the decision to inaugurate a Central Pacific drive, thus shifting from a single axis of advance to a dual one in the Pacific; (5) the worsening of command relations in the CBI theater; and (6) the failure there to undertake a large-scale Allied offensive. Because of these factors, the search for the men to complete the American high command in the war with Japan was so far inconclusive. General Archer Vandegrift, the Marines' stellar leader in the Solomons fighting, stood out among the officers who had been successful field commanders in battle and was already earmarked for larger responsibilities.

KNOWN FOR "TENACITY, COURAGE, AND RESOURCEFULNESS": VANDEGRIFT

After two years at the University of Virginia, twenty-one-year-old A. Archer Vandegrift passed the Marine Corps' entrance examination and in January 1909 was commissioned a second lieutenant. Sent to the officers' school (School of Application) at Parris Island, South Carolina, he got a quick lesson in Marine discipline. Returning late from liberty in nearby Port Royal, he was arrested, found guilty in a general court-martial, and reduced in grade, meaning that he would be a junior second lieutenant longer than most of his peers. The school commandant, moreover, gave him an unsatisfactory mark in all areas but health on his fitness report, stating for the record that he was not "fit to be intrusted with hazardous and important independent duties." In his memoirs over a half century later Vandegrift noted that King and Nimitz also had courts-martial on their records as young officers. He hoped this would buoy junior officers suffering similar mishaps and "may influence those senior officers charged with promotion to select an officer for what he is and what he is likely to be without undue weight on early recorded errors."[17]

Vandegrift rebounded strongly and graduated from the school that summer. His first assignment was a typical Marine duty of that era: providing security at the Portsmouth, New Hampshire, Navy Yard. Besides guard work, his tours of duty to 1937 included a variety of combat missions against bandits and revolutionaries in Nicaragua, Panama, Mexico, and Haiti. He also served in China twice, protecting American legations and interests in Shanghai, Tientsin, and Peking. As one historian says, "China was a nursery for the Marine Corps leadership of World War II," and seven Marines who saw duty in China between the world wars later became commandants of the Corps.[18]

Vandegrift was a colonel in command of the American Legation Guard at Peking in 1937 when he received orders to report to Corps headquarters in Washington as the military secretary to Lieutenant General Thomas Holcomb, the new commandant of the Marine Corps. With twenty-six years of service behind him, Vandegrift assumed this would be his final duty. Having known Holcomb at stations in China and Virginia earlier, he adjusted easily to the commandant's somewhat formal and intimidating manner, and he became an admirer of Holcomb's mental prowess and his administrative skills. Brigadier General Holland M. Smith, with whom Vandegrift had worked previously in developing amphibious assault doctrine and tactics, was serving as Holcomb's chief of staff. More stable under pressure than the talented but volcanic Smith, who soon took a field command, Vandegrift was promoted to brigadier general in 1940 and became assistant to the commandant.

Eager to get back with troops after four years in Washington, Vandegrift was delighted in November 1941 when Holcomb chose him to be assistant commander of the First Marine Division, then at the New River, North Carolina, training center. Major General Philip Torrey, the division commander, expected to retire in a few months; he was quickly impressed by Vandegrift's aggressive leadership over the division's training program and recommended him as successor. Holcomb appointed Vandegrift as the division commander in March 1942, and he was elevated to major general. Although by no means combat ready, Vandegrift and his division were ordered to New Zealand in May for future use in the new South Pacific Area.

Summoned to South Pacific headquarters in late June, Vandegrift was greeted by Admiral Ghormley, the area chief, who appeared unusually somber. He handed the Marine general a top-secret dispatch from the Joint Chiefs calling for an invasion of Guadalcanal and Tulagi in the South Solomons on August 1. Although the assault would be postponed a week, they still had less than six weeks' notice, which was inadequate for planning and preparing the attack. MacArthur joined Ghormley in protesting the hastily decided expedition, but King was successful in his push for it to be launched.

When Vandegrift's Marines assaulted the two islands in early August, they seized Tulagi after a short, savage fight but became involved in a four-month struggle for Guadalcanal. During this time of "incredible difficulties," says a noted historian, Vandegrift's "optimistic disposition and professional skill, supported by an able division staff, gave the 1st Marine Division a sense of hope."[19] Unfailingly confident and cool even during the worst enemy attacks on Guadalcanal, Vandegrift was respectfully called "Sunny Jim" by his Marines, the younger ones probably not learning that he had received that nickname for calmness under fire in Nicaragua three decades ago. When asked by Ghormley if his troops could hold their small perimeter during the early desperate days on the island, he responded, "Hell yes, why not?"[20] According to a student of military leadership, Vandegrift displayed on Guadalcanal an unusual "flexibility of mind" that enabled him, unlike the enemy commander and some of his American colleagues, "to throw overboard all preconceptions and to deal with the situation in its own terms."[21] Much of the hardest fighting was over when the First Marine Division was relieved in December; the reinforcing Marine and Army divisions gave the Americans a two-to-one edge in troop strength over the Japanese on Guadalcanal, where once the enemy had outnumbered Vandegrift's forces.

Ordered back to the United States for a speechmaking tour in early 1943, Vandegrift also was summoned to the White House in February where President Roosevelt bestowed the Medal of Honor on him and read the citation that praised "his tenacity, resourcefulness, and courage" in leading the Marines in the first American counteroffensive.[22] As for the public appearances the Pentagon required of him, Vandegrift was uncomfortable in that role and commented modestly to reporters that so much had appeared in the press about the Guadalcanal operations that "it seemed a kind of impertinence for me to add anything to it."[23]

When the situation had seemed at its worst on Guadalcanal in late October, Holcomb had flown to the island and, despite Vandegrift's great uneasiness about his security, had insisted on a tour of the front. When the Corps commandant and the division commander had some time alone after dinner that evening, they chatted first about sundry news of Washington and of Marine friends. Suddenly Holcomb remarked that he would be sixty-four years old next year, and, to Vandegrift's surprise, he confided: "If the President wishes me to stay on, I shall stay. . . . If he wishes me to retire, I am going to recommend you as my successor. . . . If he approves, I promise to keep you fully informed before you take over."[24] Holcomb then turned the conversation to the brazen attempts by Admiral Kelly Turner to interfere with Vandegrift's ground operations. The official Marine history states that Vandegrift's position on amphibious command relations "prevailed, and in the future the amphibious troop commander, once established ashore, would be on the same command level as the naval task force commander"—a milestone from the Marines' viewpoint.[25] The next day Vandegrift and Holcomb flew to South Pacific headquarters at Noumea, New Caledonia, to confer with Halsey and his staff. Holcomb said nothing more about the Corps commandancy during his South Pacific visit that autumn.

After his whirlwind visit to the States following the Guadalcanal campaign, Vandegrift joined his division in Australia that spring where the Marines were recuperating and training for future missions in the Southwest Pacific theater. Meanwhile Holcomb kept him closely posted, according to Vandegrift, on "the details of his office, quite often asking my concurrence with long-term officer assignments before he made them."[26] On a subsequent Pacific trip Holcomb informed him that he would definitely retire at the end of 1943. General Gerald C. Thomas, then a colonel and Vandegrift's chief of staff, remembered his saying to Vandegrift: "I talked to the President and he's agreeable. You will be my successor as Commandant."[27]

In a move to give him higher command experience, the commandant named Vandegrift commander of the I Marine Amphibious Corps, the top Marine command then in the Pacific, on July 1, 1943; he was also given his third star. At the I Corps headquarters in Noumea, Vandegrift took over from Major General Clayton B. "Barney" Vogel, whose fear of flying and some questionable command traits had not pleased Halsey. Operation Cartwheel had begun on June 30, the South Pacific forces assaulting Rendova in the Central Solomons. Vandegrift headed the I Corps through the conquest of Rendova, the tough early stage of the two-month battle for New Georgia, and the seizure of Vella Lavella.

During the assault on Vella Lavella in mid-August, Vandegrift was observing his Marines from the flagship of Rear Admiral Theodore S. "Ping" Wilkinson, the South Pacific amphibious force chief who had replaced Turner. Suddenly three Japanese dive bombers attacked the vessel, one of their bombs exploding so close to Vandegrift that his shirt, in his words, was "completely covered with black marks from the powder stains." When he went back to Noumea, he added, Halsey "gave me hell and told me not to go on any further operations where I didn't belong."[28]

Intending to bring Vandegrift to Washington that fall to orient him on the commandant's responsibilities, Holcomb assigned the I Corps to Major General Charles D. Barrett on September 15. Vandegrift, before returning to the States, was to tour Marine outfits in the Pacific, which now included the new V Amphibious Corps of General Holland Smith, scheduled to spearhead the Central Pacific's first offensive in November, the invasion of the Gilberts. In a freak accident at Noumea on October 8, Barrett fell from an upper-story window and was killed. Vandegrift was ordered back to Noumea immediately to head the I Corps, which assaulted Bougainville in the North Solomons on November 1. A week later General Roy Geiger relieved Vandegrift, who finally was permitted to journey to the States. Not until he went blind during his retirement years did Vandegrift reveal to anyone but his family and confidants that his eyesight was seriously failing by the fall of 1943. There is no indication, however, that the problem handicapped his performances in the Pacific or later in Washington.

In the office of the secretary of the navy on January 1,

1944, Frank Knox presided over the short ceremony marking Holcomb's retirement and Vandegrift's appointment as commandant of the Marine Corps. When he had come to the national capital in 1937 as Holcomb's secretary, the Marine Corps had consisted of only 18,000 officers and men; now it had 390,000, and would peak at 486,000 in mid-1945. Worn down by his seven years in the commandancy, Holcomb counseled Vandegrift before leaving: "You have a good many friends in the Corps. I only hope that when you turn your job over to a successor you have the same number. The Commandant does not make many new friends if he does his job well."[29]

For the next year and eight months Vandegrift was busy presiding over the administration, training, and myriad other responsibilities entailed in running the Marine Corps' many programs and installations, as well as its five divisions and four air wings engaged in the Pacific war. As commandant, he was responsible to the secretary of the navy, Frank Knox, until poor health forced his retirement in the spring of 1944, with James Forrestal replacing him; he was also subordinate to the chief of naval operations, who was King until late 1945 and then Nimitz. General Gerald Thomas, who directed the Division of Plans and Policies at Corps headquarters during Vandegrift's commandancy, remarked of him: "Never in my three and a half years with him there did I see him lose a battle," but he stressed that Vandegrift, King, Knox, and Forrestal "worked very, very smoothly together" regarding Marine affairs.[30] Perhaps it was fortunate that Vandegrift had to work more closely with the deputy and assistant chiefs of naval operations than with King himself.

Vandegrift made a number of trips to the Pacific, particularly in connection with the Marines' largest operations in the Corps' history—the Marianas, Iwo Jima, and Okinawa. (His son, a Marine lieutenant colonel, was wounded in both legs on Iwo Jima.) A strong advocate of Marine aviation, he persuaded Nimitz to use Marine aircraft on escort carriers for ground-support missions, and he wisely chose

Major General Francis P. Mulcahy, an outstanding air commander, to head Marine air forces in the Pacific. In April 1945, Vandegrift became the first four-star general on active duty in Marine Corps annals (Holcomb and several prior commandants having attained full general as they retired).

Continuing as commandant until the end of 1947, he spent much of the postwar portion of his leadership defending the Corps against budget cuts by Congress and against challenges by the other services to its roles and missions during the often bitter wrangles leading to the National Security Act of 1947. General Clifton B. Cates, his successor as commandant, became the beneficiary of two changes Vandegrift had fought for and not attained: elevation of the commandant to membership on the Joint Chiefs of Staff and to an administrative level in the naval establishment on a par with, rather than subordinate to, the chief of naval operations.

Through all the pressures and turmoil of wartime expansion, postwar demobilization, and national defense reorganization, Vandegrift was a formidable champion of Marine Corps interests but retained his poise and positive attitude. Many service colleagues would agree with Rear Admiral Samuel E. Morison's description of him as "a man of iron."[31] One of his Marines said that Vandegrift, who "was of old Virginia stock," came from "the mold of Stonewall Jackson. He was both wary and audacious, seldom without a plan."[32] A longtime friend who served under him in the Solomons and at Corps headquarters observed that "the most impressive trait" of Vandegrift was "his modesty topped off by his being a gentleman in the old tradition. It is difficult to reconcile these characteristics with the fact that he was a thoroughly professional fighter, an excellent tactician, a firm leader, and—most of all—a brave man."[33] Admiral Theodore Wilkinson paid him a simple but supreme tribute when he wrote in his diary on October 13, 1943, upon the Marine general's return to command the I Marine Amphibious Corps in the South Pacific: "I was glad to see him return as I have a great deal of confidence in him."[34] In the war against Japan and in the postwar struggle to save the Corps, Vandegrift was, indeed, "a Marine's Marine."

ASSIGNED "THE TOUGHEST JOB OF ANY OF OUR GENERALS": STILWELL

General Joseph W. Stilwell's favorite Shakespearean passage was from a scene in *Henry IV* in which Hotspur tells King Henry:

> *But I remember, when the fight was done,*
> *When I was dry with rage and extreme toil*
> *Breathless and faint, leaning upon my sword,*
> *Came there a certain lord, neat, trimly dressed,*
> *And as the soldiers bore dead bodies by,*
> *He called them untaught knaves, unmannerly,*
> *To bring a slovenly unhandsome corse,*
> *Betwixt the wind and his nobility.*
> *With many holiday and lady terms*
> *He questioned me . . .*
> *. . . he made me mad*
> *To see him shine so briskly, and smell so sweet,*
> *And talk so like a waiting-gentlewoman*
> *Of guns, and drums, and wounds . . .*[35]

No wonder Vinegar Joe Stilwell, as his soldiers nicknamed him, liked these lines, for Hotspur alludes to two of the four concerns that bound the American general professionally: unusual sensitivity to his soldiers' needs and unmitigated disgust for interfering, pretentious persons of high rank. He was strongly dedicated also, in his words, to striving for "China's good" at the same time that he "stood up for American interests" in Asia.[36] These four intensely felt commitments would channel his career into a complex command situation in the Second World War that brought him a measure of greatness but ended in bitterness on all sides.

By the time America went to war against Japan, Stilwell had been a soldier forty-one years. A graduate of the Military Academy in 1904, his tours of duty overseas to 1941 included two in the Philippines and three in China, as well as combat service in France in 1918. Few people knew that an explosion in World War I so impaired the vision in his left eye that, according to his wife, "he could not distinguish the fingers on a hand at three feet."[37] First visiting China in 1911, he spent a total of ten years' service there before World War II, traveling widely through the countryside, mastering the language and culture of the people, and developing an affection for the Chinese that was rare among American officers. He also was a careful observer of the training and tactics of the Nationalist and Communist Chinese armies and established personal ties with many high-level civilian and military leaders on both sides in the Chinese civil war. He was a colonel serving as military attaché at the United States embassy in Peking when the Sino-Japanese War began in 1937.

Two years later General Marshall, the new Army chief of staff who had been much impressed by him when they served together at the Infantry School in the early 1930s, recommended and obtained Stilwell's promotion to brigadier general and chose him to head the Third Brigade in Texas. The chief of staff continued to admire his work, moving him up rapidly in commands the next two years and pushing through his promotion to major general. Stilwell's outstanding leadership of the Seventh Infantry Division in the large-scale maneuvers in California in mid-1941 prompted Marshall to give him command of the III Corps. The selection was strongly favored by Major General Walter K. Wilson, the outgoing head of that corps who also was retiring; he rated Stilwell first among all the forty-seven two-star generals in the Army.

Several weeks after the Pearl Harbor attack, Marshall assigned Stilwell to the War Plans Division where he was to direct the planning for an invasion of Northwest Africa. This project was then being discussed by the Combined Chiefs at the Arcadia Conference under the code name of Gymnast, later to be changed to Torch. Although Stilwell was pleased to be working under Gee Gerow and with Eisenhower in that division, as well as to have contact with other future high commanders of the war, he was unhappy with the hypothetical nature of the Gymnast planning, which meant allowing for a variety of contingencies. He was also perturbed over the chaotic work conditions, as he indicated in a letter to his wife in late December 1941:

> *My impression of Washington is a rush of clerks in and out of doors, swing doors always swinging, people with papers rushing after other people with papers, groups in corners whispering in huddles, everybody jumping up just as you start to talk, buzzers ringing, telephones ringing, rooms crowded, with clerks all banging away at typewriters. "Give me 10 copies of this* AT ONCE.*" "Get that secret file out of the safe." "Where the hell is the Yellow Plan (Blue Plan, Green Plan, Orange Plan, etc.)?"* . . . *Someone with a loud voice and a mean look and a big stick ought to appear and yell "*HALT. *You crazy bastards.* SILENCE. *You imitation ants. Now half of you get the hell out of town before dark and the other half sit down and don't move for one hour." Then they could burn up all the papers and start fresh.*[38]

At the Arcadia session on December 29, Roosevelt, Churchill, and the Combined Chiefs agreed to the establishment of ABDACOM as the Allied command in Southeast Asia, with General Archibald Wavell as its head, and also the creation of the China theater of operations, with Generalissimo Chiang Kai-shek as supreme commander. Chiang would not be subordinate to the Combined Chiefs of Staff: "Though an Allied commander, the Generalissimo was responsible only to himself," states the official American Army history, "which made him unique among those who afterward held similar posts" set up by the Combined Chiefs.[39] Roosevelt, who fervently wanted China to make a major contribution in the war and to achieve great-power status later, suggested to Chiang that he set up a combined planning staff of Chinese, American, and British officers at once. Chiang responded in early January 1942 asking the president to appoint a senior American officer to serve as his Allied chief of staff.

The early preference of Stimson and Marshall was General Hugh Drum, then commander of the First Army and the senior line officer of the U.S. Army. He was brought to the War Department for talks with top officials about the position, but "Drum seems to have arrived in Washington," says an authoritative account, "expecting the top field command in World War II."[40] Concluding that the War Department leaders held divergent and confused views about the nature of the China mission, Drum pompously proposed that they "decide on a policy and arrange the means" before asking him to decide whether he wanted to go to Chungking.[41] At a session with Marshall on January 9, he learned that no large American ground forces would be sent to China or Burma. When he opined that his abilities would be wasted in such a post, Marshall frankly stated that he could not recommend his appointment anyway. Later discussions between Drum and Stimson convinced the secretary of war, too, that, in essence, Drum "had refused to go to China"; by January 17 Drum was no longer under consideration.[42]

Meanwhile, on the fourteenth Marshall had proposed Stilwell for the assignment. During the ensuing nine days Stimson, Marshall, and Stilwell explored thoroughly the potential problems of the mission, and many difficulties were foreseen. When asked by Marshall on January 23, "Will you go?" Stilwell replied flatly, "I'll go where I'm sent." The chief of staff responded, "Well, that's refreshing after Drum."[43] Having obtained the generalissimo's agreement to the American general, Stimson got Roosevelt's approval on the twenty-third to the appointment of Stilwell as head of American forces in the CBI theater and as Chiang's chief of staff. Nourishing no illusion about the complicated world he was about to enter, Stilwell realistically, even prophetically, wrote in his diary that night: "The old gag about 'they shall offer up a goat for a burnt sacrifice' is about to apply in my own case."[44]

Two days before departing from Washington, Stilwell was called to the White House on February 9 for a farewell session with the president. He recorded in his diary that Roosevelt was "very unimpressive" and "frothy," telling him to assure Chiang that "we are in this thing for keeps" and grandly pledging that the *Normandie,* the largest and fastest ocean liner in the world, "will be assigned to supply your new Theater."[45] Hardly had the general returned to his hotel when he learned that the *Normandie,* being refitted for military service, had burned and capsized that day at a New York pier. Looking back, Hopkins observed that this reverse "was only the first of a long series of bitter discouragements for this rugged, fearless, tactless American soldier."[46]

Promoted to lieutenant general, Stilwell arrived in Chungking, the Nationalist capital, in early March. After about a week of talks with Chiang and his top military officials he flew to Burma and took command of the Chinese troops fighting in the northern portion of that country. The Japanese offensive was already in full momentum, rolling back the British, Indian, and Chinese defenders; in May Stilwell and a remnant of his force retreated 140 miles on foot into India. For the next year and a half he worked assiduously at training and equipping Chinese ground units at his huge training center at Ramgarh in eastern India, while frequently flying to the distant British and Chinese headquarters at Delhi and Chungking for sundry meetings. In the autumn of 1943 he was given the additional title of deputy supreme commander of the new Southeast Asia Command (SEAC), which was headed by Admiral Louis Mountbatten. By then Stilwell's other positions included commanding general of U.S. Army forces in the CBI theater, chief of staff to Chiang, supervisor of lend-lease to China, American delegate on the Allied military council of the China theater, and commander of the Chinese Army units that were assigned to him by Chiang (then several divisions at Ramgarh).

In spite of his accumulation of titles, however, it was obvious to Dr. Lauchlin Currie, Roosevelt's special envoy at Chungking for a while, that the Stilwell-Chiang relationship was troubled, and he repeatedly warned Roosevelt that, instead of adding to Stilwell's responsibilities, he should be replaced. As early as September 1942, Currie told Marshall, "I am convinced that the present arrangement cannot work," for "Chiang made his resentment and bitterness clear" about Stilwell.[47] Marshall, however, staunchly defended Stilwell.

In October 1943, Mountbatten placed all Allied ground forces in Burma (or soon to be there) under the highly capable General William J. Slim, who had long commanded British troops in that combat area. Busy preparing his Chinese divisions and a small American force for offensive action starting in December, Stilwell was appointed head of the Northern Combat Area Command, comprising most of North Burma. In the complex Allied command structure Stilwell was thus subordinate to Slim in this role, but as deputy commander of SEAC he was Slim's superior.

Taking personal command, Stilwell led his largely Chinese soldiers in an advance into the Hukawng Valley of North Burma at the end of the year, triggering a series of offensive operations that culminated in the capture of the principal Japanese stronghold, Myitkyina, in August 1944. It was a remarkable triumph that some military analysts said would be impossible to achieve with predominantly Chinese troops. Also in August he was promoted to four-star general, a rank then held in the American Army only by Marshall, MacArthur, Eisenhower, and Arnold. Moreover, a few weeks earlier, Roosevelt, at the urging of Marshall and Stimson, told Chiang in rather strong terms that he should place Stilwell in command of all Chinese forces. In his message the president acknowledged that tension existed between Chiang and Stilwell, but he emphasized: "The future of all Asia is at stake, along with the tremendous effort which America has expended in that region. . . . I know of no other man who has the ability, the force and the determination to offset the disaster that now threatens China."[48] Roosevelt's reference was to a large Japanese offensive that had overrun much of East China, including several key American air bases. The turn of events, of course, was a blow to Chennault, who had crusaded for supply priority for his air force rather than for the Chinese armies, as Stilwell wanted. Chiang had supported Chennault, according to a noted historian, because he was "a popular general with links to the White House" and served as "an antidote to Stilwell, a means to outmaneuver him by dividing the Americans against themselves."[49] For a fleeting time that summer of 1944 it seemed that Stilwell's stock was on the rise. Indeed, for three weeks, while Mountbatten was in England, he even served as acting supreme commander of the SEAC, though he felt quite uncomfortable in the sea of British officers in the headquarters at Kandy, Ceylon.

President Roosevelt finally appeared to be standing behind him four-square, as Marshall and Stimson had done faithfully since he took on the CBI command. Whereas he had sloughed off Stilwell's counsel at the Trident meetings in the spring of 1943, now Roosevelt followed the general's advice and sent Chiang a virtual ultimatum that American lend-lease and other aid would be reduced or terminated unless he implemented the military reforms Stilwell proposed and named the American general as head of all his forces. Among several missions that the president dispatched to China that summer was one Stilwell strongly favored: an American military survey team was sent to the Chinese Communists in Yenan to determine the possibilities of American cooperation with and assistance to Mao Tse-tung's army in the war against Japan.

Chiang responded to Roosevelt's unprecedented pressure by requesting him to send a special envoy to "adjust relations between me and General Stilwell."[50] The president chose Major General Patrick J. Hurley, who had been President Hoover's secretary of war. He gave Hurley his directive on August 18: "Your principal mission is to promote efficient and harmonious relations between the Generalissimo and General Stilwell to facilitate General Stilwell's exercise of command over the Chinese Armies placed under his direction."[51] Hurley knew little about China and less about the ways of Chiang and his officials; the result, says one authority, was that "Chiang enveloped him in seductions and evasions."[52] According to another scholar, Hurley "quickly allied himself with Chiang Kai-shek and accused Stilwell of being crude, unreliable, and possibly disloyal."[53] Learning that Roosevelt was sympathetic to Hurley's version of the situation and was shifting positions again, Stilwell wrote his wife in early October that Roosevelt was an "old softy" who "has apparently let me down completely."[54]

Among his final maneuvers in Chungking, Stilwell appealed to T. V. Soong, one of the most influential Nationalist leaders and a Chiang confidant, for the selection of "an overall commander" of Chinese forces. The American general added frankly: "I have been delayed, ignored, double-crossed, and kicked around for two-and-a half years in my attempt to show the Chinese how they can hold up their heads and regain their self-respect. I have looked forward for 44 years to getting a chance to command American troops, and I could have had it if I had not been a real friend of China and the Chinese people."[55] By then, however, Stilwell's efforts in Chungking had become futile, and on October 11, Chiang sent an extraordinary message to Roosevelt, claiming that Stilwell's Myitkyina campaign had drained off scarce military resources that had resulted in the loss of "almost all of east China" and that "this is an hour of crisis" in China that Stilwell's elevation to command of all Chinese forces could turn into total disaster.[56] Hurley, adding his own conclusion, agreed with Chiang and pointed out that the generalissimo had forced Roosevelt to choose between him and Stilwell and that further support of the latter might lead Chiang to negotiate a separate peace with Japan. Both Chiang and Hurley called for the replacement of Stilwell by another American officer.

Roosevelt, who had played a relatively small, if final, role in the appointment of Stilwell, had been making his influence felt increasingly in the Chiang-Stilwell affair since spring of 1944. By August he had appeared to be turning away from the generalissimo and toward Stilwell, but now the mercurial Roosevelt abruptly changed again. In conciliatory language he inquired if Chiang had in mind certain officers who would be acceptable. The Chinese leader named Generals Alexander Patch, Walter Krueger, and Albert Wedemeyer. Since the first two were then leading armies heavily involved in combat, the president, on the advice of Marshall and Stimson, chose Wedemeyer, who had been engaged in staff work most of the war either under Marshall or Mountbatten. Unlikely a mere coincidence, the presidential election and Roosevelt's bid for a fourth term were upcoming in early November when the president notified Chiang on October 18, 1944, that Major General Wedemeyer would replace Stilwell but would head only American forces in China, those in Burma and India to be under Lieutenant General Daniel I. Sultan. Chennault, Stilwell's longtime nemesis, would be retained as commander of the Fourteenth Air Force, though, under pressure from Arnold, he would resign in July. In a personal memorandum shortly after getting the news of his relief from command, Stilwell was more objective than might have been expected: "Competent authority, for good and sufficient reasons, ordered my relief from duty in the CBI theater. Since I am persona non grata with the existing Chinese government, it was the only thing to do. The trouble was largely one of posture. I tried to stand on my feet instead of my knees."[57]

During the first five months of 1945, Stilwell served as commander of U.S. Army Ground Forces. In June 1945, with the fatal wounding of General Simon Buckner on Okinawa, he took charge of the Tenth Army in its final battles to secure that island. Returning to the States in the fall, Stilwell headed the Western Defense Command and then the Sixth Army. He died in October 1946.

Wedemeyer concluded after getting to know Chiang that Stilwell's opinions of the generalissimo were "unjust, uninformed, and prejudiced" and that he had been "on the border of disloyalty" to the supreme commander of the China theater.[58] But Wedemeyer and Stilwell were known to dislike each other, and, more important, Stilwell's command problems of 1942–44 had been far more complicated than merely a personal feud with Chiang. They were rooted in international and interservice difficulties that had never been resolved between the Chinese, American, and British commands and between the strategies advocated by devotees of air power or of ground offensives. The tangled Allied command structure in the region made it hard for Stilwell to carry out the variegated responsibilities of all the positions he was assigned. Roosevelt's grandiose notion of China as a great power did not jibe with the confused, divided status of the nation and with the low priority on logistics the Combined Chiefs gave to the military ventures of Mountbatten, Chiang, and Stilwell. Of course, Stilwell's cantankerousness, sarcasm, impatience, and indiscreetness contributed greatly to his troubles with Chennault, Wavell, Mountbatten, Chiang, and the chief lieutenants of "The Peanut," as he privately referred to the Chinese generalissimo. In brief, Hurley's role was one of the immediate causal factors, not an underlying one, in the recall of Stilwell.

Brigadier General Frank Dorn, Stilwell's chief of staff, strongly believed that his boss "became the scapegoat in an international tug of war in high places."[59] A scholar recently expressed a sentiment that was widespread among American military men outside the Pentagon at the time: "Much of the criticism of Stilwell should be directed against the central direction of the war in Washington" and against the leaders who had burdened him with "one impossible task after another."[60] Perhaps the chief culprit in this regard, though a firm supporter of the general, Secretary of War Stimson wrote Stilwell during a dark period in his CBI experience: "You accepted an offer of duty which lesser men would have tried to avoid and have shown the utmost courage and skill against impossible odds. Both Marshall and I think more highly of you than ever."[61] In 1946, Stimson remarked that in his opinion Stilwell "had had the toughest job of any of our generals" in the Second World War.[62] The official history of the wartime Joint Chiefs of Staff states candidly that he had been given "a mission that had been virtually impossible from the beginning."[63] The coauthors of the U.S. Army volumes on the CBI theater later wrote, "It would have been a miracle if all the potent and seething factors in this theater could have operated smoothly even if unity of thought could have guided the actions of the military leaders. But miracles were not destined to happen."[64] Major General Haydon L. Boatner, a longtime key officer in the CBI, said that the historical records should point out, "especially for the many fine men who spent years of frustration therein, that the theatre they served in was always of secondary importance and that except for 'keeping China in the war' nothing else in the CBI was vital to our winning World War II. This is especially important because of the many volumes which emphasize the controversies of the generals."[65]

Of the eighteen leaders of the American high command featured in this book, Stilwell was the only one to be relieved of his duties in World War II. But it is unlikely that any American could have succeeded in altering wartime China's fate, as the most eloquent of Stilwell's biographers attests:

> *In great things, wrote Erasmus, it is enough to have tried. Stilwell's mission was America's supreme try in China. He made the maximum effort because his temperament permitted no less; he never slackened and he never gave up. Yet the mission failed in its ultimate purpose because the goal was unachievable. The impulse was not Chinese. . . . China was a problem for which there was no American solution. . . . In the end China went her own way as if the Americans had never come.*[66]

From another perspective, Stimson observed later that although it failed "in the larger sense," Stilwell's wartime mission in China was characterized by four significant achievements: "China under Chiang *did* stay in the war; Stilwell *did* prove that Chinese troops well trained and led could match the valor of soldiers anywhere; he *did* clear the Ledo Road to China (rightly renamed the Stilwell Road); most of all, he left to the American Army a matchless record of devotion to duty and professional skill."[67] With the secretary of war's assessment even the irascible Stilwell might have agreed—grudgingly.

SIX

MEDITERRANEAN TROUBLES AND NORMANDY WORRIES

COMMAND CHALLENGES AND CHANGES
(EUROPE, MAY 1943–JUNE 1944)

It was in the Mediterranean theater that the Americans first learned to respect the German Army and its killing tools. In the strategic realm, the American military chiefs' argument for starting Overlord soon may have been sounder than the British preference for continuing in the Mediterranean until the Normandy assault could be undertaken with overwhelming firepower. But Churchill and his generals were not only haunted by the ghosts of the butchering grounds of France from 1914 to 1918 and anxious about the currently dwindling supply of British manpower; they were also genuinely awed by the great potency of the German war machine of World War II. Their concern was well founded, for later research showed, in the words of a prolific historian of the European conflict, that "wherever British or American troops met the Germans in anything like equal strength, the Germans prevailed." They were "formidable soldiers," and the German Army's principal weapons and equipment "decisively outclassed that of the Allies in every category save artillery and transport" as late as 1944. Even in artillery the Germans had in their 88-mm. dual-purpose weapon "the best gun produced by any combatant nation in the war," particularly when used against tanks.[1] Generally American commanders at the senior levels were slower than their own combat forces, much less the British, in developing a healthy fear of the Germans' fighting ability.

Nevertheless, while the American high command pushed for accelerating preparations for Overlord, Mediterranean operations indicated that the Normandy invaders would need vastly superior strength to be successful. Though gaining supremacy of the skies and seas in the region, the Anglo-American forces had required much longer to secure Northwest Africa than had been expected in the autumn of 1942 when the Torch landings were made. During the period covered in this section, from May 1943 to June 1944, the British and American armies learned some brutal lessons in Sicily and Italy in how fiercely and shrewdly the Germans could conduct defensive warfare. The disappointing progress in southern Italy prompted British leaders to revive their uncertainties about launching Overlord in June 1944, some calling for its delay until the Germans had been weakened further through strategic bombing and Soviet operations. During the twelve months before Overlord there were many sharp differences between the American and British chiefs and senior officers over issues of command and strategy, stemming, in no small measure, from their increasing wariness over the Germans' superb defensive capabilities.

The Allied conquest of Sicily in July and August 1943 was accomplished in spite of several tragic breakdowns in American interservice coordination and despite rising friction between Patton, who led the U.S. Seventh Army, and Montgomery and Alexander, who headed the British Eighth Army and the XVIII Army Group, respectively. Patton's dash to Palermo and then eastward toward Messina was spectacular at times, but the Germans, with only 60,000 troops against 467,000 Allied soldiers, conducted excellent delaying actions, culminating in a well-executed evacuation to Italy of most of the German corps. Sicily, remarks a noted American military analyst, "proved once again the strength of the

German Army and its thorough training and high degree of professionalism." Only moderately impressed by Patton's aggressive performance, he concludes that "sheer weight of men and metal overpowered the Germans in Sicily."[2] An able British student of the campaign maintains that "the sterling qualities of the Germans in defence and withdrawal" were a forewarning that "the soft under-belly of Europe might turn into a crocodile's tail," which was what soon happened in Italy.[3]

Four American ground commanders earned distinction in the Sicilian campaign despite the Germans' admirable showing: Major Generals Lucian Truscott, of the Third Division, and Omar Bradley and Geoffrey Keyes, the corps commanders; and, of course, Lieutenant General George Patton, the Seventh Army's leader who attracted much attention in both the British and American press. All four men merited special attention from Marshall and Eisenhower for larger future commands, with Patton having the edge as the most senior, the most combat-experienced, and possibly the best army-level commander of the group. But, as Patton's chief biographer observes, "just as he stood at the height of his career, an invincible and heroic figure on his way to even greater glory and fame, he suffered a crippling indignity perpetrated on him not by his American rivals, not by the British, but by Patton himself."[4]

In August, as the campaign neared its end, Patton struck two American GIs in separate incidents at Army hospitals on Sicily. Both patients were suffering from combat fatigue (shock), but Patton misjudged their situations, berated them as malingering cowards, and slapped them. Later he publicly apologized to them and to his army, while Eisenhower and Marshall pondered what to do about the gifted but flawed battle leader. He was left on Sicily and his command reduced to 5,000 troops, while Mark Clark led the Fifth Army into Italy, Bradley headed the First Army as it trained for Overlord, and other generals received choice assignments. Finally, in late January 1944, Eisenhower brought Patton to England to command the Third Army, which would not see action for another half year, and to play a key role that spring in deceiving the Germans about the Overlord invasion site. Because of Eisenhower and Marshall's wise decision to retain the impetuous Patton, the Allied offensive from Normandy into Germany would have the services of the army commander who caused trepidation in the hearts of even the best German officers.

The Allied conquest of Sicily triggered the overthrow of Italy's Fascist dictator, Benito Mussolini. The Italian government then began negotiations with the Allies through Eisenhower for an armistice, the terms of which were agreed to on September 3, the day Montgomery's Eighth Army landed on the toe of the Italian boot. Five days later the surrender of Italy was announced publicly, and the next day Major General Ernest J. Dawley's VI Corps of Clark's Fifth Army assaulted Salerno, south of Naples. Field Marshal Albert Kesselring rapidly deployed German divisions in South Italy, and for almost two weeks his defenders at Salerno not only kept Dawley's corps from breaking out of the beachhead but also threatened to force the Allied troops into the sea. Eventually the VI Corps drove inland, but the near disaster at Salerno was not an auspicious beginning for the Americans in Italy. Montgomery's slow advance northward and failure to put pressure on the Germans around Salerno offered little promise, moreover, for improving Anglo-American coordination of forces.

Clark had accepted Dawley reluctantly after General McNair, head of Army Ground Forces, proposed him to lead the VI Corps. Dawley was senior to Clark in rank and was considerably older; also, he was a good friend of McNair, Clark's former boss, and had Marshall's approval. Clark gave in on the issue after Eisenhower told him, "You are so close to McNair, it's up to you" to take Dawley. In North Africa, Clark had found it difficult to admonish the older Dawley even when he proved autocratic and his troops deficient in military discipline. Clark later said that he had not had "much faith in his capacity" long before the Salerno battle.[5] Dawley's leadership in the beachhead operation was found wanting in several respects, particularly aggressiveness. Clark personally took charge at Salerno for a while, and Eisenhower, deeply concerned about the VI Corps' ability to hold, visited there to consult with Clark, Dawley, and the division commanders. Both Clark and Eisenhower expressed growing concern about Dawley's leadership. On September 20, the last day of the Salerno battle, Clark relieved Dawley, but he was not altogether pleased that Eisenhower and Marshall agreed on Major General John P. Lucas as the new head of the VI Corps. Like Dawley, Lucas was older than Clark and was close to McNair. He had succeeded Bradley as commander of the II Corps in Sicily, but Clark had not been impressed by his performance at that level.

The Fifth Army captured Naples on October 1, only twelve days after the breakout from the Salerno beachhead, but Kesselring's forces offered mounting opposition as the Anglo-American armies pushed northward, mostly through mountainous terrain where the Germans developed powerful entrenched positions. Halfway between Naples and Rome the Fifth Army was stopped by unusually fierce resistance around the ancient Monte Cassino monastery and along the nearby Rapido River. With the Fifth Army locked in a bloody stalemate there, which proved to be the Germans' heavily fortified Winter Line, Clark became involved in several decisions in early 1944 that led to tragic episodes and much criticism, some quite unfair about his role. The most controversial decisions, to be expounded upon later, were his orders for the Thirty-sixth Infantry Division to cross the Rapido in late January, a costly operation that did not succeed; his VI Corps' amphibious assault at Anzio, also in late January, which entrapped the men in a desperate beachhead battle that lasted five months; and his approval of an Allied plan to use heavy bombers against the Monte Cassino monastery in mid-February, which destroyed the historic Benedictine structure but did not result in the Germans' withdrawal from the mountaintop.

Clark's Fifth Army did not enter Rome until June 4, eight months after taking Naples, which lay less than 120 miles south of the Italian capital. Because of the ongoing crises at Anzio and Cassino in the spring of 1944, Clark had to forgo a chance to lead the Riviera invasion, which would take place in August, and he thereby probably lost the later opportunity to command the VI Army Group in its offensive into Germany. Ultimately he would head an army group, but it would be in Italy where he would remain until the end of the European war.

Operation Shingle, the Anzio assault, was viewed in advance with unwarranted enthusiasm by Churchill, Roosevelt, and Alexander, the army group commander in Italy. Because of shortages of assault craft and supplies, as well as uncertainty that the Fifth Army could break through the strong Winter and then Gustav lines of German defenses to the south of Anzio, Clark and Eisenhower turned against Shingle and got Alexander to cancel the operation in late December. Churchill, however, promptly reinstated it. When Lucas's VI Corps went ashore at Anzio on January 22, the subsequently slow advance of the British and American divisions gave the Germans time to rush powerful forces into the Alban Hills just beyond the beachhead. The result was a critical situation for the corps that required almost continuous fire support from Allied ships and aircraft to keep the Germans from wiping out the lodgment. The VI Corps was not able to break out of the Anzio beachhead until late May and only after the Fifth Army had smashed through the Gustav Line to the south.

Lucas had had forebodings about the Anzio mission soon after getting the assignment. Referring to Churchill's disastrous amphibious plan of World War I, he wrote in his diary before leaving for Anzio: "This whole affair has a strong odor of Gallipoli and apparently the same amateur is still on the coach's bench."[6] Alexander and Clark visited him at Anzio several times, each criticizing his cautiousness and urging him to push his two divisions into the Alban Hills. Before Lucas felt he could attempt this, however, Kesselring dispatched elements of fifteen German divisions against the VI Corps. In mid-February, General Jacob Devers, who was now deputy commander of the Mediterranean theater under British General Henry "Jumbo" Wilson, visited the beachhead and conferred with Lucas and his top officers. Devers left with the conviction that the VI Corps leader was "too tired" to continue under such intense pressure. The next day Wilson, Devers, Alexander, and Clark met to consider the desperate situation at Anzio where the most menacing attack yet by the Germans had just started. The group concurred on the relief of Lucas, with the VI Corps command going to Truscott, the dashing commander of the Third Division. Clark believed that Lucas "was ill—tired physically and mentally—from the long responsibilities of command in battle." He told Alexander, however, that until the current German attack was repulsed Truscott would serve as Lucas's deputy corps commander. Clark later commented, "All Truscott had to do was make sure he had a beachhead to command when the crisis was over."[7]

By February 22, after four days of savage fighting, the Germans were hurled back. That day Clark traveled to Anzio by PT-boat, found Lucas utterly exhausted, replaced him with Truscott, and sent the relieved general to Sorrento, a resort below Naples, for several weeks' rest before returning to the United States. Clark told him that he "could no longer resist the pressure . . . from Alexander and Devers" to remove him but felt Lucas had performed as well as could be expected under the conditions. Rather puzzled by the timing, Lucas wrote in his diary that his relief occurred just when "I thought I was winning something of a victory."[8] According to Truscott, Lucas "was bitter toward General Clark and blamed his relief upon British influence."[9] After the war Alexander, who had criticized him at the time for not quickly seizing the Alban Hills, reputedly remarked that he now believed Lucas "was right to wait and consolidate." Whether Lucas could have succeeded in taking the hills rapidly is moot, but, as an authority on the operation says, "for not having tried, Lucas could not altogether, nor would he ever, be forgiven."[10]

In mid-February, while the Allied advances were stalled

at Anzio and Cassino, Eisenhower formally established Supreme Headquarters, Allied Expeditionary Force (SHAEF), in London. Its two main functions were to revise and expand the cross-channel assault planning, begun two years earlier by General Morgan's staff, and to serve as the top command post when Operation Overlord got underway. Although the eventual strength of the American forces in Overlord was planned to be much greater than the British, his strong sense of Allied teamwork made Eisenhower amenable to including on the SHAEF staff approximately equal American and British representation. As in his North African and Mediterranean commands, however, he would work with British officers in the key positions of naval, air, and ground commanders in chief, at least during the initial phase of Overlord. The XXI Army Group would be commanded by Montgomery and would consist of the British Second Army, Canadian First Army, and, for a while, Bradley's U.S. First Army. When Eisenhower moved SHAEF to Normandy, he would become ground commander in chief as well as continuing as Overlord supreme commander. Bradley would then take over the new XII Army Group, which would include the First Army, now led by Lieutenant General Courtney H. Hodges, Bradley's former deputy, and Patton's Third Army, which would constitute the main American backup force for the Overlord invasion.

By December 1943, overseas deployments of American ground, sea, and air personnel, despite the Germany-first strategic commitment, were about equal in the war against Germany and the conflict with Japan: roughly 1.8 million American servicemen were engaged in each. The buildup and reinforcement of Overlord, however, would soon make a striking difference, most of the shipments of men and materiel from America between 1944 and 1945 earmarked for the fight against Germany. The Allied forces committed to Overlord, the majority of whom were American, would be staggering to contemplate, much less to command and control. A standard reference indicates the magnitude: "The total strength of the invasion forces gathered in England was

45 divisions, totaling with supporting units about 1 million men (two-thirds American). Almost another million comprised the tremendous logistical and administrative support forces which would sustain the combat units. The supporting naval and air elements totaled almost another million men."[11]

Eisenhower and Marshall would exchange many messages over selecting the top American ground commanders for Overlord. As early as December 1943, Marshall suggested to the new Overlord chief two combinations of generals to fill the key American Army posts in Overlord: Lesley McNair to head the army group and Bradley and Devers the two armies; or Devers to lead the army group and Bradley and Courtney Hodges to command the armies. He also proposed that if Truscott did not get a corps command in the invasion of South France, he should get one in Overlord. Interestingly, three generals who would lead American armies into Germany were omitted from Marshall's elite group of that period: William H. Simpson, Alexander Patch, and Patton. Also, Bradley, already Eisenhower's favorite, was not one of Marshall's two nominations to lead the American army group to be set up in Normandy. Never one to antagonize his superior and sponsor, Eisenhower fended off an immediate decision on Marshall's alternatives by reminding the Army chief of staff, "I am not as well acquainted with McNair, Devers and Hodges as you are."[12] The great acceleration of the American buildup in England meant a busy winter and spring for Eisenhower, Marshall, Arnold, and King, along with their personnel chiefs, in choosing commanders and units down to the division level or its equivalent. In view of the time pressures and the huge number of new forces arriving weekly in the British Isles, it is not unexpected that some of the command appointments proved unwise. It is surprising, however, that so many of the new air, ground, and sea commanders proved their worth later under combat circumstances that could not have been foreseen in early 1944.

While preparations for Overlord moved at a frantic pace, Eisenhower and the Joint Chiefs had to wrestle with a host of related strategic and logistical problems. One of the most annoying as far as relations with the British were concerned was Operation Anvil (renamed Dragoon shortly before the assault), which was the invasion of the Riviera region of South France. An early American-backed version of the Anvil plan called for the landings to occur at the same time as the Overlord forces assaulted Normandy. That proved impractical, mainly because of shortages of landing craft, transports, and ground-support aircraft. Churchill stubbornly opposed Anvil until five days before the operation began in mid-August 1944, the prime minister arguing that the forces could be better used in Italy or in an invasion of the Balkans. Roosevelt, the Joint Chiefs, and Eisenhower firmly stood their ground for Anvil, maintaining that, among other reasons, it would draw German divisions that might have reinforced the Normandy defenses, it would secure Marseilles as a major port that the Allies would sorely need, and it would cut off enemy units in Central France when the Anvil and Overlord pincers met.

Eisenhower keenly wanted Truscott as an Overlord corps commander, but the brilliant combat leader was kept with his VI Corps, which would spearhead the Riviera attack and the rapid drive up the Rhone Valley late that summer. It would be mid-June, however, before Truscott got his orders, so confused was the Anvil situation; he would be under Lieutenant General Alexander "Sandy" Patch, who had served in the Solomons and had succeeded Patton as commander of the Seventh Army. Both the invasions of Northwest Africa and South France were belatedly arranged operations because commanders in high places tried to delay final approval of the operation—the American chiefs in the case of Torch and Churchill and his chiefs in the Anvil case.

Because of Combined Chiefs' decisions at Cairo in early December, the American air command in the European war underwent a number of significant changes in January 1944. Spaatz, as earlier discussed, took command of the American strategic bombing program against Germany. He managed to get along with his RAF colleagues—Marshal Harris of the

RAF Bomber Command; Marshal of the RAF Charles Portal, chief of the British Air Staff; and Air Chief Marshal Arthur Tedder, Eisenhower's close friend and deputy supreme commander of Overlord. But all four of them, along with Ira Eaker, Jimmy Doolittle, and other American air commanders, clashed with Air Chief Marshal Trafford Leigh-Mallory, the unfortunate choice as air commander for Overlord. Personality differences, together with heated disagreements over target priorities and the proper use of strategic bombers, made for an exciting, tension-filled spring for the "air barons."

For American airmen in England one of the great upheavals of the pre-Overlord period was the news that the beloved Eaker, who had led the Eighth Air Force through its darkest days, was replaced by Doolittle just when the Eighth was beginning to get the sizable reinforcements and long-range fighter escorts Eaker had pleaded for earlier. At first Doolittle was frostily received by some of the Eighth's officers, but there was so much more action that spring and so many new officers in the expanding force that the ill feelings about the change of command subsided. Besides, Doolittle proved to be both colorful and competent, if still biased against the British. Joining the Eighth in Britain was Major General Lewis Brereton's Ninth Air Force, which he had led since June 1942 when it was the Middle East Air Force. Brereton's leadership of the Ninth as the main American tactical air arm in Britain would be generally competent, erasing the taint of his role in the Clark Field fiasco of December 1941.

Probably, in part, because his good friend Jake Devers became deputy supreme commander of the Mediterranean theater about the same time he took over the Mediterranean Allied Air Forces, Eaker found his change of command less disagreeable than he expected, though continuing to be angry with Arnold, whom he saw as the culprit in his transfer from England. Eaker would turn out to be quite able in his new command, though less in the focus of public attention. Assuming commands under him in January also were Major

Generals James K. Cannon and Nathan Twining, who headed the Twelfth and Fifteenth air forces, respectively. The Twelfth now was involved mainly in tactical operations supporting ground forces in Italy, while the Fifteenth flew strategic missions deep into Central Europe from its Italian bases.

Thanks to the efforts of both the American and British planes that challenged the vaunted Luftwaffe's fighters and devastated many of the factories producing the German Air Force's planes, Allied command of the skies was achieved over the Italian front and, in preparation for the Normandy assault, over most of France and the Lowlands by late spring of 1944. Though the outcome of the air war was no longer in serious doubt, the sobering experiences at Salerno, Cassino, and Anzio left American and British commanders extremely anxious about the fiery reception that Field Marshal Rommel and his German defenders along the north coast of France had concocted for the Allied invaders. Some of the more realistic Overlord leaders feared the Normandy operation would develop into "one terrible blood-letting," which is exactly how Rommel described it afterward.[13]

When the spotlight shifted to Northwest Europe with Operation Overlord, Generals Clark and Eaker saw their respective ground and air operations in Italy getting less and less front-page attention in Allied newspapers and—of more concern to them—decreasing priorities in allocations of men and materiel. Though each was controversial in his own way, Clark and Eaker had served well on the "first team" in the war so far and would continue to perform in vital, if less publicized, roles for the duration of the conflict.

A CONTROVERSIAL "AMERICAN EAGLE": CLARK

General Mark W. Clark had two unique, if dubious, achievements among the ground commanders featured in this book: he outlived the rest and his leadership in the war was the subject of congressional hearings. In 1946 the Military Affairs committees of the U.S. Senate and House held hearings on his commitment of the Thirty-sixth Infantry Division in the bloody, unsuccessful Rapido River attack of January 1944. Clark was strongly supported by the War Department, and the hearings were terminated short of a full-scale investigation because the facts did not justify it. But none of the other high commanders provoked such a hostile reaction among his men, the hearings resulting from a resolution of the Thirty-sixth Division Association that was endorsed by the Texas Senate.

His biographer maintains that, along with Eisenhower, Bradley, and Patton, "Clark is a member of the essential quartet of American leaders who achieved victory in Europe" (though Ike and Bradley would have added Spaatz). All four were "Marshall men," whom the Army chief of staff had known before the war and was "sure of their professional efficiency and personal integrity."[14] Clark established early career ties with three of these men so important to his future: he became acquainted with Eisenhower and Bradley when they were all cadets at West Point; he got to know Marshall when both were in France in 1918; and he became a close friend of Ike when they served together in the Third Infantry Division at Fort Lewis, Washington, in 1940. The brigade commander at nearby Vancouver Barracks earlier had been Marshall, whose duties often took him to Fort Lewis, while Clark frequently had to go to Vancouver Barracks. Later Clark observed that his association with Marshall on the eve of World War II "was one of the greatest breaks I ever had."[15]

Within a year after Marshall became the military head of the Army, Clark's fortune began to rise fast. In the late summer of 1940 he was promoted to lieutenant colonel, transferred to the Army General Headquarters in Washington, and shortly became operations officer under Major General Lesley McNair, the GHQ chief of staff. Soon to be reorganized, the GHQ agency was charged primarily with organizing and training troops for combat deployments. McNair and Marshall were impressed by Clark's sharpness and organizational skill, the Army chief of staff remarking that he "played a very determining part" in the GHQ program to expand the Army. Marshall added, "As a matter of fact, the method of raising these divisions, building them up, was largely worked out by General Clark."[16] Besides earning a reputation as one of the best training leaders in the Army, Clark also won praise from his superiors for his outstanding staff planning in the Louisiana maneuvers of 1941.

Major Ernest N. Harmon, later a distinguished armored leader in the war against Germany, worked with him in the 1941 maneuvers and described him as "bright, resourceful, and diplomatic." Harmon also thought he was "an extremely handsome soldier. He stood two or three inches above six feet; his Roman nose in a bony face had real distinction."[17] Not as flatteringly, Captain Harry C. Butcher, Eisenhower's naval aide of 1942–45, described him as "tall, lanky, and sharp-nosed," while Churchill thought he resembled "the American eagle."[18]

Marshall and McNair upset some officers in the War Department by the rapid manner in which they advanced Clark's career. In August 1941 he was promoted from lieutenant colonel to brigadier general, skipping the grade of colonel. The next spring he was elevated to two-star general and appointed chief of staff of the Army Ground Forces, whose commanding general was McNair. In the meantime, Clark had been assiduously promoting the career of his buddy Ike, successfully recommending him to Marshall as chief of staff of the Third Army in the summer of 1941, as head of the War Plans Division and then the Operations Division of the War Department in early 1942, and as commander of American Army forces in Britain that May. Acting as a sponsor for Eisenhower would turn out to be exceedingly beneficial to Clark's own interests.

In May 1942, as earlier related, Marshall sent Eisenhower, Clark, and other top officers to survey conditions in England preparatory to the American buildup there for a future invasion of Hitler's Europe. Upon returning to Washington, Eisenhower recommended to Marshall that General

Joseph McNarney be named to head the American Army in the European theater and that Clark be appointed leader of the first American corps to be sent to the United Kingdom. Marshall picked Eisenhower to head the new theater, as Clark had suggested, and he selected Clark to head the II Corps, the first such unit to be deployed to England. In late June, Eisenhower and Clark established their new headquarters in London. From the start Churchill was very amiable toward the pair and, in his words, was "impressed by these remarkable but hitherto unknown men," whom he "felt sure" that Roosevelt and Marshall "intended to play a great part" in future operations against the European Axis.[19]

On August 12, 1942, the Combined Chiefs formally appointed Eisenhower and Clark as commander in chief and deputy commander in chief of Operation Torch. Actually Ike had obtained the concurrence of the British Chiefs on Clark as his acting deputy and had been employing him as such for several days before he notified Marshall and sought the approval of the U.S. Joint Chiefs. By then Eisenhower was boosting Clark as zealously as his deputy had earlier done for him. He reported to Marshall, for instance, that since Clark had taken "direct charge of all TORCH planning, a tremendous upsurge in progress has been noticeable. He is on the ball every minute and his splendid organizational sense, his fine personality and his realism all combine to make him an officer who grows steadily in my esteem and admiration."[20] Clark had been scheduled to lead the II Corps in the Torch assault in early November, but Marshall replaced him with Lloyd Fredendall when Eisenhower convinced him that Clark was needed full-time as his deputy commander.

Two weeks after the Torch landings Clark, on behalf of Ike, signed an agreement with the pro-Vichy French Admiral Jean Darlan providing, among other terms, for French military cooperation in Northwest Africa in return for the admiral's elevation to chief of state in Algeria and French Morocco. "In both Britain and the United States a howl of indignation went up at the news of Allied dealings with that 'stinking skunk,' " writes a respected historian. "This 'shameless dickering' with a notorious Quisling was an out-rageous betrayal of Allied ideals," he continues, pointing out that the British House of Commons was considering a motion not to recognize Darlan until both Churchill and Roosevelt publicly defended the deal.[21] Marshall loyally sup-ported Eisenhower and Clark in their explanation that the arrangement was a political expediency that saved the lives of American and British soldiers, but the Army chief of staff's main biographer says the Darlan affair "left its mark" on Marshall also. "The outraged explosion of many segments of American and British public opinion" continued even after the admiral's assassination in late December.[22] Fortu-nately for Clark, his promotion to lieutenant general had been approved on Capitol Hill just before the Darlan ex-citement erupted. "If I had it to do over again," Clark later said, "I would choose again to deal with the man who could do the job—whether it turned out to be Darlan or the Devil himself."[23]

Not long after the Torch landings Eisenhower got Mar-shall to approve the establishment of the Fifth Army, which was to be located at first in French Morocco both for training purposes and to deter Axis subversion in Spanish Morocco, as well as to seize the latter territory "should Spain become less than neutral."[24] Clark was given a chance to command troops on the Tunisian front in December but turned it down to get the Fifth Army command, "for which he has begged and pleaded for a long time," commented Ike at the time. Marshall, persuaded by Eisenhower, appointed Clark as the new army commander. Ike's contention was based mainly on the grounds that "the job, for the moment, is one largely of organization and training and in these fields I think Clark has no superior."[25] No sooner had Clark set up his Fifth Army headquarters near Oran than the top Anglo-American leaders gathered at Casablanca and began discussing possible summer thrusts into Sicily and Italy. In February when the Combined Chiefs named Eisenhower to head the Sicilian operation, he, in turn, proposed and Marshall appointed Patton to lead the American force, later to be designated the Seventh Army. Clark shortly became quite anxious and began to pester Ike about his role in forthcoming plans.

Looking back in May 1944, Eisenhower wrote a diary memorandum that reflected a less complimentary image of Clark than he had formerly held:

> *In considering the months of fighting by the 5th Army [in Italy], I am reminded of the attitude of that Headquarters a year ago this spring, which illustrates not only the short-sightedness of the average human but the intense personal outlook that most officers have upon even such a critical thing as war. In January, '43, when we were considering the setting up of the 5th Army, General Clark was very anxious to have that command instead of his then title of Deputy Commander-in-Chief. He was warned that the 5th Army would be a training organization for some months and nothing else, while in his position of Deputy he would probably soon get a front-line command. In fact he was offered one, which was approximately a Corps in strength, but the title of Army Commander was too attractive. Within a month after taking command of the 5th Army he and some of his staff began to plague me as to their future. They became very fearful that the war in the Mediterranean would be won and they would never get into it, although I assured them that their troops sooner or later had to get into action. I showed them that such an outcome was inescapable. Nevertheless, they were most unhappy throughout the whole spring and I had to make special efforts to keep up their morale.*
>
> *In view of the fact that this Army has been in action continuously since last September 9th, I suppose these things are forgotten by them, but they are most revealing and somewhat amusing.*[26]

Eisenhower continued to be cordial and supportive toward Clark, but after the spring of 1943 they were no longer confidants. Undoubtedly another Fifth Army officer Ike had in mind was Major General Alfred M. Gruenther, Clark's talented and ambitious chief of staff, who would become supreme commander of NATO forces a decade hence.

The strategic decisions to invade Italy and to send in the U.S. Fifth Army through Salerno in September were made not by Clark, of course, but by his Allied superiors, with Eisenhower playing a crucial part. Neither could Clark be blamed for the inadequate logistics and fire support of the operation nor, as mentioned previously, did he name Dawley as the assault ground commander with any enthusiasm. Clark's subsequent relief of the VI Corps leader, particularly when considered in the light of the Fifth Army commander's previous orders to drop the Eighty-second Airborne Division into the small, embattled beachhead and his instructions to Admiral Hewitt to prepare for a possible sea evacuation of the hard-pressed corps, made him appear to critics as mercurial, shifting between confidence and desperation during the Salerno crisis. Several reputable military historians later judged Clark severely and somewhat unfairly, one of the chroniclers charging, for instance, that he used Dawley "as scapegoat for his own panic."[27] After the Salerno battle Eisenhower cautiously confided to Marshall that Clark "is not as good as Bradley in winning, almost without effort, the complete confidence of everybody around him, including his British associates. He is not the equal of Patton in his refusal to see anything but victory in any situation that arises; but he is carrying his full weight and, so far, has fully justified his selection for his present important post."[28]

After Salerno, Clark's advance toward Rome was slowed for ten days by German resistance along the Volturno River, twenty miles north of Naples. From November 1943 until the following May, however, the Fifth Army was stopped by Kesselring's Winter and Gustav lines in the Monte Cassino-Rapido Valley region. Extremely deferential toward the British high command when he had been Ike's deputy, Clark became convinced after the Salerno action that Alexander and Montgomery were conspiring against him, especially in downplaying his leadership and his army in press releases and communiqués. As his distrust of the British grew, he became obsessed with garnering the ultimate publicity coup of the Mediterranean war, the capture of Rome. When Eisenhower relinquished the Mediterranean command and moved to London in January 1944, the overall direction of Italian operations became a virtual British monopoly, with Wilson the theater chief, Alexander the army group commander, and Montgomery the head of the largest Allied army. More important, the British Chiefs henceforth served as executive agents for the Combined Chiefs of Staff in the Mediterranean war. Churchill thus gained the main responsibility for formulating strategy for that area and doggedly pushed through his risky plan for an amphibious assault at Anzio to break the bloody stalemate farther south. Like Salerno, Anzio was not conceived by Clark; indeed, he had opposed the attack for a time. "Political rather than military considerations dominated the decision" on Anzio, he argued.[29]

If Clark himself erred regarding the Anzio operation, it was primarily at the very beginning and at the end. The selection of Lucas was his, though in fairness to Clark, the VI Corps leader had not performed unsatisfactorily since succeeding Dawley at Salerno. Clark's relief of Lucas at Anzio was criticized by his fellow American officers not so much for unfairness but rather for the Fifth Army commander's seeming obeisance to Alexander in the matter.

When the breakout from the beachhead was finally achieved in May, Alexander ordered the VI Corps, now led by Truscott, to seize the Valmontone highway junction to the east, thus blocking the German Army's key escape route from the Gustav Line. Clark, however, ordered Truscott to push his main elements north toward Rome instead, leaving the Valmontone route open for the enemy withdrawal. As a prominent historian of the campaign observes, it seems that "emotion rather than military logic was the dominant force" in Clark's decision.[30] Truscott said that he protested to Clark "in the most vigorous terms possible" but to no avail.[31] According to Truscott's chief of staff, he and the rest of the VI Corps staff "felt the same" as Truscott that "this change of direction was a horrible mistake."[32] Clark did not inform Alexander until twenty-four hours after the corps had started northward. He won the race to the strategically valueless capital of Italy, but the episode hurt his relations with Wilson, Alexander, and Truscott, and it also resulted in the German Army's escape virtually intact to new positions north of Rome. Clark later admitted, "I was determined that the Fifth Army was going to capture Rome and I probably was overly sensitive to indications that practically everybody else was trying to get into the act."[33]

When his preassault worries became real crises in late January with the VI Corps' entrapment in its beachhead and the Fifth Army's inability to link up with the Anzio force, Clark ordered Major General Fred L. Walker's Thirty-sixth Infantry Division to mount an all-out effort to cross the Rapido River and penetrate the Germans' Winter Line. Fierce enemy resistance, along with mishaps and panic by the American soldiers, turned the attempted river crossing into a disaster that cost the division nearly 1,700 casualties. Afterward Clark remarked that the fiasco "was as much his fault as any one's because he knew how difficult the operation would be," according to Walker. Subsequently Walker grew increasingly bitter toward Clark, blaming the Rapido disaster on his stupidity, incompetence, impatience, and exaggerated ambition to capture Rome. After conducting his own careful study of the records in 1946, however, Secretary of War Robert P. Patterson concluded that the Rapido operation had been "a necessary one and that General Clark exercised sound judgment in planning it and in ordering it."[34] Walker and some of the officers of the National Guard division continued to believe that Clark escaped punishment because of his support by the "West Point Protective Association."[35] Major General Everett S. Hughes of SHAEF noted briefly in his diary in July 1945: "Clark still not liked by his men."[36]

The observation, of course, needed qualification, but, as evidenced in the efforts by some of his troops for a postwar congressional investigation of the Rapido incident, his reputation among a portion of the Fifth Army had been seriously tainted.

In early February 1944, Alexander formed a provisional corps of British, New Zealand, and Indian troops under Lieutenant General Bernard Freyberg, a strong-willed New Zealander. Freyberg's corps was sent to Clark's front to help overcome the powerful defenses around Cassino. Clark resented Alexander's granting the corps autonomy from Fifth Army control, and he also soon disliked Freyberg himself, writing in his diary that the New Zealand general "is sort of a bull in a china closet."[37] Deciding that Monte Cassino was the key to control of the area, Freyberg also concluded that the old Benedictine monastery was occupied by the Germans and should be bombed. Clark was skeptical, but Freyberg said he "had no doubt. It was a military necessity."[38] Clark discussed the matter with Alexander, who got Wilson's assurance that if Freyberg considered the air attack essential, it should be undertaken. Clark became "angry" when he was "obliged to accede to the wishes of a 'British' subordinate," Freyberg, states a British chronicler, but the Fifth Army commander had several objections, including no evidence that the Germans were in the abbey.[39] Devers, Wilson's deputy, thereupon flew with a reconnaissance mission over Monte Cassino and reported that the Germans were using the monastery to direct artillery fire. Finally Clark yielded and ordered the bombing.

On February 14, 1944, 255 Allied bombers, mostly B-17s, hit the monastery with nearly 600 tons of bombs. Observing from the valley, Clark said, "I had seen the famous old Abbey, with its priceless and irreplaceable works of art, only from a distance, but with the thundering salvos that tore apart the hillside that morning, I knew there was no possibility that I ever would see it at any closer range."[40] The Germans, who had never used the monastery, now turned the ruins into a strong position that prevented the Allied capture of Monte Cassino for another three months. Ironically, Clark, who raised the chief objections to the bombing, has been most often named in history books as the one responsible for the abbey's destruction.

Back in December, Clark had been instructed by Ike to begin the planning for Anvil, the southern France invasion to be staged that summer. The next month Clark was given command briefly of the Seventh Army while simultaneously retaining his Fifth Army command. It was expected that elements of the Seventh Army would spearhead the Riviera assault. Clark, like Churchill, however, was never enthusiastic about Anvil, foreseeing it as a drain on his resources in Italy. The unexpectedly long time consumed by his army in approaching Rome led Clark and his superiors to conclude in the spring of 1944 that he could best serve the Allied cause by staying with the Fifth Army, at least until the capture of the Italian capital. Patch was thereupon named to head the Seventh Army and the Riviera operation, later renamed Dragoon.

Alexander maintained that he had to prod the Fifth Army commander into replacing Lucas during the Anzio crisis, warning Clark, "You would certainly be relieved of your command" if the beachhead situation resulted in the Allied forces being "pushed back into the sea."[41] Harold Macmillan, British political officer with SHAEF and future prime minister, said the British high command in the Mediterranean seriously considered requesting the relief of Clark that March, mainly because of widespread criticism of his leadership and of his vexatious attitude in working with the British in Italy. His removal "was contemplated," Macmillan wrote in his diary, but "it was important that this should not appear to be British in inspiration," as Wilson explained the "extremely delicate" problem. Early in April, Macmillan's diary reveals the question of Clark's replacement was still a lively one with the British Chiefs, besides Alexander and Wilson, but the general agreement was that it must "be put forward by General Devers (the American Deputy Commander-in-Chief) to Washington" in order to "avoid the story getting around that this has been done in London."[42] Although Devers seems to have concurred privately, the British scheme to get rid of Clark was dropped partly because it was leaked to the Pentagon and because it did not get the support of Churchill, who steadfastly stood by Clark throughout the war. It is little wonder that General Joseph McNarney reported to Ike after a visit to Italy in October 1944 that Clark was still "very bitter against Alexander and Devers."[43]

Clark, who has been much assailed for his supposed publicity mongering in the race to Rome, probably had some knowledge that his British superiors desired his relief, and he may have exploited the capture of Rome to insure his own continuation in a combat command, having been shuffled out of roles in both Overlord and Anvil. Clark's "greatest disappointment of the war" came in the wake of his grand entry into Rome when he lost seven divisions that were transferred from his Fifth Army for operations in France.[44] To the chagrin of some senior British officers, it was the supreme Englishman, Churchill himself, who nominated Clark that November to succeed Alexander as commander of the XV Army Group in Italy. In mid-December, Clark replaced Alexander in that position, while Alexander, in turn, succeeded Wilson as Mediterranean theater chief and Truscott took charge of the Fifth Army. Four months later Clark was promoted to four-star general, and the next month at Florence he accepted the German surrender in Italy.

That July he became commander of American forces in Austria. Two years later he took command of the Sixth Army and in 1949 of the Army Field Forces. From May 1952 to October 1953, he headed the United Nations Command and the U.S. Far East Command; in July 1953 he signed the armistice ending the Korean War. He retired from the army that autumn, later serving as president of The Citadel.

It will be long debated whether Clark was one of the great captains. In ranking the top thirty-eight American Army officers in February 1945 in the war against Germany, Eisenhower listed Clark fifth (behind Bradley, Spaatz, Walter

Bedell Smith, and Patton) and noted that he was "clever, shrewd, capable" and a "splendid organizer."[45] Field Marshal Michael Carver, a veteran of the African and Italian campaigns who became chief of the British Defense Staff in the 1970s, maintains that "Clark's greatest contribution in the war was probably not his command in Italy . . . but his part in expanding the United States Army. . . . He was the acknowledged expert in training."[46] Harold Macmillan left perceptive views of Clark in his diary from wartime visits with him in Italy. In late 1943 he claimed that Clark "is far the most intelligent American soldier I know." In early 1945 Macmillan found that the general "is still vain, but conceals this weakness more skilfully than before. He is also very ambitious."[47] Among Clark's advocates, surely the most articulate is his biographer, who asserts that "whatever his failings, he towered above his generation and helped to shape the events of his time." As a commander, his success stemmed from four principal ingredients: "He was highly intelligent and quick. He had an awesome capacity for work. He prompted the best from his subordinates. He was a master of human relations."[48] The real measure of this complicated warrior probably lies somewhere between these differing estimates.

POINT MAN FOR ARNOLD
AND SPAATZ: EAKER

On the eve of America's plunge into the Second World War, Colonel Ira C. Eaker would have been named by many of his peers in the Army Air Forces as ranking with Hap Arnold, Tooey Spaatz, and Frank Andrews as the four officers most likely to be successful at the high-command level. Only Spaatz, however, made it through the war as a distinguished air leader without becoming a casualty of sorts: Andrews was killed, Arnold suffered four heart attacks, and Eaker lost his most coveted command and suffered damage to perhaps his most valued friendship.

The crux of Eaker's leadership problem from 1942 to 1945 was that he often was cast in the role of point man for Arnold or Spaatz or for both of these superiors, who were also his close friends. Figuratively, Eaker did go first in many instances and at various levels; more significantly, in the literal sense he frequently had to be the spokesman for Arnold or Spaatz, indeed, the on-the-spot symbol of American strategic air power. Point men tend to be viewed by users as useful but expendable; such would be the fate of Eaker.

In late 1917, Eaker joined the infantry but soon transferred to the Army Air Service, earning his pilot's wings in the autumn of 1918. He was awarded the Distinguished Flying Cross twice in the 1920s: for a flight around South America and for piloting Spaatz's plane that set a world endurance record aloft. In 1936, by then a major, he made the first instrument flight across the United States. Also by the 1930s he had become a prolific writer on air power, including three books that he coauthored with Arnold. Much of their writing collaboration occurred during 1936–40 when Eaker was executive officer (and Spaatz operations officer) on Arnold's staff. Arnold became assistant chief of the Army Air Corps in 1936 and chief two years later.

During the Battle of Britain in 1940, Arnold sent Spaatz and later Eaker as observers with the RAF—"a unique and remarkable experience," commented Eaker.[49] From late 1940 until early 1942, Eaker commanded pursuit and interceptor groups at fields in California and New York, except when Arnold dispatched him on a brief mission to England in September 1941. Promoted to colonel in late December, he enjoyed a fine reputation as a commander of fighter aircraft and envisioned his future overseas in that capacity. But mainly he just wanted to get a combat command: as he confided to a superior in early January 1942, "If I could write my own orders I would have gone to the fighting theatres before this."[50]

Eaker was astounded when Arnold called him into his office on January 18 and told him he was to head the VIII

Bomber Command, the first and basic component of the new Eighth Air Force that was to be established in the United Kingdom. According to Eaker, Arnold informed him, " 'You're going over to understudy the British and start our bombardment as soon as I can get you some planes and some crews.' And I said, 'Bombers, hell. I've been in fighters all my life.' He said, 'Yes, I know that. That's what we want, the fighter spirit in bombardment aviation.' "[51] A week hence, when Eaker was promoted to brigadier general, Arnold gave him his own insignia to wear and remarked: "They were my original stars as Brigadier General and perhaps they will bring you luck. . . . They certainly have put a lot more stars on my shoulders but that does not always mean luck."[52]

Eaker arrived in England in February to set up his headquarters, but for a long time he received few men or aircraft. He personally led the first American bombing mission over Europe, which could not be mounted until late summer and consisted of only one squadron of B-17s. Meanwhile, however, he and his outfit learned much from helpful RAF leaders. He particularly praised Portal, the RAF chief, who "cooperated in every conceivable way," said Eaker.[53] Portal had a high regard for Eaker, while Harris, who took charge of the RAF Bomber Command in early 1942, liked Eaker from the start, soon regarding him as a "close" and "firm" friend who developed a belief in strategic bombing as passionate as his own.[54] When Spaatz came to Britain in July to assume command of the Eighth Air Force, he was pleased with the solid advance work done by Eaker in preparing bases and training airmen, despite severe logistical handicaps, and in cultivating harmonious relations with the British high command. As a general officer of the Eighth Air Force recalled, one of Eaker's most valuable accomplishments in England "was his handling of the British and his acquaintance with British people in power."[55]

He and Spaatz worked well together in molding the fledgling Eighth Air Force that summer and fall. Spaatz often sent him as his representative to Anglo-American strategy sessions in London where Eaker became known for his fervent defense of daylight precision bombing. Spaatz also dispatched him to Washington to argue against diverting the Eighth's aircraft to support Torch. In August 1942, Spaatz recommended to Eisenhower the promotion of Eaker to major general; he told Arnold that "Eaker's ideas of operations, etc., exactly parallel mine" and that "his responsibilities demand that rank immediately," which was soon forthcoming.[56] In late November when Eisenhower ordered Spaatz to Algiers as his air deputy, Spaatz named Eaker as acting head of the Eighth Air Force. Both airmen saw the situation as temporary, as Eaker indicated to a friend in early December: "I was very happy in the Bomber Command and very loath to leave it. Naturally I am going to do the best I can here while Tooey is away."[57]

At Casablanca in January, the Combined Chiefs concurred on the directive for Pointblank, the Combined Bomber Offensive, with the Eighth primarily handling daytime pinpoint bombing and the RAF continuing its night saturation bombing. Eaker was summoned at a critical stage in the discussion and was instrumental in persuading the British Chiefs and Churchill to alter their former preference for night missions by the Eighth. Arnold and Spaatz were delighted by his effectiveness as point man at Casablanca. Several weeks later the formal separation of the U.S. Army and Army Air Forces commands in Britain and Northwest Africa took place with Eisenhower and Spaatz assuming their new African posts, previously mentioned, while Andrews and Eaker were approved by Marshall, on Arnold's strong recommendation, to succeed them as head of ETOUSA and the Eighth Air Force, respectively.

In objecting to the continuing priority on American aircraft for Northwest African operations rather than for Pointblank, Eaker soon found himself viewed as an antagonist by some at Eisenhower's headquarters. In April 1943, he was at odds also with Arnold and Spaatz over their belief that the B-17s had sufficient defenses to be able to bomb targets deep in Germany without incurring heavy losses from enemy fighters. Eaker argued that the focus must be on destroying

German fighters both in the air and in production, and he warned that "if the growth of the German fighter strength is not arrested quickly, it may become literally impossible to carry out the destruction planned" in Pointblank.[58] That summer and autumn he sent his heavy bombers in large raids against aircraft and ball-bearing factories, especially at Schweinfurt and Regensburg, but the Eighth's losses were enormous and the bombings set back German production only temporarily. As his casualties rose to shocking levels, Eaker received increasing pressure from Arnold for better, less costly results. The Eighth's commander, in turn, grew defensive, now maintaining that German aircraft production and current fighter strength could not be wiped out until he got adequate numbers of the new long-range P-51 fighters to escort his bombers. Unfortunately, the first P-51s did not go into action over Europe until early December, by which time Eaker's days in England were numbered.

As head of ETOUSA, Andrews had supported Eaker, and when Andrews was killed in May 1943, Jake Devers, his successor, stood by the embattled leader of the Eighth, the two becoming fast friends. But Arnold's faultfinding about the Eighth's performances, ranging from maintenance to tactics, began to consume his messages to Eaker, whom he thought should be tougher in dealing with his subordinates. At one point Eaker sent him a long, moving letter in which he pointed out: "I have always felt the closest bond of friendship between us. . . . I do not feel . . . that my past service . . . indicates that I am a horse which needs to be ridden with spurs."[59] The Air Forces chief responded, "Had I not had confidence in you . . . I would never have built you up for the job you now have. . . . I am very outspoken. I say what I think and do what I think best."[60] In his ensuing messages Arnold continued his scathing criticism of Eaker and the Eighth, their long friendship threatening to crack as the two air leaders became more exhausted by their awesome work loads and pressures.

During the latter half of 1943, Arnold received strongly favorable appraisals of Eaker from a number of impressive leaders, including Portal, Harris, Churchill, Andrews, Devers, Assistant Secretary of War (for Air) Robert Lovett, presidential envoy W. Averell Harriman, and two influential American senior airmen whose judgment Arnold usually esteemed, Major Generals Hugh J. Knerr and Follett Bradley. No evidence suggests that Eaker solicited recommendations from any of them. To cite the counsel of one of the franker individuals, Bradley visited the Eighth in the summer of 1943 and reported back to Arnold: "I think Ira is doing a superb job. He needs all the backing you and the weight of the War Department can give him. He has a tremendous job and is doing it well. He needs no needling." In fact, Bradley went so far as to tell Arnold that Eaker "should be given *three stars without delay.*"[61] Late that year Eaker was promoted, but Arnold, long known for his impatience and now afflicted by a serious heart condition, seemed more interested in finding another leader for the Eighth.

In the late autumn Arnold was in the Mideast for the high-level Allied conferences at Cairo and Teheran. In side meetings during those gatherings, as well as in sessions afterward in Tunisia and Sicily with Eisenhower and his senior airmen, Arnold was involved in reorganizing the Allied and American air commands in the war against Germany. Returning to Washington, he sent a cable on December 18 to Eaker, through Devers, informing him of changes that were expected to be finalized shortly: Eaker would succeed Tedder as head of the Mediterranean Allied Air Forces, Doolittle would lead the Eighth Air Force, Spaatz would command the new U.S. Strategic Air Forces in Europe, and Twining would replace Doolittle over the Fifteenth Air Force. Eaker and Devers protested the leadership change for the Eighth but in vain, and in early January 1944 the air generals assumed their new commands, Eaker moving to his new post in the Mediterranean.

Eaker always blamed Arnold for his "undoing" and, as a noted account says, "their relations would never be quite the same again—a casualty of the hard decisions of the war."[62] In his correspondence with Eaker later, Arnold also referred to it as his decision. But determining who actually instigated the proposal to remove Eaker from command of the Eighth is difficult. Arnold's principal biographer maintains that Eisenhower, not Arnold, made the decision. In his diary Spaatz stated that he recommended Eaker's transfer to Arnold. Ike said that Arnold and Spaatz recommended it to him. Marshall, who was quite displeased at first about the episode, criticized Spaatz and Tedder for being selfish in wanting Eaker out of England before their return, and the Army chief of staff closely questioned Ike about the matter. Marshall had left on a trip to the Pacific after the Second Cairo Conference in early December and may not have been updated about the developments as quickly and fully as he wished. The official Army Air Forces history states that on December 9 Spaatz suggested Eaker's transfer to Arnold after Arnold told Spaatz he was going to be transferred back to Britain shortly. Perhaps the most reliable of the Doolittle biographies attributes the proposal to Spaatz and Tedder. A recent, well-regarded study of the American air command indicates that Eisenhower certainly supported the decision to replace Eaker with Doolittle. No matter who first proposed it, by December 18 not only Arnold but also Eisenhower, Spaatz, and Tedder all favored the change of command, though probably for different reasons.[63]

When his feelings of hurt and anger had lessened, Eaker came to realize, asserts a respected air historian, that "the importance of his new command was indeed a larger responsibility and more important to the total war effort than he had imagined," even though he had been "shorn of the air force he had built from scratch and moved downward one rung on the ladder of strategic command."[64]

Eaker did not exactly fade away during the next fifteen months as head of Mediterranean Allied air operations. For one thing, he was fully challenged in overseeing the tactical, strategic, and service commands of his Royal Air Force units and the American Twelfth and Fifteenth air forces, as well as coordinating Pointblank planning with Spaatz's headquarters. His planes had to maintain aerial supremacy over the Italian front, support the invasion of southern France, protect Allied sea lines of supply in the Mediterranean, air-drop munitions and supplies to guerrillas in the Balkans, and maintain a heavy bombardment program against targets deep in Central and East Europe. Though not involved in the decision to bomb the Cassino monastery the month after he took over the Mediterranean air command, Eaker was charged with implementing the controversial bombing of the ancient abbey. In the summer of 1944 he personally led the first shuttle bombing mission by American bombers utilizing Soviet air bases in East Europe.

Eaker and Devers, the deputy supreme Allied commander of the Mediterranean theater during January–September 1944, "made a splendid team," observed Robert Lovett.[65] Both generals got along well with the senior British officers in Italy, Wilson and Alexander. The friendship between Eaker and Devers that had developed in London grew deeper in Italy; in fact, Eaker credited him with the "peaceful times" with Arnold that followed several letters by Devers to the Army Air Forces chief.[66] When Devers was given command of the new VI Army Group in September 1944 for the offensive from the Rhone Valley into South Germany, he strongly recommended Eaker as his replacement as Wilson's deputy—that post being reserved for an American officer by agreement of the British and American chiefs. Marshall, however, insisted on Joseph McNarney, believing he would be less likely than Eaker to be influenced by the British. Earlier the American Army chief of staff had not been pleased when Eaker, Devers, and Clark all agreed with Churchill, Brooke, Wilson, and Alexander that Anvil should be dropped in favor of a trans-Adriatic amphibious assault along the Balkan coast. Marshall had chided Eaker then: "You've been too damned long with the British."[67] It must have been difficult at times for Eaker to figure out the different shades of meaning that Marshall and Eisenhower used in calling for Anglo-American teamwork.

In March 1945 Eaker received another jolt when Arnold, now slowed by multiple heart attacks, ordered him back to

Washington as deputy commanding general of the Army Air Forces, succeeding Lieutenant General Barney M. Giles, who was going to a choice job in the Pacific war. Eaker was quite angry about leaving his command; Arnold had to remind him that no good officer wanted Washington duty at such a time but it was an order. In June 1945, after Eaker had been back in Washington for several months and the war against Germany had ended, Arnold, then briefly in California, wrote him expressing insight into the great worth of Eaker to him and to the Allied air war against Germany:

I realize fully the disappointment which you felt when, due to my illness, you received the call to return from your post in the combat zone to this Headquarters. At the time when our forces in Europe were on the threshold of victory, you were forced to lay down command of the great Allied Air Forces in the Mediterranean Theater and your long and important relationship with all the Air Forces in Europe, to the development of which you made so tremendous a contribution. This to undertake a position in the War Department in Washington—which as we both know is never sought by any airman or soldier of your war experience—a call made necessary by my own absence. As a result, you were unable personally to direct and witness the end-product of the effort, the skill and the courage which you brought to the war effort in the past three years.

You have played a major role in the development and employment of the air power which brought our European enemies successively to their knees. Your sure tact and inspiring understanding of people have played an outstanding part in the welding of our effort as one with that of our Allies.

Conscious as I am of these things, I want to express to you my sincere appreciation of what you have done and are doing and my recognition of the sacrifice of

your own personal desires which accompanied your
assumption of burdens which I was forced temporarily
to lay aside.[68]

Eaker received many decorations and citations for his peace-time and wartime contributions to aviation, but this letter from his World War II commander, who had been one of his oldest friends, was precious to him because of the eighteen-month estrangement between the two. Though they were not able to resume as confidants, Eaker did remain as his deputy until Arnold retired in early 1946, and he continued in the post during the first part of Spaatz's tenure as commanding general of the Army Air Forces. Eaker retired as an officer in 1947 but continued to be active in aviation as an aircraft corporation executive, lecturer, and writer for over two more decades. "In war as in peace," one air historian rightly says of Eaker, "he was one of the few great captains of U.S. air power."[69]

SEVEN

MOUNTING THE DUAL ADVANCE TOWARD TOKYO

MIDWAR LEADERSHIP
(PACIFIC, MAY 1943–JUNE 1944)

Flaws in the American high command's conduct of the war in the Pacific did not prove as costly as they might have against Germany. This was because Japan was a less potent adversary and her farflung pelagic defense perimeter was beyond her means to guard at all points. At its zenith in early 1942 the Japanese Empire had a maximum width of 6,400 miles, while its northern and southern bounds were 5,300 miles apart. The American interservice rivalries in the Pacific and the cumbersome control system devised by the Joint Chiefs for that region, as earlier discussed, led to innumerable difficulties but none that seriously jeopardized the offensives of MacArthur, Halsey, and Nimitz. Likewise, the Joint Chiefs and their Pacific theater leaders were able to maintain the offensive momentum after Midway in spite of their failures to adhere to several traditionally cherished principles of successful warfare, especially the principle of mass, or concentration of force at decisive points; the principle of economy of force, or exertion of lesser effort against secondary objectives; and the principle of unity of command, or unified control of all planning and operations.

MacArthur believed that violation of this last principle of war had serious consequences, as he declared in his memoirs: "Of all the faulty decisions of the war perhaps the most unexplainable one was the failure to unify the command in the Pacific. . . . It resulted in divided effort, the waste of diffusion and duplication of force, and the consequent extension of the war with added casualties and cost."[1] But he did not mention that he wanted unity of command only if he were named the supreme commander or that the admirals had some justification for their opposition to placing the Pacific Fleet under him and his Army-dominated headquarters. Most students of the Pacific war probably would agree with Nimitz's assertion that the operations of his and MacArthur's forces, particularly between fall 1943 and summer 1944, demonstrated that the existing command setup had some genuine assets. Nimitz maintained, "The two Allied forces advancing across the Pacific operated as a team, each relieving the other of a portion of its burden. . . . Had there not been a Central Pacific drive to attract and hold Japanese forces elsewhere, the Southwest Pacific forces would have met far greater resistance in the New Guinea area."[2]

During the final two years of the war with Japan, in addition to the above considerations, the Americans could afford some defects in their strategic plans, interservice relations, and command arrangements because they possessed a vast and ever-growing superiority over the Japanese in virtually every category of mobility, firepower, and logistics. The most awesome display of these advantages was the powerful Fast Carrier Force of the Pacific Fleet, led by Admiral Marc A. Mitscher and alternately by Vice Admiral John S. McCain, which could roam the West Pacific for months at a time because of its efficient at-sea resupply system and could devastate land, sea, and air targets with its force of nearly 1,000 carrier planes. Another enormous edge held by the Americans was their penetration of enemy radio intelligence through the Magic and Ultra systems of intercepting and decrypting message traffic that provided American commanders with invaluable data on Japanese plans, movements, and force strengths. Also, by early 1944 American submarines were beginning to take a heavy toll of Japanese naval and merchant ships that would eventually paralyze the enemy's maritime defense system and the main lines of communication between Japan and her bases in the Pacific and on the Asian mainland.

As vital as their activities were to the ultimate defeat of Japan, however, the American officers who led the carrier, intelligence, and submarine elements in the Pacific conflict seldom had much input into strategic decision making or attained four-star rank. None was seriously considered in the Pentagon for higher responsibilities during the war, partly because such officers' specialties seemed to preclude the broadness and versatility expected of the elite of the high command, because of adverse personality traits in some cases, or because of bias among their superiors against the branches in which they excelled. The closest to gaining influential voices in top-echelon theater matters were Vice Admiral Charles A. Lockwood, head of the Pacific submarines; Rear Admiral Edwin T. Layton, intelligence chief of the Pacific Fleet; and Major General Charles A. Willoughby, MacArthur's top intelligence officer. Sometimes brilliant officers on the rise were blocked by the pettiness or jealousy of their superiors, as was the case of Commander Joseph J. Rochefort, one of Nimitz's foremost cryptographic experts and a key figure in the Midway planning. Admiral Ernest King and leaders of the naval intelligence bureaucracy in Washington not only refused to reward Rochefort for his ingenious achievements in radio intelligence but also ousted him from his unit command on Oahu when his findings proved contradictory to and more accurate than theirs on enemy attack plans. Layton remarked of his friend, "Rochefort was speared like a frog and hung out to dry for the rest of the war."[3]

The types of officers who were kept out of the top levels of the American command system also included the men who emerged as the wartime masters of amphibious warfare, which may have been the most unique contribution in the Pacific war to the evolution of military strategy and tactics.

Thanks to the farsighted research of Marine officers in the 1930s on the intricacies of amphibious fighting, a valuable body of data regarding its principles, techniques, and specialized weapons and equipment was available to American commanders early in the Pacific struggle. Of course, implementation of amphibious doctrine was a different matter, as the Tarawa assault showed in November 1943. But by the following summer Nimitz's forces in the Marshalls and Marianas, as well as those of MacArthur in New Guinea and the Admiralties, were exhibiting maturity and sophistication in amphibious operations. Admirals Kelly Turner in the Central Pacific, Theodore Wilkinson in the South Pacific, and Daniel Barbey in the Southwest Pacific, together with Army General Walter Krueger in MacArthur's theater and Marine Generals Roy Geiger in the South Pacific and Holland Smith and Harry Schmidt in the Central Pacific, became well-nigh indispensable leaders in the island operations of 1943–45 because of their understanding and skill in conducting amphibious assaults.

In Operation Cartwheel, starting in the early summer of 1943, offensive operations by MacArthur's forces along the northern coast of New Guinea were coordinated with advances by Halsey's troops in the Solomons. The two drives were intended to move northward along the lines of an inverted "V," converging finally for a joint assault on Rabaul, the great Japanese stronghold on eastern New Britain. According to the Joint Chiefs' directive, MacArthur would have strategic control of Halsey's forces until the capture of Rabaul, though the South Pacific commander would retain tactical command of operations on the Solomons' side of the combat area. Meanwhile, Blamey's Australian ground units were relegated by MacArthur to largely overland advances in the conquest of the rugged region of the Huon Peninsula in Northeast New Guinea, a prewar territory administered by Australia. By the end of 1943, MacArthur's American and Australian troops had seized the west and north coasts of the Huon Gulf and had established beachheads on the west end of New Britain. Between June and December of that year Halsey's American Army and Marine units captured New Georgia and several less strongly defended islands in the Central Solomons and gained a firm foothold on Bougainville in the North Solomons. During the first five months of 1944, after the Joint Chiefs had ordered him to bypass Rabaul, MacArthur isolated that enemy bastion with a bold move into the Admiralty Islands, north of New Britain, and then sent Krueger's Sixth Army in a leap of nearly 600 miles up the New Guinea coast to the Hollandia-Aitape area, bypassing several large enemy troop concentrations. The encirclement and isolation of Rabaul was completed that spring with Halsey's seizure of Emirau, east of the Admiralties.

MacArthur and Halsey worked extremely well together during Cartwheel, and their complex, coordinated amphibious assaults pushed the Japanese defense perimeter northward much faster than their earlier plodding campaigns in Papua and Guadalcanal. Since June 1943 their operations "had clicked off with speed and precision," states the official Army chronicle. Regarding MacArthur and Halsey, that history says that a number of Southwest and South Pacific officers "stood out prominently and later won great fame and rose to higher posts," but the two "dominated and controlled the campaigns." Although "they worked differently," MacArthur and Halsey "exhibited exceptional leadership and judgment," and "with an easy, cordial relationship, they cooperated and assisted each other."[4]

In late December 1943 Blamey informed his Australian commanders in Northeast New Guinea that MacArthur, whose growing American Army units in the Southwest Pacific forward areas would shortly outnumber the Australian forces, had decided to limit Blamey's New Guinea Force to holding operations and garrison duties in rear areas after Cartwheel. In their last large-scale offensive in New Guinea, the Australians captured the enemy stronghold of Madang, northwest of the Huon Peninsula, in late April 1944. Shortly after, MacArthur would anger the Australian high command by assigning elements of the Australian First Army to eliminate bypassed Japanese outfits in New Guinea, New Britain, and

Bougainville. Henceforth the spearhead of the Southwest Pacific theater's ground advance would be Walter Krueger's Sixth Army, while Robert Eichelberger's Eighth Army, to be formed as the second American army in that theater in the summer of 1944, would serve as the principal backup and mopping-up force in MacArthur's offensives above the equator. By then the Southwest Pacific chief also had found the naval leaders he wanted: Thomas Kinkaid to lead the Seventh Fleet and Daniel Barbey to head the VII Amphibious Force. And MacArthur now had an air leader he would not trade for any other: George Kenney, the SWPA Allied Air Forces chief, whom he assigned that summer as commander also of the U.S. Far East Air Forces, which consisted mainly of the Fifth and Thirteenth Air Forces.

Besides the phasing out of the Australians in the operations north of New Guinea, another redeployment of forces was set in motion in the late spring of 1944 when Halsey's South Pacific Area was gradually downgraded from a combat zone to a rear-area base command. The Joint Chiefs issued a directive that March calling for the transfer of South Pacific men and materiel that could be used in operations elsewhere to be completed by August. The reassignments by the Joint Chiefs included giving Halsey's six Army divisions and the Thirteenth Air Force (led by Nathan Twining to late 1943 and henceforth by Major Generals Hubert R. Harmon and St. Clair Streett) to the Southwest Pacific theater, while assigning most of Halsey's Navy and Marine sea, ground, and air units to Nimitz's theater. In the process of dissolving the South Pacific Area a number of gifted combat leaders were transferred to other war zones. In fact, ever since its creation the South Pacific had a constant flow of capable officers who, upon excelling there, were sent elsewhere, the outstanding ones including Generals Alexander Patch, Twining, and Lawton Collins, who joined the war against Germany; Lieutenant General Oscar W. Griswold, the XIV Corps commander, whom MacArthur was pleased to get; General Archer Vandegrift, who became the Marine Corps commandant; and Generals Roy Geiger and Millard Harmon, along with

Admirals John McCain, Theodore Wilkinson, Forrest P. Sherman, A. Stanton "Tip" Merrill, and Frederick Sherman, who earned further distinction in operations later in Nimitz's theater. The South Pacific chief himself, Halsey, was given command of the Third Fleet, as the Pacific Fleet's main Central Pacific force was called on alternate cruises. The same force was designated Fifth Fleet and headed by Ray Spruance on every other cruise, each of which lasted several months. Halsey's first turn in the command slot would be from August 1944 to January 1945.

Not unexpectedly, differences and misunderstandings arose between MacArthur's and Nimitz's headquarters during the reallocation of the South Pacific's resources. The two theater commanders also collided over control of the huge naval installation planned for Manus Island in the Admiralties where Seeadler Harbor was located, one of the finest and largest anchorages in the Pacific. Nimitz wanted it for the Pacific Fleet's future Central Pacific operations and stagings, while MacArthur claimed jurisdiction since it was situated in his theater. The general insisted that it was needed for the use of his Seventh Fleet and of Australian and British naval units that would be supporting his upcoming offensives. Halsey took on the mission of going to Southwest Pacific head-quarters at Brisbane to try to convince MacArthur that all American naval forces should have access freely to the Manus base and harbor. Halsey said of their Brisbane session, "MacArthur lumped me, Nimitz, King, and the whole Navy in a vicious conspiracy to pare away his authority." He observed during MacArthur's argument that "unlike myself, strong emotion did not make him profane. He did not need to be; profanity would have merely discolored his eloquence."[5] Somehow Halsey managed to persuade the upset general and without harming the warm friendship between the two strong-willed commanders.

There was no likelihood that Nimitz and MacArthur would develop the camaraderie of the Halsey-MacArthur relationship, but the POA and SWPA theater commanders had more respect for each other than most accounts have indicated.

Their first personal meeting did not occur until March 1944 in Brisbane, and in view of earlier differences their two-day conference went well until they turned to future strategic moves against Japan. Nimitz reported to King:

> He [MacArthur] seemed pleased to have the JCS directive covering the entire calendar year of 1944 because it definitely provided for his entry into the Philippines via Mindanao—a plan which is very dear to his heart. His cordiality and courtesy to me and my party throughout my visit was complete and genuine and left nothing that could be desired. Everything was lovely and harmonious until the last day of our conference when I called attention to the last part of the JCS directive which required him and me to prepare alternate plans for moving faster and along shorter routes towards the Luzon-Formosa-China triangle if deteriorating Japanese strength permitted. Then he blew up and made an oration of some length on the impossibility of bypassing the Philippines—his sacred obligations there—redemption of the 17 million people—blood on his soul—deserted by [the] American people—etc., etc.—and then a criticism of "those gentlemen in Washington who—far from the scene and having never heard the whistle of bullets, etc.—endeavor to set the strategy of the Pacific War"—etc. When I could break in—I replied that—while I believed I understood his point of view—I could not go along with him—and then—believe it or not—I launched forth in a defense of "those gentlemen in Washington" and told him that the JCS were people like him and myself—who with more information were trying to do their best for the country—and to my mind—were succeeding admirably.[6]

According to the notes of a King-Nimitz conference in early May, Nimitz averred that his "relations [are] excellent with

CINCSWPA [MacArthur]."[7] But their accord would be sorely tried in the months ahead, for a lengthy debate involving the JCS and the leaders in Brisbane and Pearl Harbor was just beginning on the merits of the top Pacific priority in the future being a thrust by Nimitz's forces into Formosa, as advocated by King, who also wanted to bypass all the Philippines, or an invasion of Luzon by Southwest Pacific forces, as MacArthur favored. In the strategic arguments Nimitz sometimes was caught in the middle because on several points he agreed with MacArthur, much to the consternation of King.

The second major axis of advance toward Japan had been opened in the Central Pacific Area in the autumn of 1943 with the invasion of the Gilberts by Marine and Army forces, backed by the fire support of Admiral Raymond Spruance's Fifth Fleet, which actually comprised the bulk of the Pacific Fleet's combat ships at the time. In what Vandegrift called "the first example in history of a sea-borne assault against a heavily defended coral atoll," American Marines paid heavily in casualties in taking Tarawa, the main battle scene of the Gilberts campaign.[8] But invaluable lessons were learned there about weapons, tactics, and fire support in amphibious warfare. Robert Sherrod, a combat correspondent present during the savage Tarawa battle, was impressed during the aftermath that the Navy and Marines' "capacity to learn, after two years of war, had improved beyond measure" and that they were "learning how to learn faster."[9] Like Rabaul, the Japanese bastion of Truk in the Carolines was neutralized and bypassed on orders from the Joint Chiefs of Staff. Instead, Nimitz sent Spruance and his Central Pacific forces to invade the Marshalls. There the enemy defenses on Kwajalein atoll slowed the soldiers and Marines, but overall the Americans' performance in securing the Marshalls was far superior to their record in the Gilberts. The official Marine account states, "Seizure of the Marshalls represented the coming of age of U.S. amphibious power."[10] The timing of this maturation was critical because that summer Nimitz's amphibious forces would be required to strike their most strategically decisive blow yet: invading the Marianas, which lay within B-29 bombing range of the Japanese home islands.

During the period from June 1943 to May 1944, the multifaceted American assaults against and penetrations of the Japanese perimeter in the Pacific were already utilizing strategies and weapons systems that General Hideki Tojo, Japanese prime minister of 1941–44, later said were "the three principal factors that defeated Japan," namely, the bypassing and neutralizing of Japanese strongholds, the enormous loss of Japanese shipping to submarine attacks, and the fast carriers' potency and staying power at sea far from their bases.[11] He might have added that the top-echelon leadership groups that MacArthur and Nimitz pulled together for their respective theater operations also contributed importantly to the Allied victory in the Pacific. On the other hand, by the midwar stage Japan had lost in action several of her finest senior commanders, including Admiral Isoroku Yamamoto, who was her greatest strategist and headed the Combined Fleet.

Fortunately Nimitz had found a four-man team of senior leaders who had shown brightly in the conquest of the Marshalls and elsewhere in Central Pacific actions by late spring of 1944 and upon whom he could rely to lead larger operations in the future: Ray Spruance, Kelly Turner, Holland Smith, and Pete Mitscher, each of whom received an additional star after the Marshalls campaign and, more important, the assurance that he would have a vital role in the Marianas operations. Nimitz had been convinced for some time regarding the command abilities of Spruance, Turner, and Smith, though the latter two could be difficult to control. Now, following Mitscher's superb handling of the Fast Carrier Force in support of the Marshalls assaults and in raids on Truk and other enemy islands, the POA theater chief was pleased with his fourth and newest addition to the nucleus of Central Pacific field commanders. Nimitz later commented, "Marc Mitscher, soft-spoken, often reticent, had little of the colorful command personality of Smith or Turner and few pretensions to the intellectual eminence of Spruance, but 30 years of intense devotion to naval aviation had fitted him uniquely to command the Navy's roving air bases of World War II."[12]

Arriving at Pearl Harbor in June 1944 from twenty months in the South Pacific, Halsey had long enjoyed Nimitz's friendship and trust. At first, however, some officers of the inner circle at POA headquarters were reluctant to accord Halsey and his lieutenants who were also ordered to Central Pacific commands the esteem given to Spruance and his main subordinates. Of the many command changes that took place in the Pacific in the late spring and summer of 1944, the most noteworthy were the shift of Halsey from heading the South Pacific Area to leading the Third Fleet and the promotion of George Kenney to command of the Far East Air Forces. Both men were charismatic, colorful, and aggressive warriors. Indeed, if the POA and SWPA theaters had candidates that could rival Patton as the American commander of large field forces in World War II who was the boldest and most forceful in leadership style, they were surely Bill Halsey and George Kenney.

THE IMPULSIVE, SWASHBUCKLING "SAILOR'S ADMIRAL": HALSEY

Headquarters of the South Pacific Area, Noumea, New Caledonia. Several months after Guadalcanal was secured, some naval veterans of that long, desperate struggle were recalling the impact on morale of the news in October 1942 that Vice Admiral William F. "Bull" Halsey had assumed command of the beleaguered American forces in the South Pacific. A young officer commented: "One minute we were too limp to crawl out of our foxholes. The next, we were running around, waving the dispatch and whooping like kids." Two Marines were soon "working up to a brawl. One of 'em was arguing that getting the Old Man was like getting three carriers and two battleships, and the other was swearing that he was worth three carriers and three battleships."[13] General Gerald C. Thomas, who had been a Marine colonel in the Guadalcanal battles, later confirmed that when his men learned that Halsey had taken charge, "it gave everybody a lift" to be under such "a down-to-earth fighting man."[14] Halsey's reputation up to that point may have been a bit overblown by the press, but he would not disappoint the hero-hungry American public nor the servicemen whom he led to subsequent victories. While some naval colleagues criticized his playing hunches and charging too audaciously in combat situations, Nimitz caught the essence of Halsey's heroic image when he succinctly described him as "a sailor's admiral."[15]

The nickname "Bull," which Bill Halsey never liked, was given to him when he was a hard-driving fullback on the Naval Academy's football teams of 1902 and 1903. It was revived by correspondents in early 1942 when he led his task force in bold raids in the West Pacific. Graduating at Annapolis in 1904 (thirty-one years after his father, a captain in the Navy), Halsey rose steadily in rank and responsibilities, proving particularly skilled in torpedo craft and destroyers. He earned the Navy Cross as a destroyer commander in World War I. A captain by 1933 with a fine record as a destroyer leader, he was chosen to attend the Army War College, having earlier graduated from the Naval War College.

Toward the end of his course at the Army War College, Halsey was offered an unusual proposition by Admiral Ernest King, who was chief of the Bureau of Aeronautics and interested in attracting capable senior officers to naval aviation. Knowing that Halsey had been interested in flying for at least seven years and had been rejected for pilot training in 1930 because of poor eyesight, King told him that he could have command of the aircraft carrier *Saratoga* if he completed the aviation observer program at the Pensacola Naval Air Station. Halsey happily agreed, but after taking the observer courses, which were in the ground-school curriculum, he somehow obtained a waiver from the Bureau of Aeronautics that allowed him to enter flight training at Pensacola.

In the spring of 1935, at the age of fifty-two, he qualified as a pilot and was awarded the coveted Navy wings insignia. Though ultimately logging over 1,500 flying hours, Halsey never attained a high degree of skill as a pilot. His Pensacola instructor, who served as his assistant operations officer in the South Pacific, recalled that student Halsey's flying in 1935 had been unique: "The worse the weather, the better he flew."[16] (Latecomers to naval aviation like Halsey and Slew McCain were regarded privately by career naval airmen as "synthetics" and never gained the esteem that veteran flyers like Pete Mitscher and Jack Towers enjoyed.)

As King pledged, Halsey was given command of the *Saratoga*, which he handled better than some air officers expected. He then proved to be an energetic and able administrator, if not one who always went by the book, in heading the Pensacola Naval Air Station from 1937–1938, earning a promotion to rear admiral. During the next two years he commanded a two-carrier division in the Atlantic. After briefly leading a carrier division in the Pacific, he was promoted to vice admiral and given command of Aircraft Battle Force in the spring of 1940, which put him over all the carriers of the Pacific Fleet. To his delight, Admiral Husband Kimmel, one of his closest friends from the Annapolis class of 1904, became commander in chief of the United States Fleet and Pacific Fleet in February 1941. The two old comrades enjoyed some happy moments together at Pearl Harbor during the ten months before the Japanese attack that doomed Kimmel's career.

During the autumn of 1941, Halsey was in command of a small task force centered on his flagship, the carrier *Enterprise*. When the Japanese struck Pearl Harbor, Halsey's task force was returning from Wake where some Marine fighter aircraft had been delivered. Scrappy and excited, he set out on December 9 to engage the Japanese fleet, but, fortunately for his inferior force, no contact was made. According to a noted naval historian, Halsey "had been slated for relief when the war started" but was retained, in part, because of his "reputation as a slugger and inspiring leader."[17]

As soon as Nimitz took over the Pacific Fleet at the end of the year, planning got underway for retaliatory strikes by several task forces against Japanese-held islands in the Central Pacific. From late January to early March of 1942, Halsey led a task force consisting of the carriers *Enterprise* and *Yorktown,* five cruisers, and ten destroyers in a series of wide-ranging raids against enemy bases in the Marshalls and Gilberts and the isolated islands of Wake and Marcus. The damage wrought by his ships and planes in these attacks was much less than early reports suggested, but the press further inflated the destructiveness of the raids and the public hailed Halsey as the first American naval hero of the war. He won more acclaim as the commander of the two-carrier task force that launched Doolittle's fabled B-25 bombing attack on Tokyo in April. Returning to Pearl Harbor, Halsey's Task Force 16 was then sent to the South Pacific to assist Admiral Frank Jack Fletcher's force in engaging an enemy fleet west of the Solomons, but Halsey's ships were still over 100 miles away when the Battle of the Coral Sea was fought in early May. A few days later Nimitz notified him to bring his force back to Oahu, the urgent tone of the message indicating to Halsey that a new confrontation with the Japanese Navy was nearing.

When he reached Pearl Harbor on May 26, an excited Halsey, knowing he was the senior admiral available, expected to lead the fleet against what radio intelligence revealed to be the bulk of Admiral Yamamoto's Combined Fleet. Instead, Halsey was ordered to the naval hospital at Pearl, and Fletcher became the senior naval leader for the impending battle of Midway. For two months Halsey had been suffering from a worsening case of dermatitis and ulcerated gums that caused much pain, extreme irritability, insomnia, and a twenty-pound weight loss. He speculated that "possibly the combination of nervous tension and tropical sun was to blame, since I had been on the bridge for six straight months." He recommended and Nimitz appointed Admiral Spruance, Halsey's cruiser division commander, to lead Task Force 16 in the coming battle. "The most grievous disappointment in my career," Halsey said in his autobiography, was missing the great engagement against Yamamoto's fleet in early June.[18] "When illness prevented Halsey from putting the capstone on his fame by commanding in the Battle of Midway, his determination to spectacularly sink the enemy was only increased," asserts his foremost biographer.[19]

For over three months Halsey was more out of the Pacific picture than he had expected: he was sent to a noted dermatologist in Virginia after the Navy doctors on Oahu could not cure him. When he was healthy again and back at Pearl Harbor, Nimitz named him temporary head of the Pacific Fleet's land-based aviation. After the Midway triumph Ray Spruance had become Nimitz's chief of staff and Thomas Kinkaid had taken command of Task Force 16. Nimitz promised Halsey that he would get back his old task force command as soon as the *Enterprise,* then in drydock for battle repairs, was ready again. Halsey was ecstatic about the chance for sea action, of course, and he was joyous also about finding his son at Pearl Harbor, an ensign assigned to the drydocked *Saratoga.* The press reports about his return and the thunderous cheers from the *Saratoga*'s crew when he visited the carrier pleased him, too, for obviously his absence had not cost him his reputation, which he now deeply cherished, as a fighting sea dog.

In the meantime the Guadalcanal operation was becoming critical, and in late September Nimitz and some of his staff flew to the South Pacific to investigate. At Noumea, Nimitz found Admiral Robert Ghormley and his officers of the South Pacific headquarters infected by defeatism, but when he flew on to Guadalcanal, over 800 miles to the north, the POA chief discovered that Vandegrift and his battling Marines were confident. Upon his return to Pearl Harbor, Nimitz decided to send Halsey, Spruance, and several other officers to the South Pacific to inspect bases and to study varied problems of that subtheater. They departed aboard a four-engine seaplane on October 14.

The following evening, while the Halsey party was stopping overnight at Canton Island, Nimitz called a meeting of staff officers at POA headquarters, largely made up of the men who had gone with him to the South Pacific recently. He candidly asked for their opinions about relieving Ghormley and about possible successors. All of them favored a change of command because a leader tougher and more inspiring than Ghormley was needed to gain victory in the Guadalcanal campaign. Kelly Turner was briefly discussed as a possible replacement, but he had clashed bitterly with the Marine leaders of the island battle. According to a reliable account, the staff conferees on October 15 generally believed that Halsey "filled the bill" but in a qualified sense: "He had the required rank and firmness and was moreover a popular leader, but he was especially needed as a carrier force commander. Besides he had had little experience as an administrator and was believed not to be at his best behind a desk."[20] Nimitz thanked his staff for their counsel and dismissed them without indicating his own position.

Early the next morning he sent a radio message to King requesting permission to replace Ghormley with Halsey; he received a quick favorable response from his superior, who previously had been crucial in advancing Halsey. Nimitz then notified Ghormley that Halsey would relieve him as commander of the South Pacific Area and South Pacific Force upon his arrival shortly at Noumea. Nimitz's sealed dispatch to Halsey was handed to him by one of Ghormley's officers as he left the seaplane on October 18 in Noumea harbor and stepped into a whaleboat to go to Ghormley's flagship nearby. Halsey twice read the message and then exclaimed, "Jesus Christ and General Jackson! This is the hottest potato they ever handed me!"[21] Even Spruance, the POA chief of staff, was taken unawares. Halsey was torn by feelings of excitement and sadness when he met Ghormley, the two having been football teammates at the Naval Academy and friends for four decades.

Ghormley left for Pearl Harbor in a few days, and, despite little orientation, Halsey plunged into his tough new challenges with his usual zest and confidence. According to

Spruance, when he asked Halsey for Kelly Turner to head the Central Pacific amphibious force, Halsey "answered back real quickly" in the affirmative, preferring to be rid of the volcanic admiral and to get the stabler Ping Wilkinson in his stead.[22] That decision and the top priority he placed on developing the airfield on Guadalcanal impressed Vandegrift and his Marines. Halsey's popularity with the Marines and the Navy in the South Pacific was enhanced also by the slogan that he ordered to be painted on buildings and hung as posters, even in heads, throughout his command: "Kill Japs, Kill Japs, Kill More Japs!"[23] And, unlike Ghormley, he often visited Guadalcanal, chatting with enlisted men and officers alike and displaying concern and trust.

Most studies of the Pacific war have maintained that Midway was the decisive point. As far back as 1943, however, Clark Lee, an astute correspondent in the South Pacific, argued that the Americans "began to take the initiative" on a permanent basis only when Halsey became the area commander.[24] The admiral's most recent and authoritative biographer, writing forty-two years later, countered the trend of writings on the topic in the interim and concluded that, indeed, the crucial episode was Halsey's entry on the dismal South Pacific scene in October 1942: "At this time of crisis Halsey arrived in the South Pacific, relieved a defeatist U.S. command, and in thirty extraordinary days completely reversed the course of the conflict, throwing the Japanese on the defensive, from which they never recovered. This was the real turning point of the Pacific war."[25] The shift in momentum involved other factors as well, but Halsey was surely the catalyst that precipitated the new vigor in the American forces. By late November they were on the offensive, to be slowed but never set back again, though the last enemy troops were not evacuated from Guadalcanal until February 1943.

Near the end of the campaign Nimitz said of Halsey: "He has that rare combination of intellectual capacity and military audacity, and can calculate to a cat's whisker the risk involved."[26] In November, Halsey was made a four-star admiral after quick action by the Navy Department, the president, and Congress that had widespread public approval. Roosevelt himself allegedly originated the move to promote him. "The fighting admiral" of previous raids exaggerated by reporters now had more than lived up to the somewhat premature accolades of the press. In his subsequent operations that drove the Japanese out of the Solomons and the islands of the eastern portion of the Bismarck Archipelago, Halsey surprised even many of his admirers by his organizational skills and judicious decision making as area commander. Admiral Ping Wilkinson, who was his deputy at South Pacific headquarters for a while, revealed in a personal diary entry of mid-March 1943 that Halsey and his staff were succeeding but not without encountering "administrative tangles caused by the topsylike growing process of the show out here. With the army, the army air force, the marines, and the navy all teaming up together out here, but all, of course, separate entities, I know something of what the circus chariot driver must experience."[27]

Halsey was proving his worth ashore as well as at sea, but some of his naval colleagues worried that he was beginning to believe his larger-than-life portrayal by the press. A respected naval scholar has written that "Halsey was very much a victim of his own publicity." Admiral Spruance, who was more remote from the press, probably had Halsey in mind when he later commented about the pitfalls of publicity for a celebrated commander: "Should he get to identifying himself with the figure as publicized, he may subconsciously start thinking in terms of what his reputation calls for, rather than of how best to meet the actual problem confronting him."[28]

As aggressive and impulsive as he was, Halsey sometimes acted on his own initiative, as when Nimitz had to remind him in 1944 that "assignments of flag officers in the Pacific Fleet, since they are of a continuing nature, must be controlled by me or by higher authority."[29] On that occasion as well as similar ones of overstepping his bounds, Halsey was not arrogant and for a while afterward became a model of contriteness. In the above case, for instance, he responded to Nimitz: "I am most apologetic for the present mix-up. I can assure you my intentions were excellent, but my execution rotten."[30] Halsey's likability and zealous determination to succeed usually kept King and Nimitz from remaining annoyed by his occasional rushing around the rules.

In May 1944, with the South Pacific campaigns completed, Halsey met with King and Nimitz in San Francisco where he learned that in June he would be relieved as commander of the South Pacific Area and, after the Marianas campaign that summer, would go to sea in command of the Third Fleet. As explained earlier, he would alternate command with Spruance actually over the principal units of the Pacific Fleet in the Central Pacific operations, the forces being called the Fifth Fleet when led by Spruance. King had begun the numerical-fleet designations in March 1943 with the Third Fleet being Halsey's South Pacific naval units, the Fifth being Spruance's Central Pacific forces, and the Seventh being the American naval units in the Southwest Pacific, led by Arthur Carpender and later Thomas Kinkaid. The Third Fleet of the South Pacific operations, however, had been a small outfit compared to the Third Fleet that Halsey took over in August 1944 for the operations in the Palaus and the Philippines. The new force comprised more than 500 combat ships that had formerly been in the Central and South Pacific units, as well as a host of new vessels that joined the Central Pacific armada from the States that summer. An officer in the Joint Intelligence Center at Pearl Harbor observed, "The chameleonlike ability of the fleet to take on the color of its commander was remarkable." Under Spruance's leadership the fleet "refused to be distracted from its objectives, and we could read its schedules and confidently plot the locality of all its forces at any hour." On the other hand, when it "went to sea under Halsey, whose staff were splendid opportunists, neither the Japanese nor the Estimate Section [at Pearl Harbor] knew what to expect."[31]

Arriving at Pearl Harbor in mid-June 1944, Halsey and his staff spent much of their time that summer planning and preparing for the naval aspects of the Palaus invasion. Meanwhile, Spruance won acclaim and some criticism for his leadership of the Fifth Fleet in the Battle of the Philippine Sea in June. Having missed all the big battles so far—Coral Sea, Midway, the Solomons series, and now this one off the Marianas—Halsey was primed for action when he took over the powerful fleet in late August. He was to play unexpected roles shortly in both strategy and naval warfare. After his carrier aircraft delivered devastating blows to enemy air strength in the Philippines in mid-September, Halsey audaciously sent a message to Nimitz urging that, in view of the destruction of Japanese air power in the area, the Palaus and Yap invasions should be cancelled and MacArthur's initial thrust into the Philippines should be an invasion of Leyte in October rather than of Mindanao, to the south. Nimitz and MacArthur were agreeable on the Leyte proposal, and it quickly won the approval of Roosevelt and the Joint Chiefs, who were then conferring with Churchill and his military assistants at Quebec. Halsey asserted later that "the new plan advanced the war two months or more."[32] Unhappily, however, the Palaus assaults were not cancelled, resulting in a costly battle for Peleliu.

In late October Halsey got his long-awaited chance to command in a major battle; it was the battle for Leyte Gulf, the largest naval engagement in history, and it resulted in swirls of controversy about Halsey that have never ceased. When MacArthur's troops invaded Leyte that month, Halsey's Third Fleet was supposed to provide air cover and its surface units were to block Japanese naval forces from breaking through to Leyte Gulf where the congested beachheads and large numbers of cargo and troop ships were vulnerable. Kinkaid's relatively small Seventh Fleet would be no match for the combined power of the four Japanese naval forces converging on the area. But Nimitz also instructed Halsey to destroy the enemy fleet if he had the chance. With dual and possibly contradictory tasks assigned to Halsey and with him reporting to Nimitz and Kinkaid to MacArthur, the American naval situation off Leyte was a disaster waiting to happen. In the ensuing Leyte Gulf battle—really four far-

General Douglas MacArthur, President Franklin D. Roosevelt, Admiral Chester W. Nimitz, and Admiral William D. Leahy at Pearl Harbor Conference, July 1944.

Generals George C. Kenney, Walter Krueger, Douglas MacArthur, and George C. Marshall meeting on Goodenough Island, east of New Guinea, December 1943.

General Thomas Blamey, General Douglas MacArthur, and Prime Minister John Curtin at Melbourne, Australia, June 1942

Fleet Admiral Chester W. Nimitz and Admiral William F. Halsey meet aboard battleship South Dakota *in Tokyo Bay, late August 1945.*

Anglo-American leaders at the Second Quebec Conference, September 1944. Seated: General George C. Marshall, Admiral William D. Leahy, President Frankin D. Roosevelt, Prime Minister Winston S. Churchill, Field Marshal Alan Brooke, Field Marshal John Dill. Standing: Major General L. C. Hollis, Lieutenant General Hastings Ismay, Admiral Ernest J. King, Air Marshal Charles Portal, General Henry H. Arnold, Admiral Andrew Cunningham.

Generalissimo Chiang Kai-shek and Lieutenant General Joseph W. Stilwell at one of their early wartime meetings, Maymyo, Burma, April 1942.

Field Marshal Bernard L. Montgomery, General of the Army Dwight D. Eisenhower, and General Omar N. Bradley celebrating the surrender of Germany, May 1945.

Lieutenant General Carl A. Spaatz arrives in England, June 1942.

President Harry S Truman, General Carl A. Spaatz, and General Ira C. Eaker at the White House.

Major General Graves B. Erskine and Lieutenant General Holland M. Smith confer on Iwo Jima, March 1945.

Lieutenant General George S. Patton, Jr., and General George C. Marshall.

Lieutenant General Mark W. Clark and General of the Army George C. Marshall reviewing Sikh troops in Italy, February 1945.

The U.S. Joint Chiefs of Staff lunch together,
October 1942: Admiral Ernest J. King, General
George C. Marshall, Admiral William D. Leahy,
and General Henry H. Arnold.

Vice Admiral Raymond A. Spruance, Admiral Ernest J.
King, and Admiral Chester W. Nimitz visit the Marianas,
around July 1944.

Rear Admiral R. Kelly Turner and Major General A. Archer Vandegrift on Guadalcanal, around September 1942.

Generals Dwight D. Eisenhower and George C. Marshall confer at Algiers, Algeria, June 1943.

ranging engagements, mostly in the Philippine and Sibuyan seas and never in Leyte Gulf—Halsey chose to chase a decoy force of enemy carriers that had few planes aboard and inadvertently allowed a strong Japanese surface force almost to reach Leyte Gulf. Only the enemy commander's ineptness and the courageous defense by small naval units not under Halsey prevented wholesale destruction of American shipping and beach positions in the Leyte Gulf area that day. Nimitz and MacArthur were merciful toward Halsey afterward, and King, asserts one source, even "attempted to shift the blame to the commander of the Seventh Fleet, Adm. Thomas Kinkaid."[33]

Halsey's decisions and actions during the battle for Leyte Gulf would be hotly debated in naval circles, the media, and historical works but without resolution of the issues. Until his death Halsey was highly sensitive to criticisms of his Leyte Gulf role. The controversy, however, tended to overshadow other flaws of his as a fleet commander that were analyzed by some scholars of naval history. He would have become apoplectic, for instance, if he had lived long enough to read the severe judgment in 1968 of the top historian of the fast carriers in the Pacific war: "Concerning the record of Halsey and McCain with the fast carriers . . . both men were inferior third-act heroes in the Central Pacific offensive and might best have served elsewhere."[34]

There were also Halsey's tragic encounters with typhoons. Two months after the battle for Leyte Gulf he led the Third Fleet into a vicious typhoon in the Philippine Sea that cost three ships and many lives. When he resumed the fleet command in May 1945, after several months at Pearl Harbor, he led the Third Fleet out of the path of another typhoon but then inexplicably turned back into it, this time off Okinawa. Vice Admiral J. J. "Jocko" Clark, one of his carrier commanders, said the destruction to the fleet "was almost the equivalent of a defeat in battle."[35] That October, only a month before he came back to the States, Halsey's fleet was battered by one of the worst typhoons of the century, though most of the ships were in port. Following the first two incidents, naval courts of inquiry investigated and sharply criticized Halsey and some of his senior officers, particularly McCain. After studying the court's findings in the June 1945 case, Secretary of the Navy James Forrestal was ready to retire Halsey and McCain. King's intervention spared Halsey, but McCain was ordered to a nonnaval post in Washington at the end of hostilities. After witnessing the Japanese surrender on Halsey's flagship, the battleship *Missouri,* in Tokyo Bay on September 2, McCain died of a heart attack en route to his new position. "It grieves me bitterly," Halsey remarked later about his "great friend" Slew McCain.[36]

The 1944 law creating the five-star ranks had authorized four generals of the army and four fleet admirals, but only Leahy, King, and Nimitz had been promoted to the latter rank by the end of the war. King and Nimitz both would have preferred that Spruance and Halsey be given the five-star rank. After wrestling with the matter for a while, King nominated both men, along with four other admirals, and passed the decision along to Forrestal. In turn, the secretary of the navy was unable to make a selection and sent the list to President Truman, who chose Halsey in December 1945. Some Spruance supporters believed that Representative Carl Vinson (Democrat, South Carolina), the powerful chairman of the House Armed Services Committee, who had come out publicly for making Halsey a fleet admiral, had significant influence on President Truman's decision. Several persons close to Truman, on the other hand, have suggested that the president may have chosen Halsey because he was the senior admiral of the two, held more responsible posts early in the war, and was the most popular naval hero of the war to the American public. The last-named factor was undoubtedly not an insignificant consideration to such a master politician, but Truman would not have been wrong in choosing either of the top candidates.

Relieved of active naval duty at his own request in December 1946, Halsey kept busy with a variety of educational, charitable, and corporate positions. Up to his final days in 1959 he could still become outraged over criticisms of his Leyte Gulf moves and of Kimmel's role in the Pearl Harbor disaster. To the end he remained impetuous, courageous, combative, adventuresome, and compassionate.

Rear Admiral Charles J. "Carl" Moore, Spruance's chief of staff, remembered him as "very excitable and very impatient" but also "considerate, friendly, and kind."[37] Admiral Robert B. "Mick" Carney, Halsey's wartime chief of staff and later the chief of naval operations, summed up Halsey as "more damned fun than a circus."[38] He was "a grand man to be with" and "a splendid seaman" who could "smack them [the enemy] hard every time he gets a chance," commented Spruance.[39] Admiral Arleigh A. Burke, a future CNO who served under Halsey in the Pacific war, said Halsey "was not brilliant" but was "a good fighter . . . [and] a great leader . . . [who] knew how to get the most out of people."[40] Halsey "was a very able officer but would take chances," recalled Admiral Russell S. Berkey, another Pacific leader.[41] According to Admiral Richard L. Conolly, who headed task forces in both the Pacific and Mediterranean theaters, Halsey was one of the top six "real tactical leaders we [the Anglo-Americans] produced in the war," the others being Generals Patton, Krueger, and Doolittle and two British commanders, Field Marshal Montgomery and Admiral Andrew Cunningham.[42] Halsey, the area commander, is solidly established as the pivotal figure of the South Pacific war. Halsey, the fleet commander, is probably destined to remain one of the most fascinating and controversial naval leaders of modern times. MacArthur may have expressed it best when he told Halsey as the admiral was about to leave Tokyo for the United States in November 1945: "When you leave, Bill, the Pacific becomes just another ocean."[43]

WELL SUITED TO BE MACARTHUR'S
AIR COMMANDER: KENNEY

Of the commanders featured herein, King, Nimitz, and Vandegrift suffered courts-martial as young officers and Halsey narrowly missed one at the height of his career, but General George C. Kenney was the only one who was almost hit with a court-martial at the crucial field-grade stage of his professional advancement. From 1927 to 1928 Kenney was a student at the Army Command and General Staff School, Fort Leavenworth. The commandant was Brigadier General Edward L. King, a disciplinarian who was especially strict about drinking among the staff and students of the school. Lieutenant General Robert L. Eichelberger, then a major and the post adjutant general, said that King, who would command the American and Filipino defenders on Bataan in 1942, "accepted the Prohibition law with grim seriousness. Anyone on the post who took a drink was personally disloyal (in his view), and anyone bringing in liquor was subject to court-martial." One evening the military police caught Kenney entering the fort with a half dozen bottles of liquor. The next day he was required to appear before Eichelberger, who recalled that Kenney, then thirty-nine years old, "assumed despairingly that his military career was ruined."[44] The adjutant general chose to tear up the summons, however, and never mentioned the incident to King. Kenney went on to graduate from the Command and General Staff School in 1928 and later from the Army War College. At Southwest Pacific headquarters sixteen years hence Kenney, the head of the Far East Air Forces, gratefully reminded Eichelberger, the commander of the Eighth Army, of the significant role he had played in his career.

Born in Canada while his parents were vacationing there in 1889, Kenney was reared in Massachusetts and spent three years at Massachusetts Institute of Technology. He left before his final year to take an engineering job. Energetic and ambitious, he was president of a small civil engineering company by the age of twenty-seven. Enlisting as a flight cadet in the Aviation Section of the Signal Corps in 1917, he earned a commission and joined the American Expeditionary Forces in France in early 1918. He flew seventy-five combat missions and shot down two German aircraft. By the end of the war he was a captain and had both the Distinguished Service Cross and the Silver Star.

Having won the respect and friendship of Brigadier General William Mitchell and his chief subordinates during the air war over France and the subsequent Rhineland occupation, Kenney returned to the States in 1919 with bright prospects in the fledgling Army Air Service (which became the Army Air Corps in 1925). He performed well in tours of duty during the 1920s that ranged from squadron commander and instructor to air inspector and production engineer. After graduating from the Army War College in 1933, he was retained on duty in Washington the next two years on the staff of Major General Benjamin Foulois, the chief of the Army Air Corps. He was alleged to have been the chief author of the McSwain Bill of 1934, an unsuccessful measure calling for an autonomous air force. When the GHQ Air Force was set up in 1935, Frank Andrews, its commander, picked Kenney as his assistant chief of operations and training. After seventeen years as a captain, he was finally elevated to major that year. When Andrews challenged the conservative views on air power of the War Department hierarchy, he and several of his staff, including Kenney, were penalized by Chief of Staff Malin Craig, who had them transferred out of GHQ Air Force headquarters and "scattered to the four corners of the country."[45]

By then Kenney had become widely known in the Air Corps for his industrious, aggressive, and innovative ways. In the 1920s he had gained distinction by developing the first fixed machine guns on wings and the parachute fragmentation bomb. An authority on the Air Corps before World War II maintains that "unlike Eaker or Spaatz or Andrews," Kenney and Arnold had been "genuinely interested in scientific development" in aeronautics since early in their careers.[46] Kenney was a vociferous champion of more funding for research and development in military aviation, and he was outspoken in urging adoption of the B-17 heavy bomber.

When Craig exiled Kenney to an inconspicuous position at Fort Benning, his isolation did not last long because later that year Arnold became the chief of the Air Corps and soon set to work getting the penalized airmen back into the mainstream. Their return to influence was made easier by Marshall's support when he became Army chief of staff. In Kenney's mind, however, there was no question about the chief credit for his renascence going to Arnold: "We were close personal friends. . . . We used to have lots of arguments, but we understood each other, we respected each other's judgment, and liked each other. Hap used to call me his 'trouble shooter.' "[47]

From 1939 to 1941 Kenney was assigned tours of duty as an observer with the Navy during maneuvers in the Caribbean, assistant air attaché at the United States embassy in Paris, and head of the Air Corps' Experimental Division and Engineering School at Wright Field in Ohio. A major when Arnold took over the Air Corps, Kenney was a brigadier general by early 1941 and was promoted to major general a year later when he took command of the Fourth Air Force on the West Coast. A measure of his worth to Arnold was the fact that the two observers the Air Corps chief sent to Europe in September 1939 were, in his words, "two of the best officers in the Air Corps," Kenney and Spaatz.[48] A naval officer who worked with Kenney in collecting data from downed German planes in France commented, "I strongly believe that Kenney's rise to the pinnacle of his brilliant career was given considerable impetus by his visit to France at that propitious time and by our joint report."[49]

MacArthur, it will be recalled, had been unhappy with Lewis Brereton and George Brett as his respective air commanders in the Philippines and Australia. After the Philippine air defenses collapsed, Brereton had been transferred to the Middle East and by the summer of 1942 was leading the Ninth Air Force. Brett had headed the air forces of the ill-fated ABDA Command in the East Indies and had then fled to Australia, subsequently being assigned temporary command of the few American forces that had reached that continent. That spring he was named the head of Allied Air Forces in the new Southwest Pacific theater.

By late June 1942, MacArthur was disgusted with the unaggressiveness and disharmony manifest in the leadership of the American-Australian air organization in the Southwest Pacific Area. He requested Frank Andrews as the replacement for Brett, but Marshall countered by offering him Kenney or Doolittle. Doolittle had been only a lieutenant colonel when he led the Tokyo raid in April and had recently been advanced to brigadier general; some senior airmen resented his rapid rise, especially since he had left the Air Corps between the wars and worked for Shell Oil. MacArthur preferred the more experienced two-star general who was then commanding the Fourth Air Force and was known to be tough and vigorous (and no great admirer of Doolittle, as the SWPA chief would learn later). When Kenney met with MacArthur for the first time, on July 30 at the SWPA headquarters in Brisbane, the theater commander launched into a long tirade against the SWPA airmen as "an inefficient rabble of boulevard shock troops whose contribution to the war effort was practically nil."[50] He demanded loyalty and results, and Kenney fervently promised both.

That night Kenney took off for New Guinea, and after several days there and at SWPA air bases in Australia he reported back to MacArthur his analysis of the problems and his proposed corrections. MacArthur was impressed by his "can do" approach to the deplorable air situation, particularly when Kenney proclaimed that his first priority would be "to take out the Jap air strength until we owned the air over New Guinea." According to Kenney, the SWPA chief "said to go ahead, that I had carte blanche to do anything I wanted to. He said he didn't care how my gang was handled . . . as long as they would fight."[51]

Kenney, who officially assumed command on August 4, quickly revamped the administration, operations, and services of the Allied Air Forces, relieving five American generals and prodding Air Vice Marshal William D. Bostock to shake up and invigorate his Royal Australian Air Force. On September 5, Kenney was given the additional duty of commanding the U.S. Fifth Air Force, formally established that day as the principal American air arm in the SWPA theater. By mid-September the Fifth Air Force's bomber command, led by Brigadier General Kenneth N. Walker, was hitting

Rabaul with the largest Allied raids yet mounted in the war against Japan. In the meantime, the fighter command of the Fifth, headed by Brigadier General Paul B. Wurtsmith, began to challenge enemy aircraft more vigorously over New Guinea. Kenney's deputy, Brigadier General Ennis C. Whitehead, was the dynamo behind much of the Fifth's successes. Kenney described him as "my strong right arm all through the war. . . . A very serious, thorough planner, with all the guts in the world. I had to practically threaten to court-martial him to keep him from going out on all the combat missions."[52] (As already mentioned, Whitehead succeeded Kenney as Fifth Air Force commander in 1944; Wurtsmith became head of the Thirteenth Air Force.)

As Allied Air Forces chief, Kenney oversaw operations by American, Australian, New Zealand, Dutch, and other national air forces, including a few Mexican squadrons toward the end of the war. At first Bostock's Australians carried about the same load of missions as the American airmen, but by late 1943 the preponderance of air strength was in the U.S. Fifth Air Force. In fact, up to March 1944 the Fifth had flown 117,076 sorties, dropped 34,249 tons of bombs, destroyed 2,172 enemy planes, and lost 524 of its own aircraft—a record of combat performance that was exceeded only by the Eighth among the eleven numerical American air forces.[53] The Fifth's operations ranged from long-distance bombing attacks against oil refineries on Borneo and shipping in the Java Sea to close-support strikes for nearly sixty amphibious assaults on New Guinea, the Bismarcks, the Moluccas, and the Philippines. The achievements of the Fifth Air Force under Kenney's leadership were many and sometimes spectacular, such as the transporting of two American regiments and several Australian units over the rugged Owen Stanley Mountains to forward areas of combat in Papua in late 1942; the virtual destruction of a large Japanese force of warships and merchantmen in the Battle of the Bismarck Sea in March 1943, the attackers effectively using a Kenney-invented technique called skip bombing; the successful airborne assault on Nadzab, Northeast New Guinea, that September in the first large-scale paratroop drop of the Pacific war; and the raids on Rabaul later that fall that often exceeded 400 bombers. By the time Kenney relinquished the command of the Fifth to Whitehead in June 1944, it had become a vaunted alternative in MacArthur's strategy to the carrier air power he had earlier tried in vain to obtain.

The redeployment of forces in the South Pacific Area that spring and summer brought into the Southwest Pacific theater the Thirteenth Air Force, the First Marine Air Wing, and several New Zealand air units, which led Arnold to approve MacArthur's recommendation for a new overall command setup. MacArthur wanted to call it the "First Air Army," but Arnold objected, and they settled on the Far East Air Forces, with Kenney to be the commander while continuing as SWPA Allied air chief. Later the Seventh Air Force of the Central Pacific Area would also come under the Far East Air Forces. Despite repeated efforts by Kenney and MacArthur to gain control of the B-29s that were deployed to the Pacific in 1944, Arnold retained command of them until mid-1945 when Spaatz, Twining, and Doolittle arrived in the Pacific to lead the Strategic, Twentieth, and Eighth air forces, respectively. As late as June 1945, when Arnold conferred with him in Manila, MacArthur still wanted Kenney over the B-29s and as overall air chief in the Pacific. Arnold recorded in his diary after their meeting on June 27: MacArthur "says that there cannot be two dominant characters in the Pacific like Kenney and Spaatz"![54]

As did MacArthur, Kenney sometimes antagonized Australian commanders and American Navy leaders in the Pacific by ignoring or contradicting their counsel in planning operations and by devoting inadequate attention toward establishing better cooperation and coordination between the various national forces, the American services, and the Pacific theaters in conducting the war with Japan. Kenney became not only one of MacArthur's confidants, but also a key strategic adviser to the SWPA chief. Indeed, MacArthur thought so highly of Kenney's grasp of strategy that he sent him to several meetings at Pearl Harbor and Washington with the Joint Chiefs of Staff and representatives of Nimitz's and Halsey's headquarters. On the trips to the national capital, usually accompanied by Major General Richard K. Sutherland, Kenney often had sessions with high-ranking officials of the War Department and even conferred with Roosevelt in private at the White House. Through the spring of 1944 he also engaged in secret talks with various conservative Republicans who were interested in promoting a MacArthur-for-President movement, which was stillborn.

Though he never ranked him at the level of Spaatz, Arnold had a high regard for Kenney and his Southwest Pacific achievements. When he congratulated Kenney in March 1945 on his promotion to full general, Arnold said: "You got there the 'fustest' with, perhaps at times, the 'leastest,' but you always got results and this fourth star only partially recognizes your achievement. You have earned it—the hard way."[55] MacArthur commented after the war, "Of all the commanders of our major Air Forces engaged in World War II, none surpassed General Kenney in those three great essentials of successful combat leadership: aggressive vision, mastery over air strategy and tactics, and the ability to exact the maximum in fighting qualities from both men and equipment."[56] The Southwest Pacific commander was impressed by what he called "Kenney's restless genius that drives him ever onward." An Australian observer in 1944 remarked, "No general in the United States Army has been more fanatically air-minded than MacArthur" after he was converted by Kenney, "an evangelist for airpower properly employed" who showed him "how to make airpower the decisive element in his operations."[57] Kenney later remarked, "As much as I respected MacArthur and liked him as a person, I've got to admit that he knew practically nothing at first about aviation. When I got out there, he didn't even want to fly." By the end of the war, however, "he had learned a lot and had gotten an appreciation of air power that was, in many respects, ahead of a lot of our air commanders."[58]

Kenney became one of the few officers from MacArthur's command to be given high-level positions by the Pentagon in the postwar period. During the years 1945–51, he headed the Pacific Air Command, the Strategic Air Command, and the Air University, as well as serving as the senior U.S. representative on the United Nations Military Staff Committee. Allegedly, Kenney and General Hoyt S. Vandenberg were the chief candidates for the post of chief of staff of the Air Force in 1948, the latter being chosen because of strong support from Spaatz, the outgoing Air Force head. Between 1949 and 1960, Kenney wrote four books, all concerning the war in the Southwest Pacific.

Little George, as the short, stocky Kenney was sometimes called in private, possessed sharply defined personality and leadership traits, as the following brief descriptions of him by some fellow senior officers in the Southwest Pacific theater indicate. On the favorable side, he was "a hard-hitting guy who would fight back," "the only one who could tell MacArthur off," "a wonderful person and a colorful personality," "a very determined, active, energetic man," "blustery but very talented as an airman," and "one of the most influential people in the theater." On the other hand, some colleagues considered him "arrogant and opinionated," "an Irish rascal," "fond of attention and flattery," and "too optimistic about the capabilities of his air forces."[59] Thomas Kinkaid probably expressed the sentiment of most naval leaders in the Pacific: Kenney "thought 'damn Navy' was one word. . . . Kenney and Halsey used to mix a lot about the operations in the Philippines."[60] In his memoirs in 1947 Halsey "violated military custom by publicly criticizing a fellow officer who was still living" when he commented on the Philippine operations of the autumn of 1944 and "Kenney's inability to give Leyte effective air support. I had to stand by and attend to his knitting for him."[61] Arnold regarded Kenney as "a real leader" of air power in the Pacific war who turned the SWPA air performances "from below average" to "excellent" and whose leadership helped to produce "the finest bunch of pilots I have seen" among the numerical American air forces around the world in World War II.[62] Major General Richard J. Marshall, the deputy chief of staff at SWPA GHQ, remarked simply, "I think he was a splendid airman for General MacArthur."[63] However they might differ on Kenney's personal characteristics and leadership style, nearly all his admirers and detractors in military and scholarly circles agree that of all the Southwest Pacific commanders Kenney had the greatest input, for better or worse, on MacArthur's strategic thinking during the war against Japan.

EIGHT

LEADING THE FINAL CAMPAIGNS AGAINST GERMANY

FROM NORMANDY TO THE ELBE
(EUROPE, JUNE 1944–MAY 1945)

Most of the fundamental decisions on high command and strategy in the war against Germany had been set by the time of the Overlord attack. The advance up the Italian boot was to continue but with diminishing resources, despite British interest in using Italy as a springboard for thrusts into the Balkans or the Danube Valley to preempt Soviet moves there. For two years the British peripheral strategy in the Mediterranean had largely determined Anglo-American operations, while the American preference for a concentrated cross-channel assault in France had been put off. With the shift in the balance of military power within the Grand Alliance by late 1943, however, Britain was compelled to yield the reins of strategy making, and the already emerging superpowers, America and the Soviet Union, set about implementing their commonly held strategy for defeating Germany: massive pincers closing from the east and west, with a virtual holding line to the south and no front to the north. Thus, the strategic priorities Churchill had proposed for advances into Hitler's heartland through North Italy and Norway were summarily dismissed.

During the final eleven months of the European fighting the pattern of Allied strategy affected the American high command in significant ways, forcing the British to recognize the Americans as dominant in decision making within the Combined Chiefs and the European theater command and elevating the American commanders in Northwest Europe to positions of power and prestige superior to their own colleagues in the Mediterranean and Pacific theaters. Eisenhower and his top commanders now not only controlled the largest American ground and air forces ever assembled but also were on the threshold of becoming a dominant influence on American military policy and strategy for decades to come. In fact, with Eisenhower in the White House and Marshall heading the State and Defense departments later, their impact would be strong on postwar foreign policy, too. In retrospect, the "European generals" of the American Army became so influential that it did not seem surprising when Ike's wartime chief of staff, General Beetle Smith, was named head of the Central Intelligence Agency during the Korean War.

From the summer of 1944 to the German surrender the following spring, Marshall, Arnold, Eisenhower, and their principal advisers and personnel chiefs became conduits through which were channeled a huge flow of American commanders at the division level and above into the European theater. By August 1944, American senior officers chosen by Marshall and Eisenhower had served in command of two armies, seven corps, fourteen infantry divisions, seven armored divisions, and two airborne divisions in the ground operations in Normandy. Their appointees in the top ground commands were much more numerous in ETO by the next spring, for the American forces in the drive from Normandy into West Germany had grown in troop strength to nearly three times that of the combined British, Canadian, and French armies on their flanks. Moreover, almost 16,000 of the 28,000 Allied combat aircraft over Europe by then were American, with a roughly corresponding superiority in numbers of American air commanders at the group and wing levels and higher.

The men who led the main American ground and air organizations in the European operations of 1944–45 were, for the most part, senior officers who had graduated from West Point and who had personal ties with Marshall, Arnold, Eisenhower, or one of their confidants. The personal factor turned out to be both an asset and a liability in identifying the best possible leaders. Most of the senior ground commanders proved to be professionally competent but cautious, restrained, and uncreative in the exploitation of their forces' mobility and firepower. George Patton at the army level and Lawton Collins in corps leadership were conspicuous exceptions. The American leaders in the last European campaigns, moreover, did not generally demonstrate much appreciation of logistics or communications intelligence, and they tended to be intimidated by the real or alleged prowess of the Germans, though not usually reacting as carefully as their British counterparts. And the top-level Americans in the ETO command structure often appeared naive or unconcerned about the diplomatic, political, propagandistic, economic, or other nonmilitary ramifications of their military plans and operations. In their defense, however, it must be added that from the levels of Marshall and Eisenhower downward the senior American commanders were largely bereft of guidance on nonmilitary issues from 1944 to 1945, even though the Allied coalition was crumbling and postwar aims were of great concern to the British and the Soviets.

For the past four decades the writings on Allied strategy making and high command in the European war have been replete with scathing criticisms, most of the barbs aimed at the Americans. Churchill said, "The American clear-cut, logical, large-scale, mass-production style of thought was formidable," but he lamented the Americans' low priority on political factors.[1] British and German critics especially have been harsh in criticizing the American commanders' heavy reliance on overwhelming might and little use of innovative tactics. A noted military scholar recently concluded that in confrontations between American and German troops in World War II the American leaders sought successful outcomes that could be produced "largely by machines" in superior numbers and by "the greatest possible firepower" in contrast to the German commanders' reliance on maximum, high-caliber "fighting power" from their soldiers.[2] The leading historian of the last two decades on the American Army declared in his recent study of the ETO commanders of 1944–45 that the principal traits of the American leadership in the advance across northern France and into West Germany "add up to unimaginative caution. American generalship by and large was competent but addicted to playing it safe."[3] On the other hand, Tooey Spaatz, Jimmy Doolittle, Ira Eaker, and their strategic air commanders appeared to become more emboldened in sending their bombers in larger and larger waves and over greater distances to devastate German cities. By the final months of the European war some American bombing missions seemed to be aimed as much at breaking German civilian morale as at attacking military targets—long a practice of the RAF that Americans had earlier found repugnant.

The Overlord invasion of Normandy was, by far, the largest and most crucial Allied venture of the Second World War. Churchill called it "the most difficult and complicated operation that has ever taken place," while, as a prominent military analyst remarked, "it was for the Third Reich the beginning of the end."[4] Despite flaws in planning and execution, Eisenhower and his Allied forces achieved success in the powerful but very risky assault against the German defenses along the English Channel. He wrought minor miracles in overseeing the final assembling and launching of the gigantic Overlord armada, and after more than four decades he still appears to have been the officer best suited to ensure that the top-level Allied command team worked together well enough to achieve the final victory. As for his shortcomings in Overlord, Ike did not provide adequate planning for what would likely occur once the troops were established ashore, his SHAEF planners having focused on the amphibious assault and not on the advance inland through the difficult bocage (hedgerow) country. Also, in waiting until early September to move his headquarters to Normandy and to assume direct command of the Allied ground forces, Eisenhower forfeited the opportunity to provide his moderating personal influence on the fast-deteriorating relations between Bernard Montgomery and the American commanders in the beachhead.

Omar Bradley was stable and dependable as the U.S. First Army's leader in Normandy, but he was unable to develop an effective, harmonious relationship with Montgomery, his temporary superior. At first he was hesitant in challenging the hypersensitive, vain British leader, and, according to an authority, "Montgomery's conservatism and Bradley's reluctance to press the issue" led to "the failure to seal the Argentan-Falaise pocket," with large German forces escaping from the trap during the Allied charge out of the Normandy beachhead in August.[5] Patton's forceful leadership of the Third Army in its spectacular turning movement at Avranches during the Allied offensive and in his units' rapid advance to the Seine River bore out Ike's earlier perseverance and faith in him as an inspired and inspiring combat leader. Major General Lawton Collins, the VII Corps commander, shone brilliantly in the Contentin Peninsula and Cherbourg operations, but though he would continue to provide stellar leadership in later battles, he would never move farther up the wartime command ladder. His superiors took notice of his command talents, as well as those of several other outstanding corps leaders, such as Major General Matthew B. Ridgway of the XVIII Airborne Corps, but when new armies were added later in the European campaign they were passed over for the commands in favor of more senior and conservative officers. Courtney Hodges, Bradley's deputy who took his place as head of the First Army when the latter took over the XII Army Group in August, was a notable case of the bypassing of vigorous, combat-proven younger officers in favor of older generals with key personal connections who could be counted upon to provide good, if not superior, leadership. Another case in point was Gee Gerow, who led the V Corps on Collins' flank in Normandy. Personally close to Marshall, Lesley McNair, and Eisenhower, he would deliver less than distinguished command performances then and later; nevertheless, he would be elevated to command of an army in the closing stages of the European fighting.

Although several chances to trap retreating German units were missed in the Riviera-Rhone operations (Dragoon) that began in August, the senior American commanders in southern France were more than adequate in overcoming the relatively weak German defenses—Alexander Patch, who led the Seventh Army, and Jake Devers, who, beginning in September, commanded the VI Army Group, which included the Seventh Army and General Jean de Lattre de Tassigny's French First Army. The real gem of Dragoon, however, was Lucian Truscott, already a veteran combat commander of great distinction who now led his VI Corps in slashing, fast-moving attacks striking inland from the Riviera that left the German defenders reeling or isolated. Like Collins, the dashing Truscott was retained under conservative superiors who did not fully utilize his genius for battle. Eventually he would succeed Mark Clark as the Fifth Army commander in Italy, but gifted, bold officers like him, Collins, and Ridgway should have been brought into the higher-command echelons earlier to offset the caution, intimidation, and old-boy ties of some of the generals who were already there.

The American operations from Normandy to the meeting with the Soviets at the Elbe River deep in Germany were characterized by the attrition of a number of senior officers who were in high-level positions or who seemed to be promising candidates for such posts. Brigadier General Theodore Roosevelt, son of the former Republican president and a fighter known for his courage in Tunisia and Sicily, died of a sudden heart attack shortly after landing in Normandy. The miserable showings in battle of the Ninetieth Infantry Division in its Overlord missions in June and July led Bradley to replace Major Generals Jay W. MacKelvie and Eugene M. Landrum as successive commanders of the listless outfit. Finally that summer Major General Raymond S. McLain assumed the divisional command and quickly provided the spark that restored the Ninetieth's morale. "When McLain left the 90th the following October to take command of a corps," said Bradley, "his successor inherited one of the finest divisions in combat on the Allied front."[6] Lieutenant General Lesley McNair, the nearly deaf commander of U.S. Army Ground Forces, was killed in late July near St. Lo, France, when he was visiting a sector of the American Ninth Infantry Division that was mistakenly bombed by American planes. Rear Admiral Don P. Moon, who led a task force in the Overlord invasion, committed suicide a few days before the exhausted, depressed officer was to head a naval unit in the Dragoon amphibious assault in August. Major General Maurice Rose, who made the U.S. Third Armored Division into one of the best tank outfits of the war, was shot to death while trying to surrender to a German soldier after being trapped in a combat action in Germany the next March.

As has long been a favorite maneuver in duplicity, some senior officers were shifted to higher-level posts that really afforded them less power. Lieutenant General Lewis H. Brereton became one such pawn after too many personal clashes and controversial episodes: he had been MacArthur's air chief when the Japanese devastated Clark Field on the first day of the war; he had ordered the raid on the oil fields and refinery at Ploesti, Rumania, in August 1943, which caused little damage to the facilities but enormous losses for his Ninth Air Force bombers; and he had ordered the bombing mission on the Normandy front the next summer that killed McNair and over 100 American soldiers. Brereton, whose leadership of the Ninth Air Force had been criticized by colleagues on other grounds also, was then given command of the new First Allied Airborne Army, which was organized primarily for Operation Market-Garden, the ill-fated assault by British and American paratroop and glider forces around Arnhem, Holland, that fall. Actually the planning of the operation and the basic control of the main forces in the attack were under British commanders, so Brereton's role in Market-Garden was marginal, though he bore some of the taint of the bungled mission. The next spring his duties in the airborne operation supporting Montgomery's grandiose crossing of the Rhine were also nominal, with Montgomery and his British airborne corps commander paying little heed to him. Meanwhile, Major General Hoyt S. Vandenberg, Arnold's and Spaatz's favorite air officer then on the rise and a future Air Force chief of staff, had taken charge of the Ninth Air Force, providing sounder leadership and more effective communication with American and British commanders in ETO.[7]

The breakout from the Normandy beachhead and the rapid pursuit of the Germans across northern France produced a contagious euphoria among most Anglo-American officers and many predictions of Germany's imminent collapse. Instead, the German forces, under excellent field leadership, regrouped with amazing resiliency, while the Allied armies found themselves running out of munitions, fuel, and supplies and unable to press their attacks before the Germans became entrenched in defensive positions along the German border. The reasons for the logistical paralysis that hit the Allied forces that autumn were many and complex. An important factor was Montgomery's slowness in taking Antwerp and clearing the nearby Schelde estuary to provide a major port near the front. Also, there were problems in the administration stateside of the U.S. Army Service Forces, which was headed by General Brehon B. Somervell, an imperious and overly ambitious officer who was involved in empire building as well as logistics. The head of Eisenhower's Services of Supply in ETO was Lieutenant General John C. H. Lee, a martinet who was in good stead with Somervell and whose autocratic rule over his agency led supply officers in the field to nickname him "Jesus Christ Himself Lee." According to Eisenhower's chief chronicler, "Lee was the cause of one of Eisenhower's rare outbursts of anger against Marshall" when, on Somervell's suggestion, Marshall obtained Lee's promotion to three-star rank without consulting Ike.[8] The host of problems associated with supplying the ETO's huge forces were never solved altogether, though perhaps the basic reasons were the inadequate education in logistics of the whole officer corps and the American Army's relatively sudden growth from a small constabulary type of force into a very large organization deployed in overseas combat.

Although it was rumored for a time that Somervell desired and might obtain the position of Army chief of staff if Marshall had been chosen to head Overlord, neither officers in logistics nor those in intelligence normally had much voice in the high echelons of the ETO command. The worst failure in intelligence occurred in December 1944, not long after the supply emergency: Eisenhower, Bradley, Montgomery, and their army commanders were caught by surprise when Hitler hurled his last great offensive into the Ardennes Forest sector of the front in Belgium. The Battle of the Bulge also reemphasized the sorry, often petty state of Anglo-American command relations that Montgomery seemed to enjoy exacerbating, the extraordinary gifts of Collins as a combat leader, and Patton's uncanny ability to achieve hard-hitting mobility and to make dramatic headlines with his Third Army.

In the wake of the repulse of the German offensive in the Ardennes, there were recriminations of the bitterest sort exchanged by top ETO generals as well as within the Combined Chiefs of Staff regarding the conduct of the costly battle. For a brief time the British chiefs and Churchill floated the idea of making Alexander the Allied ground forces commander for the drive into Germany, with Eisenhower retaining his loftier and less-battle-involved post as theater commander. Not only was the proposal dropped but Ike was ultimately given a freer hand than ever in running the European theater, in part due to the ailing health of President Roosevelt. The U.S. Army's former chief historian observes that "General Eisenhower was given more and more responsibility for political decisions, or fell heir to them by default. Lacking clear and consistent guidance from Washington, he made decisions on the basis of military considerations."[9] Thus Eisenhower approved a broad advance into Germany by his various Allied armies rather than the narrow northern thrust by the British XXI Army Group, the former approach being militarily sounder but the latter possibly enabling the Western Allies to outrace the Soviets into Berlin.

In truth, neither Eisenhower and his commanders nor the leading Western statesmen were able to adjust fast enough in the rush of events in the spring of 1945 to transform the Allied wartime strategy, which had been successful militarily, into a peacetime coalition strategy that could reconcile the political differences of the alliance partners. "The war outran the strategists and the statesmen," as one authority maintains, adding that "the Second World War represented a shift in the international balance of power, for which a coalition strategy fashioned for victory provided no real or grand solutions."[10] Ironically, eight years later, Eisenhower as president would have to wrestle with East-West problems in Europe that were emerging during 1944–45 but were set aside for later resolution due to the exigencies of military operations at the time.

Bradley, the commander of the American First Army and XII Army Group, and Patton, the leader of the U.S. Third Army, were not operating from 1944 to 1945 at the level of the makers of grand strategy, but their actions impinged upon the larger military picture and also upon nonmilitary developments that would affect the future of Europe. Thus their titles belie the broad significance of their roles in the final year of the war. In addition, these two generals provide a sharp and revealing contrast in styles of military leadership. Whatever the shortcomings of the American method of selecting high commanders, it is a tribute to the wisdom of Marshall and Eisenhower that they found the right niches in the war with Germany for such different leaders as Bradley and Patton.

IKE'S "MASTER TACTICIAN":
BRADLEY

On February 12, 1941, Lieutenant General Erwin Rommel landed at an air base near Tripoli, Libya, and set forth to lead the German Afrika Korps in the desert war against the British. Meanwhile in England, Lieutenant General Bernard Montgomery, a division leader at Dunkirk the previous spring, now commanded his first corps. At Fort Benning, Georgia, Brigadier General Courtney Hodges headed the Infantry School, while Brigadier General George Patton was acting commander of the Second Armored Division at the same post. On that twelfth day of February in Washington, Lieutenant Colonel Omar N. Bradley, the lowly assistant secretary of the General Staff of the War Department, received congratulations from family and friends, for it was his forty-eighth birthday. He had pulled more than his share of non-troop assignments; he had missed duty with the AEF in World War I, indeed, never serving outside the States in his career. His route to promotions was slow, with his rising to major in 1918 but not reaching lieutenant colonel for another eighteen years. He commanded few infantry outfits and none larger than a regiment. But his career was about to change—and fast: less than four years hence, Bradley would command an army group of over 1.3 million soldiers, including Hodges' and Patton's armies, that would advance into Germany alongside Montgomery's less powerful army group against enemy forces bereft of the leadership of Rommel, who had killed himself.

Of humble origins in Missouri, Bradley won an appointment to the U.S. Military Academy and became a cadet not out of a strong ambition to be a soldier but, as one scholar explains, "because it was a place where a young man with a desire for an education but without the means to finance it could get highly acceptable training without cost."[11] Together with Eisenhower, a Kansan who had entered West Point for the same reason, Bradley graduated in 1915 in "the class that the stars fell on." For the next fifteen years his tours of duty were routine; the high point was his second-place ranking, behind Gerow, in the advance course at the Infantry School in 1925. Later he would excel as a student at the Command and General Staff School and the Army War College. A turning point in his career occurred in 1929 when he became a tactics instructor at the Infantry School. The assistant commandant and head of the academic program was Colonel George Marshall, who soon elevated him to chief of the Weapons Section—"the highest possible personal honor" at the institution, according to Bradley.[12] Marshall secretly made notations on Bradley in his little black book of brief remarks about officers whom he considered superior. (His list included also among the Infantry School faculty such future leaders as Joseph Stilwell, Matthew Ridgway, Lawton Collins, and Bedell Smith.) Marshall found Bradley to be masterful in his understanding and teaching of tactics, as well as "conspicuous for his ability to handle people and his ability to do things carefully and simply."[13] In late 1936 when Bradley wrote to congratulate him on getting his first star, Marshall replied prophetically: "I very much hope we will have an opportunity to serve together again. I can think of nothing more satisfactory to me."[14]

Two years later Bradley reentered Marshall's world, this time in Washington, where Marshall, now a lieutenant colonel, was assigned to the G-1 Section (personnel and administration) of the General Staff and Bradley was deputy chief of staff of the Army. In 1940, Marshall, as chief of staff, ordered Bradley to his office as assistant secretary of the General Staff. Subsequently Brigadier General Robert Eichelberger, superintendent at the Military Academy, requested Bradley's transfer to West Point as commandant of cadets, but Marshall was measuring him for other responsibilities. The Army chief of staff surprised Bradley by appointing him instead to the much more important and prestigious post of commandant of the Infantry School. When Bradley arrived at Fort Benning in late February 1941 to succeed Courtney Hodges, who became the chief of infantry, he received a telegram notifying him that the Senate had just approved his promotion from lieutenant colonel to brigadier general. With Marshall's powerful sponsorship, he was finally on his way upward.

As became true of other promising officers, the pace of his advancement accelerated following America's entry into the Second World War. In late December 1941, Marshall named him commander of the Eighty-second Infantry Division, which would win fame upon its alteration to an airborne unit. After six months of leadership that impressed Marshall and Lesley McNair, Bradley was transferred to command of the Twenty-eighth Infantry Division, a National Guard outfit that was encountering some problems in training and morale; under him the foundation was laid for the division's favorable showing in Europe. On his fiftieth birthday, February 12, 1943, Bradley received a message from Marshall: "It is only fitting that your birthday should precede by only a few days your transfer to command a corps which comes as a long-delayed acknowledgment of your splendid record with the 28th Division."[15] Four days later Bradley, then at his division's training camp in Florida, had orders assigning him to head the X Corps stationed in Texas.

The same day, however, he got a telephone call from McNair's G-1 at Army Ground Forces headquarters notifying him that he was going overseas. Bradley said he was "flabbergasted" and explained that he had orders to assume command of the X Corps, whereupon the personnel chief at the other end of the line responded, "Oh, that was yesterday." For security reasons, his assignment could not be revealed then, but he was to report to the War Department the next day where he would be briefed. When Bradley inquired about whether to bring clothing for cold or for hot weather, the G-1 tipped him off: "Remember your classmate? You're going to join him."[16] Bradley immediately realized he meant Ike's Torch command in Northwest Africa. As he packed later, his feelings were ambivalent. He would be disappointed to lose the chance at his first corps command if the new assignment turned out to be a staff desk job at Torch headquarters. Whatever the position, however, he was pleased with the direction in which he was headed: "For the first time in 32 years as a soldier, I was off to a war."[17]

When he talked to Eisenhower between sessions of the Casablanca Conference in January, Marshall proposed that he add an officer as his special representative, or his "eyes and ears," to tour the frontlines and report on the situation. At the time Eisenhower was overburdened with political and diplomatic problems as well as military ones and felt "out of touch" with his field officers.[18] Actually Patton had recently been designated as his deputy, and Truscott had been added to the staff in charge of an advance headquarters. Many years later Bradley was still puzzled over why he also was needed there at the time: "I cannot imagine why Marshall proposed yet another man on the battlefront, and the record is not clear on the point. Perhaps Marshall was tactfully seeking a way of reinforcing Ike on the battlefield with professional generals skilled in infantry tactics, without actually saying so."[19] A few days before Rommel struck the Americans at Kasserine Pass on February 19, Ike sent Marshall a list of thirteen officers suitable to him for the new post. Marshall proposed Bradley from the group, Eisenhower quickly agreed, and Bradley was soon on his way, landing at Algiers on February 24.

After three days of indoctrination at Torch headquarters, Bradley, who had just been promoted to major general, was sent by Ike to the Tunisian front to confer with the officers and men of the battered II Corps. When Eisenhower replaced Fredendall with Patton as head of the II Corps in early March, he also appointed Bradley as deputy commander of the unit, informing Marshall at the time that Bradley "has been a godsend in every way."[20] The principal Marshall biographer observes, "Of all the officers sent to Eisenhower by Marshall none brought stronger recommendations than Bradley," who had earned the chief of staff's support on the basis of "steady performances of high quality."[21] The recommendation of Bradley for the deputy slot, however, came from Patton, whose motive was not the purest, according to a leading historian: "Patton for his part, not wanting a free-ranging emissary of the Supreme Commander peering over his shoulder, persuaded Eisenhower to make Bradley the deputy corps commander, though Bradley retained the right to represent Eisenhower."[22] When Patton left the corps to begin preparing his new army for the assault on Sicily, he recommended and Ike appointed Bradley to command the reinvigorated II Corps in mid-April. After aggressive performances by the outfit in the final battles in Tunisia, Bradley, who was promoted to lieutenant general in June, led the II Corps in the conquest of Sicily, demonstrating sure and steady control in combat and sound logistical management in contrast to the flamboyant style and sometimes reckless moves of his superior, Patton, who headed the Seventh Army in the campaign.

At the end of August 1943, Marshall, who had considered Clark and Patton also for the position, picked Bradley to command the First Army in Operation Overlord. Clark was then preparing to lead the Fifth Army in the Salerno invasion; unless there was a dearth of leaders, it seemed wise to let him develop in that role for a while, but the First Army commander would be needed in England soon to begin organizing and training. Contrary to popular accounts, Marshall did not know about Patton's slapping incidents on Sicily at the time he selected Bradley. When the Army chief of staff informed Ike that he had chosen Bradley to head the First Army, Eisenhower, who had received early reports about Patton's misbehavior at the hospitals, responded enthusiastically: "Bradley is a standout in any position and is running absolutely true to form. . . . Of the three, Bradley is the best rounded in all respects, counting experience, and he has the great characteristic of never giving his commander one moment of worry." In the last clause he obviously had Patton's recent outbursts in mind that Marshall and the world would soon learn about. He added that he was "distressed at the thought of losing Bradley because I have come to lean on him so heavily in absorbing part of the burdens that otherwise fall directly upon me."[23]

In early September when Bradley received his orders and left Sicily for England, he was instructed to establish not only First Army headquarters but also an army group headquarters, the latter to be activated in Normandy the next summer. For a time Marshall mulled over the qualifications of Devers and McNair for the permanent command of the army group. After Ike arrived in London in January, however, the chief of staff formally appointed Bradley as the XII Army Group commander, the organization to begin functioning after the Third Army joined the First in the Overlord campaign. Though Patton's formal selection to head the Third Army came later, it was being discussed then and may have been a factor in Marshall's choice of Bradley for the army group command, according to what he remarked to his Operations Division chief, General John E. Hull: "Patton . . . is too impetuous. He needs a brake to slow him down. . . . He always needs someone just above him, and that is why I am giving the command to Bradley."[24] Until Bradley moved up to head his own army group, he would be under Montgomery, the British XXI Army Group leader—an ill-conceived arrangement that bore the seeds of discord from the planning stage onward.

Courtney Hodges, another favorite of Marshall's, was named as Bradley's deputy commander over the First Army. They organized their headquarters staff from personnel who had served with Bradley earlier in the Mediterranean and officers from the First Army staff in the States. Hodges was older than Bradley and Eisenhower, had been dismissed from West Point for academic failure, had subsequently risen through the ranks from private, and had won distinction in combat in World War I. Similar to Bradley, he had built a reputation as "a calm, careful tactician," but some officers "had doubts" about his abilities as an army-level leader after his lackluster performance in commanding the Third Army in the States.[25] (Yet, says one authority, Hodges was "given the understanding that he would command First Army when Bradley took over 12th Army Group," which is what happened in August 1944.[26])

In the advance from Normandy into Germany, Bradley's XII Army Group was in the center, with Montgomery's XXI Army Group on its northern flank and Devers' VI Army Group to the south. Under Bradley were Hodges' First Army, Patton's Third Army, Simpson's Ninth Army, and, in the spring of 1945, Gerow's Fifteenth Army. Though known for being judicious and even-tempered, Bradley sometimes had difficulty controlling Patton, who could "slip his leash" and act irresponsibly at times, notably in his ill-fated Hammelburg raid in March to rescue his son-in-law. All in all, however, their friendship and working relationship stood the tests of the campaign well, and in the last months they often teamed up to protest to Ike about his alleged favoritism toward the British. Montgomery was the chief thorn in Bradley's side during the XII Army Group's operations; later he branded the Britisher as "an arrogant egomaniac," but during the war he usually shared such sentiments only with Patton and close friends.[27] "I witnessed a first sign, but not the last, of Bradley's irritation with Montgomery," recalled General Collins, when they clashed over projected phase lines for the Normandy advance during Overlord planning sessions in April 1944.[28] When Monty ceased to command all Allied ground forces at the end of August 1944, Churchill elevated him to the rank of field marshal, for which there was no American equivalent; Bradley was not yet a full general. "The P.M. [prime minister] intends this to show that he is not being demoted by being made co-equal with General Bradley," so wrote Churchill's secretary in his diary.[29] In truth, Monty never viewed any Americans as his equal, whatever their ranks or titles.

For a while in early 1945, the long and deep friendship between Bradley and Eisenhower seemed in danger. During the Battle of the Bulge, upon Montgomery's urging, Ike temporarily transferred Simpson's and Hodges' armies to the British XXI Army Group. The First Army was returned to the American XII Army Group soon after the Ardennes battle, but Bradley became outraged when Eisenhower let Montgomery retain the Ninth Army until after the British offensive crossed the Rhine in March. Major General Francis W. "Freddy" de Guingand, Monty's chief of staff, later wrote that he "liked the quiet and confident way" of Bradley and "felt very sorry" for him during that period, "for I had a great affection for this modest soldier."[30] According to a staff member close to Ike, Bradley "showed open resentment" and "displayed real anger" over the Ninth Army issue, while Eisenhower, in turn, was "most hurt" by this "personal wound" from "one of his closest friends" and "the most co-operative of all field commanders."[31] In one of their many private grievance sessions during the final months of the war, Bradley confided to Patton that "the biggest mistake SHAEF [Eisenhower] has yet made" was loaning the Ninth Army indefinitely to Montgomery, while Patton countered that, in his opinion, "the biggest was when Gen. Eisenhower decided to turn the 1st Army north to help Montgomery at the end of Aug., and as a result stopped the 3rd Army and prevented the capture of Berlin early in Sept."[32] Bradley and Patton both detested the alleged waffling by Eisenhower regarding the broad-front advance, for sometimes he seemed to lean toward Montgomery and Brooke's single-thrust strategy and temporarily gave logistical priority to the British army group. When there was some talk about Montgomery possibly being made Allied ground forces commander again in 1945, Bradley threatened to resign—and Patton said that he would, too. Bradley's relations with Ike improved greatly when Simpson's army was finally returned to his group.

At what he called "a terrible meeting" of the Combined Chiefs of Staff on Malta in February, Marshall fiercely defended Eisenhower and Bradley against criticisms by the British Chiefs, who, he said, "were much worried by the influence on General Eisenhower by General Bradley," which would have seemed farfetched to Bradley and Patton at the time.[33] Like Marshall, of course, Eisenhower had long been a steadfast believer in Bradley. In early 1944, Ike had written his son, John, a cadet at West Point: "One thing that has struck me very forcibly . . . is the frequency with which one finds the older officer of today to be merely a more mature edition of the kid he knew as a cadet. . . . General Bradley's present position, for example, could have been predicted accurately by anyone that knew him well 30 years ago."[34] Ike had pressured Marshall many times to have Bradley promoted to four-star rank, which was finally done in late March 1945. In support of his recommendation that spring, Eisenhower told the chief of staff: "His handling of his army commanders has been superb and his energy, commonsense, tactical skill and complete loyalty have made him a great lieutenant upon whom I can always rely with the greatest confidence. I consider Bradley the greatest battle-line commander I have met in this war."[35] Years later Eisenhower remarked of him: "Throughout the war he was not only an outstanding commander, but he was my warm friend and close adviser. . . . Bradley was the master tactician of our forces and in my opinion will eventually come to be recognized as America's foremost battle leader."[36]

In his memoirs General Lucius D. Clay said of Bradley: "I know of no greater soldier ever produced from our army." Commenting on that judgment years later, Clay remarked, "I used the word 'soldier' when I wrote that deliberately. . . . He didn't have the ability of the negotiator, he didn't have the grasp of the political facts of life which General Eisenhower had, but he did understand and know what you had to do to have a good army."[37] Major General Elwood "Pete" Quesada, who provided vital tactical air support for Bradley's ground forces across Northwest European battlefields, found Bradley to be "the easiest person in the world to work with. He was unbelievably cooperative, with a very thorough understanding of the problems of others, and whereas his subordinate commanders would be indignant when these isolated tragedies and misfortunes would occur [of American aircraft attacking friendly ground units], he was sympathetic to my contention that it was a two-way street" in coordinating ground-air support.[38]

After the war Bradley headed the Veterans Administration until early 1948 when he became Army chief of staff, succeeding a "delighted" Ike, who had strongly recommended him to President Truman.[39] A year later he became chairman of the Joint Chiefs of Staff, a post he held until the end of the Korean War in the summer of 1953. Subsequently he became board chairman of Bulova Watch Company, as well as holding directorships in several other corporations.

In September 1950, through Truman's influence, Congress passed and he signed into law a bill promoting Bradley to five-star rank. The president swore him in as the youngest and last of the five-man group of generals of the Army in a White House ceremony the day after he had sworn in his new secretary of defense, George C. Marshall. A few months later Eisenhower and Montgomery would become the first commander in chief and deputy commander in chief of NATO forces.

Many contrasts between Bradley and Patton have appeared in print, but one of the most perceptive yet least known comparisons of the two officers was written by Colonel W. H. S. Wright, a War Department staff officer visiting American headquarters at Bristol, England, four days before Overlord was launched. Wright reported to Secretary Stimson that while in the Bristol headquarters he had

> *a good chance to see and talk to Gen. Bradley, Gen. Hodges and on one occasion, Gen. Patton. All are confident, sold on the scheme of the assault and anxious to go. There is no half-heartedness. . . .*
>
> *Gen. Bradley is cool, logical, measured and sure of himself and his force. His staff have complete confidence in him. . . . They all are completely devoted to Gen. Bradley. . . .*
>
> *Gen. Bradley and Gen. Patton present an interesting contrast when they are together and yet they have certain qualities in common. They apparently get along very well together and understand each other thoroughly. Gen. Bradley gives the impression of a general who succeeds by reason of calmness, logical decisions and meticulous care in preparation. Gen.*

Patton gives indications of great élan, desire to close
with the enemy and dynamic personal leadership. They
have in common the qualities of inexorable drive and
will to win, and great staying qualities.[40]

THE AMERICAN COMMANDER
WHOM THE GERMANS
FEARED THE MOST: PATTON

The Olympic Games, Stockholm, July 1912. George S. Patton, Jr., a twenty-six-year-old second lieutenant who was three years out of West Point, represented the United States in the grueling pentathlon, which consisted of swimming, steeplechase riding, fencing, crosscountry running, and pistol shooting. His point total for four of the events put him in first place, but two inexplicable misses of the target left him twenty-first in the shooting competition. It was a shock to him and his supporters because he was an expert marksman. Some believed, says one source, that the two shots the judges failed to find "passed through holes previously made in the bull's eye and therefore did not register, which was entirely plausible."[41] His proudest moment was in giving the French fencing champion his only defeat in the Olympics. (Later he continued his fencing studies at the leading French school, at Saumar, where he was named "Master of the Sword," the first American soldier to hold that coveted title.) As he crossed the finish line in the crosscountry race, in which he was third, he fainted and did not regain consciousness for several hours. His final ranking in the pentathlon was fifth among forty-two competitors. Reporters at the Olympics praised him for the "incredible" all-out effort he gave in each of the five events. The senior officer over the military members of the American Olympic team reported to the War Department that Patton "made a most excellent showing . . . and deserves great credit for the enthusiastic and exhaustive way in which he prepared himself for this very difficult, all-round competition."[42] Hard work, sound preparation, fierce demands of himself, occasional wildness, intense will power, craving for appreciation, and obsession with winning—all these traits were evident in Patton as an Olympic athlete, and they would characterize his extraordinary performance three decades later in the Second World War.

Wealth, aristocracy, and distinction in military, political, and commercial affairs were the family legacy of Patton. He was reared on a well-to-do ranch in California, and he married into a rich Massachusetts family. Cultured and versed in the graces of high society, he was one of few American Army officers to enjoy independent wealth. His fortune enabled him not only to entertain lavishly and to keep a stable of fine horses but also to act at times with less inhibitions than fellow soldiers who had no livelihood other than the military. While working zealously at his profession as a young officer, he also set about cultivating influential people, including Chief of Staff Leonard Wood and Secretary of War Henry Stimson, under both of whom he served as aide-de-camp in Washington at various times during 1911–13. Unlike officers with modest incomes who dreaded tours of duty in the high-cost environs of the national capital, he considered Washington to be "nearer God than elsewhere and the place where all people with aspirations should attempt to dwell."[43]

For the Mexican Punitive Expedition of 1916–17, Major General John J. "Black Jack" Pershing secured Patton's services as aide, getting him transferred out of a cavalry regiment in Texas. During the operations below the border Patton killed three Mexican soldiers in a firefight—an unlikely chore for an aide—and, more vital to his future, developed a cordial relationship with Pershing. When he was appointed head of the American Expeditionary Forces in the spring of 1917, Pershing chose Patton again as his aide for the venture in France. Aware after a few months on the Continent that Patton was restless to get into combat, Pershing offered him an infantry battalion to command, but the ambitious young captain turned it down and asked the general to recommend him for the American armored force about to be organized.

Considering it "a thing of destiny," Patton, with Pershing's powerful backing, became the first officer assigned to the new U.S. Army Tank Corps in November 1917.[44] In the ensuing twelve months he organized and headed the American tank training center in France and brilliantly led the AEF tank units in the St. Mihiel and Meuse-Argonne campaigns, in which he was wounded. He proudly wrote his wife after the St. Mihiel victory: "I was the only officer above the rank of major on the front line, except [Brigadier] General [Douglas] MacArthur, who never ducked a shell."[45] When he returned to America in 1919, he held several battle decorations and the rank of colonel.

With the postwar slashes in the military budget Patton, like many other good officers, was reduced in rank; he was returned to his permanent rank of captain and would not attain the level of colonel again until mid-1938. Also, the Tank Corps was placed under the infantry, so he transferred back to his original arm, the cavalry. During the years between the world wars he served in a series of "apparently aimless assignments," though he also graduated with distinction from the Cavalry School, the Command and General Staff College, and the Army War College.[46] Sometimes he was too impetuous or impatient with the complacency of the peacetime military establishment. For instance, when he was on the headquarters staff of the Hawaiian Department in 1928, the commander said of him in his efficiency report that Patton "would be invaluable in time of war but is a disturbing element in time of peace"—an evaluation Marshall and Eisenhower would agree with seventeen years later.[47]

At the time that Hitler's panzer divisions rolled into Poland in 1939, Patton was commanding Fort Myer at Arlington, Virginia, where his main duties were ceremonial, such as staging shows by the horse cavalry for congressmen and other dignitaries from the other side of the Potomac. That spring Marshall, the acting chief of staff, stayed with him for a while when his quarters at Fort Myer were being renovated. Patton thought he had charmed Marshall, and when Marshall moved up to full general and permanent chief of staff in

September, Patton sent him a set of sterling silver stars, four for each collar. Marshall thanked him politely for the gift as well as his earlier hospitality but said nothing to encourage a closer relationship. More disconcerting to Patton, who was an expert in flattery, Marshall kept him at Fort Myer while filling numerous posts in the fast-expanding Army with younger officers. As his biographer suggests, the destiny-smitten Patton, who was eager to get an armored command, was left to wonder why he was seemingly being ignored: "Was Patton too old at 54? Was he too wedded to the horse cavalry? Was Marshall testing Patton's patience? Did . . . Roosevelt think that Patton's political connections through his wife with Republicans . . . were too close? Was Patton too flamboyant, too outspoken?"[48]

Actually Patton had been receiving favorable attention in high Army circles for some time. Like Marshall, he had the blessing of Pershing, the living patron saint of the Army. He had published over a dozen solid articles in the *Cavalry Journal* on innovations in cavalry tactics and weapons. He had become one of the rare Army officers knowledgeable about amphibious warfare, had gained a mastery of military history, had delved deeply into ground-air coordination in combat (even earning a pilot's license in the process), and, most significantly, had kept abreast of developments in armored doctrine and tactics, as well as tank designs. He did not know that Marshall held him in high regard, as Marshall confided to his executive officer in the War Plans Division, Lieutenant Colonel Gee Gerow: "Patton is by far the best tank man in the Army. . . . I realize he is a difficult man but I know how to handle him."[49] Pershing, of course, and Eisenhower, who had once been in the Tank Corps, were among the few others who recalled Patton's armored leadership in World War I, but they would constitute a potent minority as far as Patton's professional future was concerned.

When the Armored Force was created in the summer of 1940, Major General Adna R. Chafee, Jr., its commander and an old friend of Patton, recommended his promotion and assignment to lead an armored brigade. Also, Patton was asked for by Major General Charles L. Scott, head of the Second Armored Division and another comrade of many years. Stimson, the recently appointed secretary of war, fondly recalled his former aide and supported him, as did Pershing, who thought Patton's role in leading the AEF tanks had been invaluable. Marshall agreed with their assessments, and in July Patton was transferred to Fort Benning to command the Second Armored Brigade of Scott's division. When Patton sent a note of thanks to the chief of staff, Marshall replied: "I thought it would be just the thing you would like most to do at the moment. Also, I felt no one could do that particular job better."[50]

Demonstrating hard-driving, inspiring leadership and a sure grasp of all things related to tanks, Patton rose fast thereafter. That fall he moved up to brigadier general and acting head of the division. He was promoted to two-star rank and named commander of the Second Armored Division in April 1941. The next January he became head of the I Armored Corps, and that April he took charge of the new Desert Training Center in California. His mission at the center was to prepare American troops, mainly armored and mechanized, for fighting in the arid regions of North Africa alongside the already engaged British Army. He drove himself and his men relentlessly, conducting arduous and complex exercises, experimenting with new tactics and weapons in armored operations in the desert, and improving techniques in combined arms warfare. According to his chief biographer, he imparted "high enthusiasm and morale to men working in unusually rugged field conditions, . . . participated in every exercise, activity, and training task," and "concentrated on teaching his men to kill efficiently, instinctively."[51] Since Chafee's death from cancer in August 1941, Patton more and more stood out as "the army's leading tanker."[52]

In July 1942 Patton was summoned to the War Department and informed by Joseph McNarney, Marshall's deputy chief of staff, that he might lead the Moroccan assault in Operation Torch that fall if he could work with the resources allotted to that force. Patton looked over the plan and brazenly told McNarney that he would need more men and materiel than had been projected. McNarney discussed Patton's response with Marshall, who promptly sent him back to California. The next day Patton called McNarney and said he "could do the job with all the forces your stupid staff is willing to give me. . . . I'm eating crow. . . . Can I have the job after all?" When McNarney told Marshall, the chief of staff ordered Patton back to Washington and remarked with a smile, "You see, McNarney, that's the way to handle Patton."[53]

Three weeks before his Western Task Force departed from Virginia for the invasion of French Morocco in early November, Patton visited Pershing, who was then at Walter Reed Hospital in Washington. In his diary that evening he recorded some of the old and ill AEF commander's words: "I can always pick a fighting man and God knows there are few of them. I am happy they are sending you to the front at once. I like Generals so bold that they are dangerous. I hope they give you a free hand."[54] Unfortunately, his isolated Torch mission did not afford Patton much opportunity to lead in battle. The French defenders offered brief but stiff resistance, then agreed to a ceasefire; the main action against the German and Italian forces would come in Tunisia, far to the east. For the next few months Patton, as the senior Allied officer in the area, took on occupation duties as well as continuing to train his troops and to guard against possible Axis raids from Spanish Morocco. In the wake of the Kasserine defeat, Eisenhower named the restive Patton to take over the defeated II Corps in March 1943. In short order Patton revitalized the outfit, led it to victory in several battles, and then turned it over to his deputy, Bradley. Promoted to lieutenant general and chosen to head the American troops in the summer invasion of Sicily, Patton was transferred back to French Morocco to organize and prepare the units that would later be designated the U.S. Seventh Army. His short-lived but aggressive appearance on the Tunisian front mightily impressed both Bradley, his II Corps successor, and Eisenhower, his friend from their days in the old Tank Corps, though Patton, who was amiable toward both, remained unpersuaded that either man knew much about battle.

As originally planned, the British Eighth Army under Montgomery was to have the paramount role in the Sicilian invasion in July, driving up the east coast to Messina and cutting off the Axis defenders from withdrawing across the narrow strait to Italy. Patton's Seventh Army was given the subsidiary task of protecting the British left flank as Monty's troops advanced northward. Strong enemy defenses, however, temporarily halted the British, so Patton quickly sought and obtained permission to launch an offensive toward Palermo, on the northwest coast of the island. Taking that city on July 22 after a wild dash by his units, Patton then turned his offensive eastward along the north coast and, despite several near disasters in small amphibious assaults, seized the port of Messina on August 17, robbing Montgomery of the chief glory of the campaign and inaugurating a bitter feud between the two men.

En route, however, Patton had gotten himself in deep trouble with Ike, too, by slapping two hospitalized American soldiers. Eisenhower chastised him severely in private and made him apologize to his army, but argued in favor of retaining Patton in discussions with Marshall and succeeded for several months in keeping the story out of the media. When the public finally learned that autumn about Patton's indiscretions, there was some pressure on Capitol Hill and the Pentagon for his removal. But Marshall supported Ike's judgment as to Patton's future value as a combat leader, so he was retained on duty in Sicily, though his responsibilities were greatly reduced and he strongly sensed his exiled status. Yet Patton never lost his belief that he had a larger role still ahead, as he wrote his wife in December from his isolated post on Sicily: "I have not had a very happy time. . . . I am a better general as a result of it. . . . I have a destiny and I shall live to fulfil it."[55]

Meanwhile, Marshall and Eisenhower had been exchanging numerous messages about forthcoming Anglo-American command changes, occasioned in part by Ike's Overlord appointment and the subsequent acceleration of preparations for the cross-channel assault. In all the various command combinations they discussed, Eisenhower steadfastly clung to the need for Patton, repeatedly emphasizing, as summarized by a reliable historian, that "the important consideration was to be sure to use Patton as an Army commander somewhere." Ike gave Patton a rating of "superior" for his performance from June through December 1943, ranked him fifth in "effectiveness" among the twenty-four lieutenant generals he was acquainted with, and described him as "outstanding as a leader of an assault force," though he was "impulsive and flamboyant in manner" and "should always serve under a strong but understanding commander."[56] General Everett Hughes, of SHAEF, wrote mischievously in his diary in early January 1944: "Devers says Patton thru. I guess the reason that D. [Dwight Eisenhower] doesn't want to take a chance on backing P. [Patton] who may win the war but do it in a manner not acceptable to D.'s press."[57] Like many other rumors that circulated through SHAEF, this one proved to be far from the truth. About that same time, Marshall and Eisenhower finally concurred on the best possible command arrangements involving Americans in ETO and MTO posts, and they agreed on Patton as an Overlord army leader but under Bradley, his former deputy, who was expected to provide the "strong but understanding" guidance he required.

In late January 1944, Eisenhower summoned Patton from Sicily to Britain where he was informed that he was to be the acting head of the U.S. Third Army, which was to follow Bradley's First Army into Normandy that summer and to become part of Bradley's XII Army Group later. In his first address to his Third Army staff, Patton was "pungent and to the point," said one of his intelligence officers. He concluded: "If you don't like to fight, I don't want you around. You'd better get out before I kick you out. But there is one thing to remember. In war, it takes more than the desire to fight to win. . . . You must also have brains. It takes brains and guts to win wars."[58] During the last week of March, Patton officially became the commanding general of the Third Army, by which time he already had his troops deeply involved in a rigorous training program. For a long time he was also used in Operation Fortitude, an Allied deception plan that deluded the Germans into thinking he was going to lead an army group in a cross-channel assault near Calais, which resulted in the stationing of a large German force along that portion of the French coast, far north of the projected Overlord landing sites. The hoax continued to work amazingly well even after the Normandy beachhead was established in June.

Keeping Patton's whereabouts and real mission secret was no mean feat in view of his unpredictable behavior. In April, for instance, he created excitement in the press and great anxiety for Ike by expounding on his notion of postwar Anglo-American global domination in a speech before a service club in Knutsford, England. Ike reported the Knutsford affair to Marshall and said he was "seriously contemplating the most drastic action." Subsequently, Eisenhower informed the chief of staff that "on all of the evidence now available I will relieve him from command," then discussing the merits of Courtney Hodges and Lucian Truscott as Patton's possible successor. But a few days later, in early May, Ike changed his mind about retaining the "admittedly unbalanced but nevertheless aggressive" Patton.[59] Again, Ike resorted to a severe reprimand in private, bluntly condemning Patton's "impulsiveness," his "dramatizing" of himself, his "indiscretions," and his "all-around judgment" and warning that the next impetuous action or statement would mean "instant relief from command." Movingly contrite and repentant in Ike's presence, Patton wrote in his diary: "These constant pickings are a little hard on the nerves, but great training."[60]

When Patton was sent to Normandy in early July 1944, a month after D day, the Overlord forces were still penned in their narrow beachhead and a virtual stalemate existed.

Late that month, however, Bradley's First Army forces achieved a breakthrough in the German defenses near St. Lo. After briefly leading two corps in the attack, Patton took over his Third Army, which became operational in France on August 1, the same day Bradley activated the XII Army Group and Hodges succeeded him over the First Army. At the time, observes a noted military historian, "the situation could not have been more fluid, a condition that could not have been more suitable for Patton's military talents."[61] He quickly transformed the penetration into a wild, free-wheeling breakout that forced the Germans into a general retreat from the Normandy defenses and turned into a temporary rout. Sending one of his corps to seize Brittany, to the southwest, and the other three eastward toward Orleans and the Seine, Patton undertook several envelopments that trapped some fleeing Germans and, with better cooperation from his superiors and the British and Canadian armies, might have decimated more of the enemy forces.

By the end of August he was masterminding Third Army operations over a five-hundred-mile stretch of France, extending from the port of Brest on the Atlantic to the Meuse River near the German border. Heavily relying on the fighter bombers of Brigadier General Otto P. Weyland's XIX Tactical Air Command to cover his open flanks in the Third Army's dash across France, Patton drove his forces boldly into Lorraine and the Saar Valley. Finally, shortages of petroleum, ammunition, and other supplies, along with worsening weather, halted his remarkable advance that autumn. Powerful fortifications, particularly around Metz, also contributed to the pause in his offensive. Patton's forte lay in exploiting opportunities for rapid maneuver and mobility; his tactics in taking unavoidable strongpoints like Metz were more conventional and less imaginative.

He was preparing a new assault against the German defenses along the Saar in mid-December when the surprise enemy counteroffensive began in the Ardennes, well to the north of his Third Army. Under severe winter conditions and a host of logistical nightmares, Patton, in one of the most spectacular movements of a large army in history, turned three of his corps from an eastward to a northward advance and led them into the Battle of the Bulge, relieving the surrounded American troops at Bastogne and helping to turn the tide in the gigantic Ardennes operation.

In the spring of 1945 he led his Third Army into southern Germany, crossing the Rhine in late March and then thrusting his units, often at a pace of over thirty miles a day, into Austria and as far east as Pilsen in Czechoslovakia. His magnificent leadership of the Third Army from the Normandy breakout to the German surrender in May was marred only by his disastrous Hammelburg raid. Another disappointment for him near the end of hostilities was Ike's prohibition against his capturing Prague, the Czech capital. Patton remained convinced that he could and should have seized Prague despite the Yalta agreement in February placing Czechoslovakia in the postwar Soviet occupation zone. Reviewing his operations since July 1944, Patton observed, "In every case, practically throughout the campaign, I was under wraps from the Higher Command. This may have been a good thing, as perhaps I am too impetuous. However, I do not believe I was, and feel that had I been permitted to go all out, the war would have ended sooner and more lives would have been saved."[62]

According to his close friend, Everett Hughes, Patton, as early as February 1945, was desirous of getting "a job in the Pacific" after the defeat of Germany.[63] But when Marshall asked MacArthur that June to choose the next army commander in the Pacific war from the chief of staff's list of four "available" officers, MacArthur's "preference" ranking was "first Stilwell, second Patch, and third Truscott," with no mention of Patton, the other general on the list.[64] Earlier MacArthur had commented to General Bob Eichelberger, his Eighth Army leader, that he would not have Patton as an army commander because he "could do brilliant things but was erratic to say the least."[65]

After the European fighting ended, Patton's Third Army became the occupation force in eastern Bavaria. Soon he again was involved in controversy, this time for disagreeing with occupation policies, especially those forbidding his troops' fraternization with Germans and prohibiting the use of Nazis in administrative posts. In early October, Eisenhower's patience finally wore out and he relieved Patton of command of his beloved Third Army, replacing him with Truscott. Patton was given the Fifteenth Army, which had entered combat in the final weeks of the war and now was engaged in preparing histories and tactical studies of ETO operations. In early December he broke his neck in a highway accident near Mannheim. He was hospitalized in Heidelberg where he died thirteen days later at the age of sixty.

Six months earlier Bradley had commented in his efficiency report on Patton: "Colorful, courageous, energetic, pleasing personality. Possesses high degree of leadership, bold in operations, has fine sense of feel of enemy and own capabilities. An outstanding combat leader."[66] General Thomas Handy later maintained, "Patton could get more out of officers and men than any other commander."[67] Major General John H. Chiles remarked, "How would you compare Bradley and Patton? If either of them had tried to act like the other one, he would have flopped."[68] According to Alexander, "Patton was a thruster, prepared to take any risks" and was "America's best fighting general."[69] Major General Hubert Essame of the British Army stated, "In mobile operations he outshone with startling brilliance in imagination, technique and achievement his Allied contemporaries." General Hans Speidel, the exceptionally gifted chief of staff to Rommel and a distinguished NATO commander later, remarked, "He was the only Allied general who dared to exceed the safety limits in the endeavor to achieve a decision."[70] Another German general said that to him and his colleagues Patton was "the most feared general on all fronts" because of his "daring and unpredictable" tactics. Field Marshal Gerd von Runstedt, longtime German commander in chief on the Western front, put it succinctly: "Patton was your best."[71] Eisenhower commented, "No one but Patton could exert such an extraordinary and ruthless driving power at critical moments or better demonstrate the ability of getting the utmost out of soldiers in offensive operations."[72]

Colonel Charles R. Codman, Patton's senior aide from 1943 to 1945, believed that "the key to General Patton's success" lay in "the unabashed enthusiasm, more, the passionate ardor for every aspect and manifestation of his chosen medium." In a letter to his wife on August 8, 1944, he captured the essence of Patton the warrior in describing some of the general's reactions during the previous week when the explosive breakout by the Third Army from Normandy was starting:

The Old Man [Patton] has been like one possessed, rushing back and forth up and down . . . occasionally darting out to haul an officer out of a ditch in which he has taken refuge from a German plane, or excoriating another for taping over the insignia on his helmet. "Inexcusable," he yells. "Do you want to give your men the idea that the enemy is dangerous?" Pushing, pulling, exhorting, cajoling, raising merry hell, he is having the time of his life. . . .

A few days ago, in Avranches itself, we were blocked by a hopeless snarl of trucks. The General . . . sprang into the abandoned umbrella-covered police box in the center of the square, and for an hour and a half directed traffic. . . .

We have been bombed, strafed, mortared, and shelled. The General thrives on it. Yesterday . . . we were speeding along . . . a bad stretch of road from which our bulldozers had recently pushed to either side the reeking mass of smashed half-tracks, supply trucks, ambulances, and blackened German corpses. Encompassing with a sweep of his arm the rubbled farms and bordering fields scarred with grass fires, smoldering ruins, and the swollen carcasses of stiff-legged cattle, the General half turned in his seat. "Just look at that, Codman," he shouted. "Could anything be more magnificent?" As we passed a clump of bushes, one of our concealed batteries let go with a shattering salvo. The General cupped both hands. I leaned forward to catch his words. "Compared to war, all other forms of human endeavor shrink to insignificance." His voice shook with emotion. "God, how I love it!"[73]

In bearing with his flaws and entrusting him with command of the Third Army, Eisenhower and Marshall had known their man: Patton was hard to control, but no other American general seemed so born to war. It was with good reason that some of his men called him "Old Blood and Guts," and not always affectionately. "A throwback to the Teutonic knight, the Saracen, the Crusader," observes Patton's main biographer, "he was one of America's greatest soldiers, one of the world's great captains. We were lucky to have him on our side."[74]

NINE

THE LAST FIFTEEN MONTHS OF THE PACIFIC WAR

FROM BIAK AND SAIPAN
TO TOKYO BAY
(PACIFIC, JUNE 1944–SEPTEMBER 1945)

The United States Joint Chiefs of Staff had been given the responsibility for the strategic direction of the Pacific war, as decided by Roosevelt, Churchill, and the Combined Chiefs of Staff in the spring of 1942. Henceforth the American high command seldom compromised with its allies in determining such matters, leaving the Chinese and the Australians particularly offended by its unilateral control of plans and operations against Japan. The fronts in China and Burma got less and less attention in American planning as the offensives in the Pacific grew in size and decisiveness. Nevertheless, the advances across the Pacific by Nimitz's and MacArthur's forces were made much easier (indeed, possible) by the fact that large Japanese forces had been stationed on the Asiatic continent until the end of hostilities. Nearly sixty percent of the 3.2 million Japanese troops stationed outside the home islands were still deployed in China and Manchuria as late as August 1945. If not often on the offensive, the Chinese tied down much of the enemy's ground power that otherwise might have been brought to bear against the American advances in the Pacific. Australia, in turn, provided the indispensable base of operations for the Southwest Pacific offensive, as well as support with forces and materiel.

The final defeat of Japan was accomplished largely through tenuous understandings and compromises between the leaders of the services in the American military establishment. "Yet for the United States," observes a noted historian, "the record of the Pacific War is not so much a story of how the services forgot their differences but rather of the ingenuity displayed by service leaders in devising courses of action which allowed them to get on with the war without having to settle those differences."[1] The dual axis of advance was maintained until the end by way of MacArthur's Southwest Pacific offensive, spearheaded by Army and Army Air Force units, and Nimitz's Central Pacific drive, largely comprised of Navy and Marine forces. Neither theater chief was as adept at compromise as Eisenhower, but somehow they made the divided command system work to their mutual advantage at the most critical times.

The discussions and studies by commanders and planning staffs at the theater and Pentagon levels on how to defeat Japan ultimately came down to very predictable positions in view of the fierce interservice rivalries: the Army Air Forces' leaders believed strategic air bombardment could bring Japan to her knees without an invasion of the home islands; the top admirals all were convinced that naval blockade and coastal bombardment of the home islands would force Japan's surrender without resort to ground assaults; and the Army's senior commanders maintained that a large-scale invasion was unavoidable. According to the Army's official history, "To the Army staff, at least, mass invasion seemed the quickest way, indeed the only way, in which Japanese capitulation could be assured. It was also undoubtedly the costliest way both in human lives and resources, and the way that would require the most extensive redeployment of the forces from Europe."[2] Ultimately, the air and sea power strategies were implemented on a limited basis, but enormous ground invasions of the home islands were in preparation when the sudden surrender occurred. The decision by Japan's leaders to capitulate, however, was brought about, in large measure, by two developments not altogether factored into the interservice debates and compromises: the use of the atomic bombs and the lightning Soviet offensive into Manchuria, China, and Korea during the last days of the war.

During the period from June 1944 to August 1945, MacArthur's Southwest Pacific forces completed the conquest of the strategically most important enemy-occupied areas of the theater and further crippled Japan's military forces and raw-material lifeline. After a savage battle for Biak, an island off Dutch New Guinea, MacArthur's American armies—the Sixth, led by Walter Krueger, and the newly formed Eighth, headed by Bob Eichelberger—proceeded to secure the rest of New Guinea in the summer of 1944. Southwest Pacific forces seized Morotai, in the Moluccas, in September, and a month later MacArthur accompanied the armada that invaded the Central Philippines, with Krueger's army assaulting Leyte under cover of ships and planes of Bill Halsey's Third and Tom Kinkaid's Seventh Fleet. In December the Eighth Army took charge of the Leyte operations, which lasted until spring. In the meantime, Krueger's divisions took Mindoro, just south of Manila Bay, and in early January 1945 invaded Luzon. For the next eight months the Sixth Army would be heavily engaged there, including a month-long battle for Manila and a strong redoubt in the northern mountains that lasted until the war's end. That spring and summer, too, Eichelberger's army, supported by Kinkaid and Daniel Barbey's naval forces and Ennis Whitehead's Fifth Air Force, conducted a series of fast-moving amphibious assaults that liberated the southern Philippines. Blamey's Australian forces meanwhile captured the coastal regions of Borneo and mopped up enemy remnants on New Guinea, New Britain, and Bougainville. Except for the additions from the deactivated South Pacific theater, these final campaigns in MacArthur's area were staged without further large-scale reinforcements, the bulk of American deployments in men and materiel concentrated on the war against Germany from 1944 to 1945. MacArthur's senior commanders remained in place for the most part during this period, though in the summer of 1945 Courtney Hodges and other generals from the European theater were beginning to arrive for the projected operations against Kyushu that fall.

In the war against Japan, Generals Walter Krueger, Bob Eichelberger, Thomas Blamey, George Kenney, and Whitehead and Admirals Kinkaid and Barbey were as instrumental to the victorious operations as were commanders like Omar Bradley and Mark Clark in American campaigns against Germany, but the former, who were the key Southwest Pacific field commanders, were rarely mentioned in the news and remain relatively obscure leaders. To a great extent, the absence of their feats in communiqués and dispatches was due to MacArthur's enormous egotism and his public relations officers' obsession with slanting the news to portray him as the only noteworthy commander in the Pacific. Such slights eventually embittered several of MacArthur's lieutenants, notably Eichelberger. Often very critical of his ground commanders, particularly Blamey and Krueger, and sometimes exasperated by Admiral Kinkaid, MacArthur had generous praise for his air leaders, especially Kenney. The only new candidate for a senior slot to gain his favor during the final fifteen months was Lieutenant General Oscar W. Griswold, the hard-driving head of the XIV Corps in Southwest and earlier South Pacific operations. MacArthur wanted him as his next army commander but had to settle instead for Stilwell.

By the last phases of the war MacArthur had become persuaded that Marshall and Eisenhower, together with several of their subordinate generals in the War Department and in SHAEF, were conspiring to handicap him logistically and strategically in his leadership in the Pacific struggle. He once confided to Eichelberger that "there was a crooked streak in Ike and George Catlett Marshall which would show up in a long war."[3] Roosevelt became another adversary to MacArthur, and the general showed more than a little interest and disingenuousness in a still-born MacArthur-for-President movement in early 1944. Truman's naming him, on the advice of Marshall, as head of all U.S. Army forces in the Pacific in April 1945 and as supreme commander for all the Allies in the Japanese surrender and subsequent occupation did not ameliorate MacArthur's sense of exclusion from the inner circle of the American military hierarchy that was evolving toward the end of World War II and that seemed ready to control U.S. defense policy in the postwar era.

Whereas MacArthur's relations with Marshall were formal and distant, Nimitz enjoyed much closer personal and professional ties with his superior, Ernest King. MacArthur and Marshall met only once during the war years, but Nimitz and King had over twenty conferences, usually at Pearl Harbor or San Francisco. Frequently domineering and sometimes brutally critical toward his admirals, King undoubtedly made Nimitz wish at times that the chief of naval operations showed less interest in Pacific affairs.

Central Pacific operations from June 1944 onward were highlighted by successful American campaigns in the Marianas (Saipan, Tinian, and Guam) in the summer; in the Palaus that autumn, though the enemy stronghold on Peleliu, in retrospect, should have been bypassed; and the two final and very costly operations in Nimitz's theater, on Iwo Jima from February to March 1945 and on Okinawa from April to June. The Pacific Fleet also took on the Japanese Navy in two large naval-air engagements during this period that left the latter virtually decimated: the battles of the Philippine Sea, featuring Ray Spruance's Fifth Fleet in June 1944, and of Leyte Gulf, won by Halsey's Third and Kinkaid's Seventh Fleet that October. Actually, however, Charles Lockwood's submarine force continued to sink more enemy ships than did all the POA and SWPA air and surface forces combined. Lockwood surely must rank as the most forgotten senior commander of the Pacific war. On the other hand, one of the most heralded from the fall of 1944 hence was Major General Curtis E. LeMay, who, in effect, became the field commander of the B-29 bombing offensive against Japan, though Arnold continued to head the force as agent of the JCS. The long-range "Superfortresses" struck Japan from bases in China and later in the Marianas, and by the spring of 1945 their fire raids had burned huge areas of the downtown and harbor districts of most large Japanese cities. In the final months the enemy home islands were also attacked by Third Fleet planes and ships, along with Kenney's land-based aircraft.

From the Saipan assault in the Marianas in June 1944 to the Japanese capitulation in mid-August 1945, Nimitz's principal lieutenants were Admirals Spruance and Halsey, the fleet commanders; Admirals Kelly Turner and Ping Wilkinson, the amphibious naval force leaders; Admiral Lockwood, head of the submarines; and Marine Generals Holland Smith, Roy Geiger, and Harry Schmidt, the amphibious corps commanders. Redeployments from other theaters brought Admiral Bruce Fraser's Royal Navy fleet into the Central Pacific operations in early 1945, despite King's opposition, and added three air leaders from the European war, Generals Spaatz, Twining, and Doolittle, who respectively took charge of the Strategic Air Force, the Twentieth Air Force, and the reconstituted Eighth Air Force (now armed with B-29s). At the same time General Hodges and advance elements of the First Army began arriving in the West Pacific to join the buildup for the Kyushu and Honshu invasions. The only senior American commander killed during the last fifteen months of the Pacific fighting was General Simon Buckner, who died in action on Okinawa in June 1945.

The strategic issue in the war against Japan that occupied the Joint Chiefs and their planners in 1944 was whether Formosa, the Chinese coast near Amoy, or Luzon was the best invasion target before ground assaults on Japan. With the large Japanese offensive in the Canton-Hankow region of South China in the spring and summer of 1944, the Washington planners ruled out further consideration of a landing on the coast of China. By the late spring, moreover, both Marshall and Arnold believed that MacArthur's proposal to seize Luzon was not strategically wise and would entail a lengthy, high-casualty campaign, as King had long argued. At a conference at Pearl Harbor in July 1944, however, MacArthur seemed to win over Roosevelt and Leahy to his position, arguing on political and humanitarian, as well as strategic, grounds. Already having JCS authorization to invade Mindanao and Leyte, the SWPA commander pressed long and hard for the recapture also of Luzon, which operations would give him the key islands in the north, central, and south parts of the Philippines and better ensure his liberation of the rest of that American territory. After further studies and debates in late summer and early fall on the Luzon-versus-Formosa issue, the Joint Chiefs finally decided that the conquest of Formosa was not feasible because of insurmountable logistical difficulties. With Roosevelt's approval, they then issued a directive in early October authorizing MacArthur to add Luzon to his forthcoming objectives. MacArthur assured the JCS that within two weeks after his troops landed on Luzon they would have control of Manila. But the capital was not secured until two months after the amphibious assault on the island, and, as it turned out, the Luzon campaign would be the longest and costliest of the Pacific war for American ground forces, as critics had feared would be the case. There was little evidence, however, that an invasion of Formosa would have been less formidable.

As planning for the final defeat of Japan was accelerated in late 1944 in the Pentagon and at the Pacific theater headquarters, it became obvious that a new directive would have to be issued or MacArthur's operations would be terminated with the conquest of Luzon because the northern boundary of the SWPA theater ran just above the Philippines. Army leaders were concerned that if the current POA boundary were retained Nimitz would be in charge of the invasion of Japan, with the large Army ground and air forces of MacArthur's theater being entrusted to the admiral for the assaults on the enemy home islands. Naval leaders, as before, refused to consider MacArthur for a long-talked-about supreme command post in the Pacific because it would give him control over the vaunted Pacific Fleet. As discussed earlier, the matter was resolved by the Joint Chiefs in early April 1945 with the issuance of a new directive on Pacific command, mainly with the impending invasion of Japan in mind. MacArthur was to command all U.S. Army forces in the Pacific and Nimitz all American naval forces there, with both retaining their theater commands. Most important for what was looming as the grand finale, MacArthur would head ground operations and Nimitz naval ones in joint missions, such as the Kyushu assault. A week before the Japanese surrendered in August, Secretary of the Navy James Forrestal was preparing to try to persuade Truman to appoint Nimitz, Marshall, or Eisenhower in that order, rather than MacArthur, to serve as an overall commander for the invasion of Kyushu, which, he said, was "far too important a matter . . . for pride of Service to enter" or for the SWPA chief to head.[4]

Arnold had renewed his proposal for a single air commander for the Pacific, but in July 1945 the Joint Chiefs approved instead his next plan, which provided for the creation of the U.S. Army Strategic Air Force, Pacific, to be headed by Spaatz and to include Twining's Twentieth and Doolittle's Eighth Air Force.[5] MacArthur, Nimitz, and even Stilwell had previously tried to get control of the much-sought B-29s; the new air command arrangement continued to forestall such control. A foremost historian of the Pacific conflict concludes, "Thus, when the war with Japan came to an end, the [American] forces in the Pacific were organized into three commands, with the strategic bombardment force in a position of near equality with the Army and Navy forces." The various efforts since Pearl Harbor to achieve unity of command in the Pacific "had failed, and even the unified commands set up in 1942 had been abandoned under the pressure of events."[6]

The long-festering differences between Stilwell and his main CBI antagonists—Chiang Kai-shek, Chennault, and Mountbatten—reached a climax in the latter half of 1944 with his successful invasion of North Burma and the failure of Chinese defenses against the Japanese drive in South China. Chiang reported to Roosevelt that Stilwell's success had been achieved at the cost of much of South China and that the crusty general was impossible to deal with, whereupon Roosevelt recalled Stilwell in October. General Al Wedemeyer, his successor in China, managed to get along with the Generalissimo, but no military reforms were forthcoming, no large-scale Chinese offensive was mounted in the remaining months of the war, and the Nationalist regime's relations with the Chinese Communists worsened. The forces of Chiang and of Mao Tse-tung appeared to be maneuvering more for postwar positions against each other than for wartime advantages against the Japanese. By early 1945, says a respected scholar, Roosevelt "no longer received any significant advice on China from Marshall and Stimson, since the War Department generally had lost interest in China."[7] The official chronicle of the Joint Chiefs states flatly that the CBI theater's "contribution did not balance the effort expended. . . . The political commitment [by the United States government] to continue to support China was an unrewarding drain on military resources."[8] Like the Korean and Vietnam morasses, the CBI was not a good breeding ground for great captains, who seem to thrive on potentially decisive situations. Even Claire Chennault, once the popular hero of Flying Tigers fame, saw his career deteriorate in China; he was replaced rather ignominiously only weeks before the Japanese surrender.

The postwar U.S. Strategic Bombing Survey concluded that even if the atomic bombs had not been dropped on Hiroshima and Nagasaki, Japan would have capitulated in a few more months anyway because of "the devastating impact" on the Japanese economy and morale of the B-29 bombing offensive.[9] Curtis LeMay, who led the XXI Bomber Command's B-29 campaign (and became a postwar chief of staff of the Air Force), preferred at the time not to employ the atomic weapon: "I think it was anticlimactic, in that the verdict was already rendered."[10] In his view, as well as that of many other Army Air Forces leaders, the B-29s' conventional bombing raids had been instrumental in forcing Japan's capitulation. A distinguished Army historian, however, points out that "the strategic bombing of Japan became effective only after sea-air-ground offensives had brought the B-29's within range of the home islands, shorn away its new empire, and defeated its Navy and air force; and only after submarines and the naval blockade had strangled its shipping and war economy."[11]

The multiple factors and numerous compromises that characterized the victory over Japan were epitomized in the Tokyo Bay ceremony on September 2, 1945, marking Japan's official surrender. General MacArthur signed the surrender document as the supreme commander for the thirteen Allied powers at war against Japan, but in fact he also symbolized the unexpectedly large roles of the U.S. Army and Army Air Forces and of the Southwest Pacific theater in that conflict. Admiral Nimitz signed for the American government, yet he also represented in reality the U.S. Navy and Marine Corps, as well as the Pacific Ocean Areas, including its North, Central, and South Pacific subtheaters. And the battleship U.S.S. *Missouri,* where the august ceremony took place, represented not only American sea power and industrial superiority but also the unassuming exhaberdasher from Independence who was the new commander in chief of the United States, President Harry Truman.

Although the dispute still rages as to the most decisive factor in the war with Japan, the triumph was attained by massive doses of American combined arms firepower, along with significant assistance from the United States' allies. Two of the most distinguished American commanders serving in the Pacific were General Holland Smith, the aggressive, fiery head of the Fifth Amphibious Corps and of the Fleet Marine Force, Pacific, and Admiral Ray Spruance, the brilliant, urbane leader of the Fifth Fleet. Very different in personality and leadership traits, they successfully commanded some of the most powerful striking forces ever assembled.

AMPHIBIOUS EXPERT
AND VOLATILE MARINE
LOYALIST: SMITH

"What are the Marines?" twenty-two-year-old Holland M.
Smith naively inquired of his congressman in late 1904. After
graduating from the University of Alabama Law School the
previous year, Smith had been unhappy in his father's legal
firm and had gone to Washington to seek a commission in
the Army. He learned at the War Department that no new
officers would be commissioned for over a year. His Alabama
congressman then suggested the Marine Corps and went on
to tell him about "its history and functions." Smith remembered his "little lecture on the street outside the War Department" as "the most convincing I have ever heard . . . a
gem of extraordinary lucidity and conviction. His talk immediately won me over." They promptly went to the Navy
Department and found that the Marines were "looking for
some boys from the South to complete the proper geographical distribution of commissions," said Smith.[12] He passed
the Corps' entrance examination and was commissioned a
second lieutenant in March 1905 and assigned to the School
of Application, the basic officer training program at the Marine Barracks at Annapolis. Thus began the forty-one-year
career of Smith as a Marine, during which he would become
known as "the father of modern amphibious warfare" and
would command "more men in battle than any other Marine
general" in the Corps' annals.[13]

Smith was one of the tiny minority of American senior
commanders of the Second World War who experienced
combat before 1941. He was involved in his first firefight as
a company commander during the Marines' intervention in
the Santo Domingan revolution in 1916. A major with the
Fourth Marine Brigade in the AEF two years hence, he was
decorated for heroism in leading a company in the battle of
Belleau Wood and later served at corps level in the Aisne-
Marne, St. Mihiel, and Meuse-Argonne campaigns in World
War I. After serving in the postwar Rhine occupation force,

he underwent various tours of duty in the States, afloat, and abroad in the next seventeen years, his most significant assignments being as a student at the Naval War College, the first Marine on the Joint Army-Navy Planning Committee, and an innovative developer of Marine amphibious exercises and training sites.

In the spring of 1937 Colonel Smith was assigned to Marine headquarters in Washington as director of operations and training and as assistant to the new commandant, Major General Thomas Holcomb. Three years later he was promoted to brigadier general and given command of the First Marine Brigade at Quantico, Virginia. Subsequently he led the Atlantic Fleet's landing exercises in the Caribbean, impressing General Holcomb and particularly Admiral King with his mastery of amphibious tactics. When the brigade was enlarged in early 1941 to become the First Marine Division, Smith was retained as the head. Later that spring he took charge of the Marine training base at New River, North Carolina, and shortly after he was picked by King to head the new I Corps (Provisional) of the Atlantic Fleet, which consisted of an Army and a Marine division. In June this command was redesignated the First Joint Training Force, with Smith still in charge and now a two-star general; its basic mission was to prepare Marine and Army troops for amphibious assaults with the Atlantic Fleet. Missing out on the much-desired Guadalcanal command, which went to Archer Vandegrift, Smith was sent to California in September 1942 to head the Second Joint Training Force, which was readying ground forces for amphibious operations in the Pacific. In that capacity he was responsible for much of the advance training of the troops involved in the reconquest of the Aleutians from May to August of 1943, and he accompanied them as an observer in the landings on Attu and Kiska.

That spring Smith was disappointed again when General Barney Vogel was chosen to lead the Marines in the impending operations in the Central Solomons. Although excelling in his valuable role as an assault training leader, Smith was growing worried about his chances of getting a field command. His anxiety stemmed, in part, from his arrest in San Diego in February for "hit-and-run and drunken driving" after striking a sailor with his automobile, breaking his leg, and not halting until forced to by a motorcycle policeman. The district attorney did not file charges, however, explaining that the sailor had been jaywalking and the general's drunkenness could not be proven. "Some members of his staff," states Smith's biographer, "were convinced that Admiral King, and perhaps even the President himself, intervened in the incident on Smith's behalf."[14]

When Nimitz came to San Francisco late that spring for a meeting with King, Major General Omar T. Pfeiffer, then a colonel on the POA war plans staff, recalled that Smith, who was "champing at the bit" to get into combat, "made contact with me and asked whether I would introduce him to Adm. Nimitz. I was pleased to do this, and it was at this time that Gen. Smith sold himself to Adm. Nimitz as an amphibious commander."[15] Nimitz took Smith with him on a tour of South Pacific bases in June, and though not very amiable toward the Marine general, the POA chief informed him during their flight back to Pearl Harbor, "I am going to bring you out to the Pacific this fall. You will command all Marines in the Central Pacific area." Smith later observed that he had felt "increasingly depressed" that spring and regarded Nimitz's decision as "the turning point" in his wartime career.[16]

With the establishment that summer of the Fifth Fleet, commanded by Ray Spruance, and the V Amphibious Force, led by Kelly Turner, Smith became, in the words of one authority, "apparently, the unanimous choice of the higher portion of the chain of command for the job of commander, V Amphibious Corps. He was considered a tough man for a tough job."[17] Spruance and Turner specifically requested him, and his appointment by Commandant Holcomb had the approval of Nimitz, King, and Knox. A noted historian of the Corps, however, points out that Nimitz went along "with some reluctance," probably due to Smith's reputation for irascibility in working with other services' commanders.[18] Admiral Turner, who could be as fiery and impatient as Smith, foresaw friction between them but assured Holcomb that "necessarily, there are personal adjustments to be made, but they will be made." Holcomb remarked to one of his staff officers: "The reason I am appointing Smith is that there's going to be a lot of trouble with the Navy over rights and prerogatives and such things and Holland is the only one I know who can sit at the table and pound it harder than a naval officer."[19]

In November 1943, at the age of sixty-one, Smith led the V Amphibious Corps in the capture of the Gilbert Islands, with the Second Marine Division taking strongly defended Tarawa and Major General Ralph C. Smith's Twenty-seventh Infantry Division seizing nearby Makin. Holland Smith was upset by the slow advance of Ralph Smith's Army troops against the lesser enemy resistance on Makin. The Marine general, whom the press earlier had nicknamed "Howlin' Mad," was critical also of the preassault bombardment by ships and aircraft, which he considered inadequate, and he later argued that Tarawa should have been bypassed in view of its minor strategic value. Despite growing tensions over personality differences and contrasts in amphibious techniques, Smith and Turner, with Spruance sometimes acting as mediator, worked well enough together to plan and lead the conquest of the Marshalls in early 1944, a series of much-better-executed amphibious assaults mainly on the atolls of Kwajalein and Eniwetok by Army and Marine divisions. Elements of the Twenty-seventh Division participated in the latter operation and were more satisfactory than earlier to Holland Smith. He was promoted to lieutenant general that March, becoming the only Marine on active duty to achieve that rank aside from Holcomb and Vandegrift.

Operation Forager, the invasion of the Marianas that summer, was the largest Allied campaign yet mounted in the Pacific. Smith was appointed commander of all ground forces in Forager and would personally lead the V Amphibious Corps in the assaults on Saipan and Tinian, with Geiger's

III Amphibious Corps seizing Guam. The Marine and Army troops under Smith's overall command in Forager totaled nearly 130,000 and included five divisions. The initial Forager amphibious assault was in mid-June against Saipan, with the Second and Fourth Marine and Twenty-seventh Infantry divisions invading the heavily defended island. At the height of the battle for an interior area the troops called "Death Valley," Ralph Smith's Army division was slowed by fierce enemy fire and precariously exposed the flanks of the Marine outfits on either side. Holland Smith ordered him to get his soldiers moving to close the gap in the center of the line, but the Twenty-seventh Division made little progress and suffered heavy casualties in Death Valley. After discussing the command situation with Spruance and Turner and obtaining their concurrence on the need for new leadership for the Twenty-seventh Division, Holland Smith relieved Ralph Smith, turning the Army unit over to Major General Sanderford Jarman. It was another six days, however, before the valley was taken.

The relief of an Army general by a Marine general was shocking to the already ragged interservice relations in POA; it precipitated an ugly controversy between Army, Navy, and Marine leaders at the time and was fully aired in the press, especially the Hearst newspapers that promoted MacArthur as Pacific supreme commander to avert such episodes. Lieutenant General Robert C. Richardson, head of Army forces in POA, was outraged, accepting as wholly valid the charge by Ralph Smith that Holland Smith was "prejudiced, petty and unstable" in dealing with Army troops; both generals maintained that Army units should never serve under him again.[20] In a more judicious tone years later the official Army history concluded that Holland Smith "had good reason to be disappointed with the performance of the 27th Infantry Division" at the time, but it "remains doubtful" that the removal of its commander was "wise" since it "appears to have done nothing to speed the capture of Death Valley."[21] Marine leaders backed Holland Smith's authority to relieve the Army general and his judgment in doing so.

At the root of the still much-discussed affair were differing Army and Marine assault tactics and long-standing service biases, as well as many earlier misunderstandings over orders between the two Smiths from Makin onward.

In the aftermath Ralph Smith was quietly transferred to an attaché post in Paris, while Holland Smith was returned to Pearl Harbor to head the new Fleet Marine Force, Pacific, a command position that did not involve control over Army forces, and Major General Harry Schmidt took over the V Amphibious Corps. Holland Smith was "present superfluously in his last combat command as Commanding General, Expeditionary Troops," in the Iwo Jima battle, but Schmidt was the actual field commander in the three-division operation.[22] Often appearing morose to officers who knew him well, Smith found it difficult to adjust to his desk job at Pearl Harbor in the next few months. From his viewpoint neither Nimitz nor Vandegrift was supportive, so he was not surprised in early July 1945 when he was relieved of his command over the Fleet Marine Force, Pacific, with Geiger named as his replacement. A leading historian points out: "By moving Holland Smith up to the command of FMF Pacific, Vandegrift could minimize the chances for further [interservice] friction. . . . Smith had become a liability to the Corps, which he never could accept or forget."[23] Thus, like Eaker and Stilwell, Smith had to face disappointment in his professional fortunes during the final stages of World War II.

Upon returning to California that summer, he took over the Marine Training and Replacement Command. He retired the following spring at the age of sixty-four, but he remained argumentative and cantankerous in discussing the Pacific assaults. Two years later, in 1948, he published his memoirs, *Coral and Brass,* which was a vitriolic diatribe criticizing many of his wartime colleagues and defending his own actions as virtually infallible. A longtime member of his staff observed that *Coral and Brass* "should never have been written because we knew that he was a finer, bigger, greater man than that book portrayed him to be."[24] Smith's biographer declares, "Unfortunately, the relief incident [on Saipan] and the allegations in *Coral and Brass* have come to overshadow Smith's pivotal role in the development of amphibious warfare and his contributions to victory in the Pacific."[25]

Contemporary opinions of Smith vary as widely as his moods. Robert Sherrod, a veteran correspondent of the Marines' island battles, points out that although Smith was "colorful" and "beloved by the Marine Corps," the hard-pushing, disputatious general "assumed the aspects of a barnacle, so far as much of the regular Navy was concerned. He spoke his mind whenever he saw something wrong."[26] King, who supported Smith and admired his aggressive spirit, remarked once to Vandegrift: "The trouble with Holland Smith is that he's like Stilwell in China. All he wants to do is fight."[27] Spruance seemed to get along passably with him, but Rear Admiral Charles J. "Carl" Moore, his Fifth Fleet chief of staff, pronounced Smith to be "a sorehead, indignant and griping about everything."[28] Rear Admiral Harry W. Hill, one of Turner's amphibious task force commanders, described Smith as "a rough, tough leader itching for a fight with the Japs. Naturally, he was hard to work with. No one ever accused him of brilliance, but everyone quickly learned that he had many positive ideas of his own."[29]

General Clifton Cates, a Marine colonel under Smith who later became the Corps commandant, found him to be quite personable and remarked, "I think his nickname of 'Howlin' Mad' is a misnomer because he wasn't as near tough as people thought he was."[30] A noted naval historian contends, however, that he and Terrible Turner lived up to their nicknames when they worked together, for "between two such hot-headed characters . . . there were bound to be many stormy scenes."[31] Despite their tense wartime relations Turner insisted in 1960 that Smith "was a marvelous offensively minded and capable fighting man" and that he still believed the testy Marine had been "the best man" to head the V Amphibious Force.[32] Nimitz's view of Smith apparently deteriorated during the war. General Gerald Thomas, who served on Smith's staff, was convinced that "Nimitz did not back him up" except sometimes "in his fights with Kelly Turner."[33] Smith ultimately felt that Nimitz was against his participation in the Central Pacific offensive. Following the Army and press furors over the relief of Ralph Smith, even Admiral King, according to a reliable source, "was displeased by Nimitz's failure to take a stronger stand" in Holland Smith's behalf.[34] The POA commander in chief, who could be icily objective in judging officers, may have been looking toward the larger campaigns still ahead when interservice coordination could be crucial.

No doubt, Smith will continue to be one of the most controversial commanders of the Pacific war, but some of his contributions to the Allied triumph over Japan and to the postwar evolution of the Marine Corps are firmly established. He was a dedicated pioneer in developing fundamental aspects of amphibious warfare in doctrine, tactics, weapons, and equipment between the world wars, and in the early part of World War II he became the foremost organizer of training in that mode of combat, besides later commanding some of the greatest amphibious assaults of the conflict. A respected study of the amphibious operations of 1942–45 contends that Smith "played the leading part in forging a fighting amphibious team that made possible the eventual successful landings in both the Atlantic and the Pacific."[35] Throughout his long career he stood up vigorously for a larger role for the Marine Corps in American defense policy and for improvement of its status and recognition within the naval establishment. His main legacy to the Corps, as his biographer rightly asserts,

> *was the aggressiveness in battle, the willingness to close with the enemy that he instilled in his officers and that was then infused in all ranks and organizations under his command. . . . Among the subordinates who imbibed that spirit from Smith was every man who served as commandant for twenty years after the war. . . . Through these men and countless others, the aggressiveness and esprit de corps which Holland Smith*

fostered, demanded, and embodied was preserved and transmitted to future generations of Marines. That was his legacy to the Corps he had served so long and which he loved so well.[36]

COOL, CAREFUL, AND CUNNING: SPRUANCE

After the discouragements he encountered at Annapolis it is a wonder that Raymond A. Spruance stayed in the Navy. As a midshipman he did not seem a likely future leader of sailors in battle: according to the Naval Academy annual, he was a "shy young thing" with "the innocent disposition of an ingenue." Although he graduated in 1906 with a strong academic record and possessed a superior intellect, he "hated the Naval Academy," says his main biographer, "and vowed never to return. He deplored its academic standards and disliked its military routine." He was uncomfortable not only at the hallowed school but also aboard a tossing ship. The school yearbook portrayed him as "a faithful supporter of the lee rail on all summer cruises" whose "dialogues with the wild waves were serious serials with semi-hourly installments." Indeed, nearly four decades later sailors on the Fifth Fleet flagship in rough seas in the Central Pacific noticed that their commander, Admiral Spruance, usually stayed in his cabin. Many speculated that the mysterious, reclusive fleet leader was meditating on his next move in the naval war against Japan. Certainly that was often the case, but an authority reveals another reason for his seclusion: "Spruance stayed sick in heavy weather throughout his career."[37] He did not fit the stereotype of the seadog, but this bright, shy, often seasick man would be ranked as one of the greatest fleet commanders of all time.

Spruance was not fully committed to a naval career until he served successfully and happily on a battleship with the "Great White Fleet," the sixteen-battleship force that President Theodore Roosevelt sent on a world cruise from 1907 to 1909 to show off American naval strength. Lieutenant Spruance got his first command in 1913—an old destroyer based in the Philippines. His friendship with Ensign Charles J. "Carl" Moore, his engineering officer, began then. On his next assignment Spruance became a close comrade of Lieutenant Kelly Turner while serving together on a battleship. Missing out on duty with the Anglo-American Grand Fleet in World War I, Spruance, though promoted to commander in 1918, became depressed about his meager salary and nearly resigned his commission. By the early 1920s, however, his outlook improved when he held a destroyer command with the Pacific Fleet and got to know his division leader, Commander Bill Halsey. Though very different in personal and professional styles, Spruance and Halsey developed a warm mutual admiration, and Halsey's encouragement helped Spruance through some low periods.

While on his fifth command, a destroyer in European waters, Spruance suffered a seeming career setback when he was officially reprimanded in 1926 for negligent supervision of a ship steward who was caught embezzling commissary funds. However, Vice Admiral Philip Andrews, the head of American naval forces in Europe under whom Spruance had earlier served as assistant chief of staff, regarded him as a promising officer, so he "pulled strings," according to a reliable source, and helped Spruance to get a fresh start as a student at the prestigious Naval War College at Newport, Rhode Island.[38] He found the faculty and courses stimulating, and upon graduating in 1927, he would mature into one of the Navy's sharpest thinkers on tactics and strategy in naval surface warfare. He would return to the Naval War College for three more tours of duty: twice as a faculty member before World War II and as president in the postwar era.

His most important ship command came in early 1938 when Captain Spruance was given the battleship *Mississippi.* He proved outstanding in commanding the big vessel on cruises and exercises in the Pacific, Caribbean, and Atlantic for almost three years, during which he also inspired and drove his crew to first places in gunnery and communications and second in engineering in fleet competitions. "Spruance was regarded as a superb shiphandler and a quiet, conscientious, competent skipper," states an expert on him.[39] He was promoted to rear admiral in December 1940 at the age of fifty-three; by then he had served over thirty-seven years in the Navy, of which half had been aboard ships. In view of his susceptibility to seasickness, his attainment of flag rank had been an especially personal triumph because it required high-caliber performances over long periods at sea.

He was somewhat disappointed, in fact, to draw shore duty as his next assignment in February 1941, but it turned out to be challenging and significant work. He was charged with establishing and heading the Tenth Naval District, with headquarters at San Juan, Puerto Rico; he was responsible for the buildup of naval bases and forces in the Caribbean defense area, including the eastern approaches to the strategically vital Panama Canal. During fleet landing exercises off Puerto Rico and nearby Culebra, he renewed his ties with Turner and became acquainted with Brigadier General Holland Smith, who, according to one study, "quickly impressed" him with his amphibious mastery, so "the admiral tucked Smith's name away for future reference."[40]

Nimitz was responsible for one of Spruance's most timely breaks when, as the Navy's personnel chief, he assigned Spruance, with Knox's approval, to command a cruiser division that was part of Halsey's task force of the Pacific Fleet. In thus detailing him, Nimitz turned down a request for Spruance from the Bureau of Naval Ordnance. So when war broke out, instead of being stuck far away in the Washington naval bureaucracy, Spruance found himself already in the combat theater, having assumed command of the four-cruiser division at Pearl Harbor in September 1941. Another fortunate turn for him was that he and his ships were at sea west of Oahu when Japanese bombers struck the fleet at its anchorage that December.

After nearly thirty-nine years in service he experienced his first battle action when Task Force 16 and its Cruiser

Division 5, as Halsey's and Spruance's units had been designated, undertook raids on Japanese bases and shipping in the Marshalls and Gilberts from January to March 1942. Spruance, whose flagship was the cruiser *Northampton,* also led his cruisers with Halsey's force when it advanced across the North Pacific and launched the first raid on Tokyo in April. Task Force 16, including Spruance's ships, was then dispatched to the South Pacific but arrived too late to assist Frank Jack Fletcher's Task Force 17 in the Coral Sea battle in early May.

When Task Force 16 returned to Pearl Harbor late that month, Halsey was quickly hospitalized, as mentioned earlier. Spruance did not learn of this until he was summoned to Nimitz's office where the Pacific Fleet chief also informed him that, upon Halsey's recommendation, he was being assigned as acting head of Task Force 16; that when Task Force 17 soon arrived, Fletcher, the senior of the two, would assume overall command of their combined forces for the impending engagement off Midway against the Japanese Navy; and that after the battle Spruance would become Nimitz's chief of staff. "About to fight the most crucial sea battle of the Pacific war," says Spruance's principal chronicler, "and knowing he soon would come ashore, perhaps for the duration of the war, Spruance left Nimitz's office with mixed emotions."[41]

The Battle of Midway lasted three days, June 4–6, 1942, but on the first day Japanese air attacks upset the American command plan: Fletcher's flagship, the carrier *Yorktown,* was so badly damaged that it had to be abandoned, with Fletcher moving to a cruiser and turning over tactical command to Spruance. According to Vice Admiral Emmet P. "Savvy" Forrestel, then a captain and Spruance's operations officer, Fletcher yielded command because he realized that "carrier operations can best be controlled from a carrier."[42] Coolly directing operations from his flagship, the carrier *Enterprise,* while often meeting disapproval from some of the staff he inherited from Halsey, Spruance led the American Navy to one of its greatest triumphs and dealt the Japanese

Combined Fleet a crippling blow to its strength in carriers and especially in first-rank pilots.

Always reticent to advertise his own feats, Spruance afterward gave credit for the Midway victory to Nimitz's genius, the superior American naval intelligence system, and good fortune. Nimitz, in turn, extolled Spruance as "a fine man, a sterling character and a great leader . . . [who] did a remarkable job. Nothing you could say about him would be praise enough." The citation for the Distinguished Service Medal that Spruance received stated, in part, that "his seamanship, endurance and tenacity in handling his task force were of the highest quality."[43] Later he was criticized by some as unduly cautious because he terminated the pursuit of Admiral Yamamoto's ships before achieving total destruction. Subsequent evidence indicated, however, that Spruance had been wise in ending the battle when he did because his pilots were exhausted, his destroyers were low on fuel, and a probable ambush lay ahead by Yamamoto's still powerful surface fleet supported by aircraft based on Wake Island. Two decades after the war Nimitz reiterated the judgment of most students of the Pacific war that Spruance's leadership in the great battle of June 1942 had been crucial, "for that action at Midway enabled us to take future offensive actions" that led to Japan's defeat.[44]

From June 1942 to August 1943, while Halsey and MacArthur captured headlines in leading early counteroffensives, Spruance served Nimitz efficiently as his chief of staff, though in virtual oblivion. He became Nimitz's main adviser and confidant, and he administered the headquarters staffs at Pearl Harbor of his superior's two large commands, the Pacific Fleet and the Pacific Ocean Areas theater. Nimitz even had him move into his house, the two officers spending not only a large portion of their work time at headquarters, but also eating their meals as well as taking hikes and swims together. Forrestel believed Nimitz was attracted to Spruance because the latter was "an experienced strategist, a sound, logical thinker with War-College-trained reasoning, a good listener, a clear talker, an analytical mind able to detect flaws in others' reasoning."[45] To his surprise, Spruance became absorbed in the staff job, particularly the input he had into planning operations, and he discovered Nimitz's rich qualities as a friend and superior: "I could not have had a finer, more considerate, more able and more fearless man to work for than Admiral Nimitz. It was a privilege to serve under him."[46]

In late spring of 1943, anticipating the Joint Chiefs' approval of their plans for a Central Pacific axis of advance, Nimitz and King often exchanged messages and sometimes personally talked about the top command posts for future offensives. During one of their hikes that May, Nimitz remarked to Spruance that "some changes in high command" would be forthcoming but that he was needed to continue as chief of staff. Spruance responded humbly, "The war is the important thing. I personally would like another crack at the Japs, but if you need me here, this is where I should be." The next day, however, Nimitz told him: "Spruance, you are lucky. I decided I am going to let you go after all."[47] But the POA commander flew off to a conference with King in San Francisco without giving Spruance any inkling of what future job he had in mind. On May 30, while the San Francisco talks were underway, Spruance received a dispatch from the Navy Department notifying him of his promotion to vice admiral. When Nimitz came back to Pearl Harbor in early June, he informed Spruance that King had approved him as commander of the new Central Pacific Force, which was to comprise all Navy, Marine, and Army units in that sub-theater (to be redesignated Fifth Fleet in 1944). According to King in his memoirs, by that stage of the war Spruance "was in intellectual ability unsurpassed among the flag officers of the United States Navy."[48] In July the JCS approved the POA operational plan for seizing the Gilberts and asked for Nimitz's proposals for the invasion of the Marshalls in early 1944. Spruance was detached as Nimitz's chief of staff and assumed command of the fledgling Central Pacific Force in early August 1943.

As his key lieutenants Spruance selected, with the approval of Nimitz and King, three old friends, Captain Carl Moore as chief of staff, Captain Savvy Forrestel as operations officer, and Rear Admiral Kelly Turner as amphibious force commander. To head the amphibious corps, or ground troops, he chose Major General Holland Smith, whom he admired but who actually was better known by Turner. Not versed in naval aviation well enough to recommend, Spruance yielded to Nimitz, another nonaviator, who chose Rear Admiral Charles A. "Baldy" Pownall to lead the carrier force.

From the start of his new command Spruance faced static from naval aviation leaders at Pearl Harbor and Washington as well as in the Pacific Fleet because, like Nimitz, he allegedly believed that carrier air power's role should be reduced to supporting amphibious assaults rather than unleashing carrier strike forces as potent offensive weapons on their own. Moreover, as a noted historian points out, "since the principal punch of the new fleet would presumably be provided by carriers, most naval aviators assumed that the appointment would go to one of themselves."[49] Vice Admiral Jack Towers particularly appeared to resent the supposedly minor influence of naval air commanders in running the Pacific war, and, exceedingly ambitious, he wanted for himself command of the Central Pacific Force. Sometimes Spruance provided fuel for his critics among the airmen, for instance, when he was so slow in coming to appreciate and trust Pete Mitscher, his gifted leader of the fast carriers. Also, Spruance "had but one aviator on his staff," notes a critical historian, and that officer was used for "nuts-and-bolts chores," his rank being "very junior to the rest of the staff."[50] Nimitz and King loyally supported Spruance most of the time against disaffected air leaders, who also were not averse to remarking unfavorably about the two senior naval chiefs' understanding of carrier warfare.

At least Spruance and his officers became more knowledgeable about and skilled in amphibious warfare in their thrusts from the Gilberts to the Marshalls and on, by summer

1944, to the Marianas. In the third week of February 1944, Spruance was promoted to four-star admiral. On the occasion Nimitz wrote him that he had "proved so great a master of the bold use of naval forces" that he was confident a "brilliant future" lay ahead—surely well meant but whimsical, as if for a just-proven commander rather than for the victor of Midway and conqueror of the Gilberts and Marshalls.[51] Each assault seemed to be executed a bit more efficiently than the previous one, though by the invasion of Saipan the Japanese opposition was the fiercest yet encountered. That assault precipitated the second major naval engagement in which Spruance would emerge as the triumphant but cautious commander: the Battle of the Philippine Sea, June 19–20, 1944, in which most enemy aircraft were destroyed but the bulk of the Japanese fleet escaped when Spruance chose to protect the American assault shipping off Guam, his primary mission, instead of pursuing the enemy vessels to the west. Some postwar evidence was uncovered to support his judgment, but many contemporaries, such as Mitscher, and a number of naval historians remain unconvinced of his wisdom on that occasion. The foremost recent historian of the Pacific war, for example, maintains that Spruance made "a poor choice" in deciding "to risk his carriers rather than the forces off Saipan," because the loss of carriers would have been "far more disastrous for the Marianas operation than the loss of some transports."[52] Spruance easily rivaled Halsey in the legacy of controversial decisions he left for future arm-chair strategists and tacticians to debate.

General Holland Smith and other Marine commanders were incensed by Spruance in February 1945 for cutting the length of the Fifth Fleet's pre-assault bombardment of Iwo Jima to three days instead of abiding by the ten days' preparation they had urged. Spruance reduced it in order to send Mitscher's carriers and several battleships to attack enemy air forces and bases in Japan that, he felt, would otherwise reinforce the Iwo garrison. The Marines especially resented his decision because he had been an ardent proponent of assaulting rather than bypassing the island during earlier planning sessions and because of the very heavy Marine losses in securing Iwo Jima. Curtis LeMay, by the way, had been instrumental in persuading Spruance that Iwo was of vital strategic value to the B-29 bombing offensive against the enemy home islands. Even Spruance's chief biographer, who is generally sympathetic toward him, admits that, regarding his decision to reduce the Iwo Jima bombardment, "whether Spruance was right or wrong never will be satisfactorily answered."[53]

When his forces assaulted the powerful stronghold on Okinawa that spring, Spruance, in turn, became the critic after he called upon Kenney and LeMay for support from the Army Air Forces and, in his opinion, received little help. Kamikazes appeared in unprecedented numbers, and the Fifth Fleet picket ships had to bear the brunt of their attacks. One of the suicide planes crashed into the cruiser *Indianapolis,* Spruance's flagship, the explosions penetrating deep below the main deck and ripping two large holes in the hull. Unharmed, Spruance oversaw early damage operations calmly and then moved his flag to the battleship *New Mexico.* Later he narrowly escaped death when another kamikaze dove into the *New Mexico* and caused nearly one hundred fifty casualties in the explosion near the bridge. Altogether the kamikazes wrought more destruction to the Pacific Fleet than the enemy had accomplished in any previous battle. Spruance became "embittered by what he considered to be the worst performance ever by the Air Force in support of the Navy," states an authority. When after two months of the savage Okinawa campaign Halsey relieved him, thus ending his final war command, Spruance caustically told his successor that, instead of attacking the kamikazes, the Army planes had "destroyed a great many sugar mills, railroad trains, and other equipment."[54]

During the final year or so of the Pacific war, it will be recalled, Spruance and Halsey, together with their respective staffs, had alternated in running the Pacific Fleet in its Central Pacific operations. While the commanders and their staff officers changed with each major cruise, as did the fleet's designation as Fifth (Spruance) or Third (Halsey), the makeup of the huge armada in ships and personnel otherwise remained largely the same except for its steady growth. Some of the most perceptive contrasts of Spruance and Halsey have come from men who served under both admirals. Many sailors tended to prefer Halsey because he was more gregarious, casual, dramatic, and visible in contrast to the introverted, aloof Spruance. Even Moore, Spruance's chief of staff and good friend, admitted that in working with Spruance "you had to adjust yourself to his pecularities," for he "was a queer egg in many ways."[55] One noted naval historian observes: "Officers were sharply divided with respect to the two admirals' command styles. Many preferred Spruance's detailed advance planning and . . . his minutely thought-out operations. . . . Other officers preferred Halsey's imaginative improvisations." He found that "Spruance's partisans were likely to brand Halsey's command procedures sloppy and reckless," but, on the other hand, "admirers of Halsey called Spruance's style overcautious and inflexible."[56]

In November 1945, Spruance relieved Nimitz as commander in chief of the Pacific Fleet and of the Pacific Ocean Areas. Ironically, Towers, his old nemesis, succeeded Spruance as head of the Fifth Fleet and, four months hence, of the Pacific Fleet and POA theater. From the spring of 1946 until his retirement in the summer of 1948, Spruance served as president of the Naval War College. One account claims he produced a "revitalized curriculum," but a foremost naval scholar maintains that Spruance "still ignored aviation" in the changes he made in the college's program.[57] In early 1952, President Truman called him out of retirement to become ambassador to the Philippines, a post he held judiciously for the next three years, which was a turbulent era in that nation's history. He died in 1969 and was buried beside his close friends Chester Nimitz and Kelly Turner in a cemetery overlooking San Francisco Bay.

During the Second World War, Spruance shunned publicity and Halsey seemed to crave it. It is unfortunate that during the postwar period there has been no rectification of acclaim for these two gifted admirals, for Spruance has continued to be virtually unknown to the American public. Nearly all descriptions of him by contemporaries mention his introverted nature, though few peers regarded it as a liability. In a typical account he was portrayed as "a man of quiet and modest personality but possessed of great powers of organization and outstanding resolution in moments of crisis."[58] Nimitz described him as a "reserved and self effacing man" who demonstrated "wisdom and tact . . . skill and courage" during "his extraordinarily successful naval career."[59] Rear Admiral Samuel Eliot Morison remarked, "When we come to the admirals who commanded at sea, and who directed a great battle, there was no one equal to Spruance [in World War II]. Always calm, always at peace with himself, Spruance had that ability which marks the great captain to make correct estimates and the right decisions in a fluid battle situation."[60]

In the aftermath of the surrender of Japan, Spruance regrettably missed out on much public acclaim and also was bypassed for chief of naval operations and for five-star rank. According to Spruance's biographer, King "would have endorsed [him] for CNO had it not been for Spruance's nearing mandatory retirement age." King refused to choose between Spruance and Halsey for the one fleet admiral position left unfilled in late 1945 and recommended both, pointing out each's assets and flaws. In nominating Spruance to Secretary of the Navy Forrestal for a fifth star, King commented succinctly, "As to brains, the best man in every way."[61] This was surely true, and Spruance would have liked King's emphasis on that trait, but the unassuming, intellectual admiral had many qualifications as a great naval captain that could not be permanently diminished by his contemporaries' failures to accord him fame, a fifth star, or the CNO post. As his main biographer expressed it: "Transcending his other virtues . . . was his fighting spirit. . . . A complex and fascinating man, he was an enigma to everyone. Above all, he was a master of the art of naval warfare."[62] Simply yet profoundly, Nimitz concluded that he was "an admiral's admiral."[63]

TEN

POLITICS?

Since only a few of the eighteen top American officers of 1941–45 had personally commanded in battle before World War II, how did these men attain their high commands? Was their rise based on factors other than merit? Such a question implies that their selections involved politics in a less than admirable sense of the word.

The conventional, primary meaning of the term "politics" is "the art or science of government." While the military establishment is a fundamental part of the federal government, that affinity has not been the focus of this work. The much-used secondary definition as "the activities or affairs of a government, politicians, or political party" has not been foremost either, though Roosevelt, the wartime commander in chief, was simultaneously the nation's consummate politician, and at least two of the featured officers, Douglas MacArthur and Ike Eisenhower, were viewed during the war by some factions of the Republican and Democratic parties as prospective presidential timber. Other meanings of the term have negative connotations, but, by and large, the senior military and naval officers examined in this book did not reach their top positions during the war by deceitful or conniving means. Rather, the evolution of the United States high command of 1941–45 concerned politics in less sensational ways: through the relations and competition between men involved in roles of power and leadership.[1]

Without exception, these eighteen leaders seemed to have achieved their positions of high command by being the best qualified and most experienced officers available for the jobs at the time. (This does not mean that they were superior to their counterparts in the Allied and Axis high commands, nor are they necessarily worthy of inclusion among the great captains of history. A number of them, however, still appear outstanding among the senior commanders of that and other modern wars. But, of course, like the determination of classics among books, the passing of time will be the final sifter among the generals and admirals who demonstrated leadership genius.)

The commanders emphasized herein were men of considerable seniority in age, years of service, and dates of rank as general or flag officers. At the time of the entry of the United States into World War II, their average age was fifty-five. William Leahy was the oldest at sixty-six, with Ernest King next at sixty-three and then MacArthur at sixty-one. The two youngest were Mark Clark and Ira Eaker, each forty-five years old. Four reached the statutory retirement age of sixty-four during the war and were granted active-duty extensions by the president: Leahy, King, MacArthur, and Marshall. By December 1941, the average time in service of the group was thirty-five years, with Leahy having served the longest at forty-six years, followed by King at forty-four years and Halsey and Stilwell at forty-one years. Two of the officers had retired before the Pearl Harbor attack: MacArthur in December 1937 and Leahy in August 1939, to be recalled to active duty in July 1941 and June 1942, respectively.

In spite of their relatively long careers prior to World War II, most of them had been penalized by the slow promotion system, aggravated by niggardly defense appropriations, during the era between the world wars. Four years was the average time of the eighteen men in rank at general or flag level prior to December 1941. MacArthur led the group by far with twenty years as a general officer, with Leahy a distant second at twelve years (excluding their retirement periods). Ten of the eighteen officers had been at general or flag rank for two years or less by the time of the Pearl Harbor raid. When these factors are considered, together with the earlier attainment of the services' top posts by MacArthur and Leahy, it is easier to comprehend the deference and respect extended to them by their colleagues during the war years even when they disagreed. Only one of the group, Eaker, had not attained the level of general officer before the United States entered the war. By the time hostilities ended in 1945, seven of the men would hold five-star rank, and the other eleven would be four-star officers, with two subsequently gaining a fifth star.

Before World War II the main routes to commissioning in the Army and Navy had been through the Military and Naval academies, but with the vast wartime expansion of the officers corps the graduates of the academies became a tiny minority of the total officers of the Army and Navy. Nevertheless, the West Point and Annapolis graduates were dominant at the general and flag levels. For example, a dependable source states that "in World War II West Pointers—about 1 percent of the total officer corps—held 57 percent of the division and higher commands and comprised 83 percent of the Army's generals, 65 percent of its lieutenant generals and 55 percent of its major generals."[2] All five of the admirals who are featured herein were Annapolis graduates. They finished at the Naval Academy within seven years of each other, so several were midshipmen at the same time and surely heard of their recent predecessors. All but Kenney, Marshall, and Eaker of the eleven Army (and Army Air Forces) generals were graduates of West Point. Several of them were cadets together and knew of the others. Archer Vandegrift and Holland Smith attended civilian universities and then passed Marine Corps entrance examinations before their commissioning, but their paths soon crossed on tours of duty in the small Corps before the First World War. Of course, the careers of the eleven Army and five Navy officers became increasingly intertwined as they advanced in their respective services, for their officer corps, too, were relatively small, particularly at the field grade and higher. Besides meeting and renewing friendships on tours of duty, whether in an Army garrison in the Philippines or aboard a battleship with the Pacific Fleet, these men became members of an elite but unofficial fraternity of survivors of the services' promotion and assignment systems when they were selected to attend the Army Command and General Staff College, Army War College, Naval War College, or the lesser service and branch schools. By the late 1930s, in other words, these eighteen men with their average of more than thirty years' service were friends or acquainted with each other in nearly all cases. The frequency of personal and professional contacts between them has been one of the most obvious themes running through this study.

Service with the American Expeditionary Forces in France or with the Anglo-American Grand Fleet in the North Sea during World War I is on the record of twelve of the eighteen officers, though not many of them actually participated in combat. Nine of the officers engaged in combat operations elsewhere in the pre-1941 period, usually in Latin America or the Philippines. Several won battle decorations and at least three were wounded, with MacArthur leading in both categories with a bushel of medals and combat citations and two wounds in France, besides nominations for the Medal of Honor for heroism in Mexico and France. In fact, by the late 1930s MacArthur was the only one of the eighteen to approach Pershing as a "household name" to the public.

The length of time that the eighteen officers remained in their highest command positions of World War II averaged thirty-five months. Their individual tenures, however, are skewed by the fact that some obtained the posts prior to the outbreak of war and several retained the positions into the postwar period. The longest tenures were those of Arnold as head of the Army Air Forces (earlier Army Air Corps), eighty-six months; Leahy as presidential chief of staff and acting JCS chairman, eighty-one months; and Marshall as Army chief of staff, seventy-five months. The shortest tenures in their top wartime roles were Clark as head of the XV Army Group, five months; Bradley as commander of the XII Army Group, nine months; and Smith as leader of the Fleet Marine Force, Pacific, twelve months. Comparisons of their highest tours of duty are complicated also by differing interpretations of the priority of various commands. For instance, Eaker regarded his command zenith as head of the Eighth Air Force, not as commander of the Mediterranean Allied Air Forces; and Smith considered his top role as head of the V Amphibious Corps, not as commander of the Fleet Marine Force, Pacific, to cite only two cases in point. Nevertheless, the method or methods used in deciding the men for the high command slots, however informal, inconsistent, and poorly documented, appears to have worked rather well if judged by their longevity in the positions, as well as their successes. Only Stilwell was relieved and transferred to a lower post, but his post-CBI jobs in heading Army Ground Forces and then the Tenth Army surely do not diminish his professional record or his esteem in the War Department.

In the stipulated, as against standard, definition of high command used in this work, the featured officers were chosen from those who, with the exception of Patton, advanced to echelons above the command of an army, air force, or fleet of numerical designation. The portraits of the eighteen commanders therefore have stressed how they attained their posts above those levels. But at least four of the subjects ascended to even loftier positions later in the war: Eisenhower moving from the Torch to the Overlord supreme command, King from chief of naval operations to commander in chief of the U.S. Fleet as well, MacArthur from commander of U.S. Army Forces, Far East, to head of the Allied Southwest Pacific theater, and Nimitz from leader of the Pacific Fleet to commander also of the Pacific Ocean Areas. Indeed, in several instances the picture turned more complex, for example, MacArthur becoming supreme commander for the Allied powers in accepting Japan's surrender and in controlling the occupation of that nation.

By the termination of World War II, several of the featured commanders were no longer in the top positions they had attained during the war, though, as earlier mentioned, the priority of the post was subject to interpretation. Stilwell, Eaker, and Smith certainly considered their status lower at the end of the war than at their wartime zenith, and within five months of Germany's surrender, Patton surely felt he had been reduced in position in being transferred from command of the Third Army to head of the Fifteenth Army. Even his appointment as acting commander of U.S. Forces in the European theater in the autumn of 1945, between Ike's departure and McNarney's assumption of the permanent command, did not assuage Patton regarding his command reduction. Also, Clark may have felt he exercised more power as commander of the U.S. Fifth Army than later as army group head.

Only one of the eighteen commanders, Marshall, was seriously considered for a higher post—Overlord—that he was not given. On the other hand, at least four of the featured officers were in jeopardy of losing their high commands but managed to retain them: Arnold because of his multiple heart attacks, Halsey because of his mishandling of the Third Fleet on several occasions, King due to his personal and policy clashes with Forrestal, and Clark owing to differences with his British colleagues in Italy. In addition, some historians maintain that Eisenhower's SHAEF position was not at all secure by January 1945, but the principal evidence does not seem conclusive on that point. Generally, the security of these eighteen men in their high commands is one of the few common threads running through the book. Indeed, it is rather surprising in view of the instability and turbulence of the times and the lack of order and precedence in the nature of the high command system.

All eighteen men demonstrated great versatility in their leadership abilities not only before and during the Second

World War but also in the critical postwar era when the challenges of the strange new Cold War put a premium on high commanders with broad knowledge and flexible minds. Except for the several who died or retired in ill health in the wake of the war against the Axis, the American high commanders of 1941–45 went on to key leadership roles in both military and civilian realms, serving with distinction as service chiefs, JCS chairmen, occupation administrators, educational leaders, business executives, ambassadors, State and Defense secretaries, and president of the United States. In their individual ways these generals and admirals cast long shadows into the future, especially through the legacy of leadership models they provided for generations of officers to come.

They left not only the records of their command decisions and actions but also words of wisdom about the nature of successful high command. Eisenhower, for instance, in December 1942 confided to a friend:

> *Through all this, I am learning many things. One, that waiting for other people to produce is one of the hardest things a commander has to do. Two, that in the higher positions of a modern Army, Navy and Air Force, rich organizational experience and an orderly, logical mind are absolutely essential to success. The flashy, publicity-seeking type of adventurer can grab the headlines and be a hero in the eyes of the public, but he simply can't deliver the goods in high command. On the other hand, the slow, methodical, ritualistic person is absolutely valueless in a key position. There must be a fine balance—that is exceedingly difficult to find. In addition to the above, a person in such a position must have an inexhaustible fund of nervous energy. He is called upon day and night to absorb the disappointments, the discouragements and the doubts of his subordinates and to force them on to accomplishments which they regard as impossible. . . . To find a few persons of the kind that I have*

roughly described above is the real job of the commander.[3]

Brigadier General S. L. A. Marshall, one of the most esteemed American officer-historians and astute scholar of military leadership, observed regarding the great captains the United States has produced:

> *Some almost missed the roll call, either because in early life their weaknesses were more apparent than their strengths, or because of an outward seeming of insignificance, which at first fooled their contemporaries. . . .*
>
> *No two of them are strikingly alike in mien and manner. Their personalities are as different, for the most part, as their names. . . .*
>
> *Part of their number commanded mainly through the sheer force of ideas; others owed their leadership more to the magnetism of dynamic personality.*
>
> *In a few there was the spark of genius. All things seemed to come right with them at all times. Fate was kind, the openings occurred, and they were prepared to take advantage of them.*
>
> *But the greater number moved up the hill one slow step at a time, not always sure of their footing, buffeted by mischance, owning no exalted opinion of their own merits, reacting to discouragement much as other men do, but finally accumulating power as they learned how to organize the work of other men. . . .*
>
> *There is not one perfect life in the gallery of the great.*[4]

Between these reflections by two wizened soldiers there lies much of the essence of success in high command. It is noteworthy that both officers referred to an ongoing learning process: Eisenhower admitting as Torch supreme commander, "Through all this, I am learning many things," and Marshall perceptively capturing the politics of high command in "accumulating power as they learned how to organize the work of other men." Perhaps this was the key common trait in all eighteen commanders: throughout their long and varied careers they never ceased trying to learn more about the nature of war and the conduct of men in battle.

ABBREVIATIONS

AAFWWII	*The Army Air Forces in World War II*
ABC	American-British Conversations
ABDACOM	American-British-Dutch-Australian Command
AEF	American Expeditionary Forces
AFHQ	Allied Force Headquarters
AFPAC	United States Army Forces in the Pacific
CBI	China-Burma-India theater
CCS	Combined Chiefs of Staff
CINCSWPA	Commander in chief, Southwest Pacific Area
CMH	United States Army Center of Military History, Washington, D.C.
CNO	Chief of naval operations
CUOHC	Columbia University Oral History Collection, New York, New York
DAMB	*Dictionary of American Military Biography*
DMBP	Douglas MacArthur Biographical Papers, Special Collections, Mitchell Memorial Library, Mississippi State University, Mississippi State, Mississippi
ETO	European theater of operations
ETOUSA	European theater of operations, United States Army
G-1	Personnel and administration section (or chief)
G-2	Intelligence section (or chief)
G-3	Operations and training section (or chief)
G-4	Supply section (or chief)
GHQ	General headquarters
HIWRP	Hoover Institution on War, Revolution, and Peace, Stanford University, Stanford, California

HUSMCOWWII	*History of U.S. Marine Corps Operations in World War II*
HUSNOWWII	*History of United States Naval Operations in World War II*
JCS	Joint Chiefs of Staff
LC	Library of Congress, Manuscript Division, Washington, D.C.
MCHC	United States Marine Corps Historical Center, Washington, D.C.
MMA	MacArthur Memorial Archives, Norfolk, Virginia
MSU	Special Collections, Mitchell Memorial Library, Mississippi State University, Mississippi State, Mississippi
MTO	Mediterranean theater of operations
NA	National Archives, Washington, D.C.
NATO	North African theater of operations
NATOUSA	North African theater of operations, United States Army
NHC	United States Naval Historical Center, Washington, D.C.
OCS	Office of the Chief of Staff, United States Army
OHC	Oral history collection
PDDE	*The Papers of Dwight David Eisenhower*
POA	Pacific Ocean Areas
PRAHC	*Papers Relating to the Allied High Command, 1943–1945*
RAF	Royal Air Force
RG	Record group
SCAP	Supreme Commander for the Allied Powers, Japan
SEAC	Southeast Asia Command
SHAEF	Supreme Headquarters, Allied Expeditionary Force
SWPA	Southwest Pacific Area
USAFFE	United States Army Forces in the Far East
USAWWII	*United States Army in World War II*
WPD	War Plans Division, United States War Department

NOTES

CHAPTER ONE
PREPARING
FOR WARTIME COMMANDS

1. Maureen Mylander, *The Generals: Making It, Military Style* (New York, 1974), p. 66.
2. William D. Leahy, *I Was There: The Personal Story of the Chief of Staff to Presidents Roosevelt and Truman Based on His Notes and Diaries Made at the Time* (New York, 1950), p. 283.
3. Ibid., p. 138.
4. Searle F. Charles, "Harry L. Hopkins," in *Franklin D. Roosevelt: His Life and Times—an Encyclopedic View*, eds. Otis L. Graham and Meghan R. Wander (Boston, 1985), pp. 184–85.
5. Ernest J. King and Walter M. Whitehill, *Fleet Admiral King: A Naval Record* (New York, 1952), p. 367.
6. John F. Shiner, *Foulois and the U.S. Army Air Corps, 1931–1935* (Washington, D.C., 1983), p. 254.
7. DeWitt S. Copp, *A Few Great Captains: The Men and Events That Shaped the Development of U.S. Air Power* (Garden City, N.Y., 1980), pp. 344–45.
8. Henry H. Arnold, *Global Mission* (New York, 1949), pp. 152–53.
9. DeWitt S. Copp, *Forged in Fire: Strategy and Decisions in the Air War Over Europe, 1940–45* (Garden City, N.Y., 1982), p. 97.
10. Arnold, *Global Mission*, p. 170.
11. Lt. Gen. James H. Doolittle, Interview (1960), II: 22, 23, CUOHC.
12. Gen. Thomas D. White, Interview (1960), IV: 4, CUOHC.

13. Arnold, *Global Mission*, p. 194.
14. Forrest C. Pogue, *George C. Marshall*, 3 vols. to date (New York, 1963–73), II: 84–86; Arnold, *Global Mission*, pp. 163–64.
15. Maj. Gen. Henry H. Arnold to Maj. Gen. Frank M. Andrews, July 28, 1941, Frank M. Andrews Papers, LC.
16. Thomas M. Coffey, *Hap: The Story of the U.S. Air Force and the Man Who Built It, General Henry H. "Hap" Arnold* (New York, 1982), p. 365.
17. Forrest C. Pogue, *George C. Marshall: Global Commander* (Colorado Springs, Colo., 1968), p. 10.
18. Rose P. Wilson, *General Marshall Remembered* (Englewood Cliffs, N.J., 1968), p. 199.
19. Leonard Mosley, *Marshall: Hero for Our Times* (New York, 1982), p. 117.
20. Pogue, *Marshall*, I: 314–15.
21. William Frye, *Marshall: Citizen Soldier* (Indianapolis, Ind., 1947), pp. 246, 248.
22. Col. George C. Marshall to Gen. John J. Pershing, Jan. 16, 1939, in George C. Marshall, *The Papers of George Catlett Marshall*, ed. Larry J. Bland, 2 vols. to date (Baltimore, Md., 1981–86), I: 684.
23. Pogue, *Marshall*, I: 327.
24. Marshall, *Papers*, I: 713.
25. Pogue, *Marshall*, I: 329–30; Mosley, *Marshall*, p. 128; Frye, *Marshall*, p. 251.
26. Pogue, *Marshall*, I: 348, 349.
27. Ibid., III: 585; Mosley, *Marshall*, p. 521; Pogue, *Global Commander*, p. 5.
28. Gen. of the Army Dwight D. Eisenhower, Interview with D. Clayton James (1967), p. 75, DMBP.
29. Gen. Thomas T. Handy, Interview with D. Clayton James (1971), pp. 23, 24, DMBP.
30. Gen. Harold K. Johnson, Interview with D. Clayton James (1971), pp. 42, 43, DMBP.
31. Prime Min. Winston S. Churchill to Pres. Franklin D. Roosevelt, June 6, 1943, in Warren F. Kimball, ed., *Churchill and Roosevelt: The Complete Correspondence*, 3 vols. (Princeton, N.J., 1984), II: 232.
32. Brig. Gen. Frank McCarthy to D. Clayton James, July 20, 1985, DMBP.
33. Katherine T. Marshall, *Together: Annals of an Army Wife* (Atlanta, Ga., 1946), p. 9.
34. Adm. Richard S. Edwards to Fleet Adm. Ernest J. King, Aug. 11, 1951, Ernest J. King Papers, LC.
35. Pogue, *Marshall*, III: 231.
36. Gen. of the Army Dwight D. Eisenhower to Marshall, May 8, 1945, in *PDDE*, VI: 14.

CHAPTER TWO
ADJUSTING TO COALITION WARFARE

1. Maurice Matloff and Edwin M. Snell, *Strategic Planning for Coalition Warfare, 1941–1942. USAWWII* (Washington, D.C., 1953), p. 123.
2. Thomas B. Buell, *Master of Sea Power: A Biography of Fleet Admiral Ernest J. King* (Boston, 1980), pp. 276, 281.
3. Morris Janowitz, *The Professional Soldier: A Social and Political Portrait* (Glencoe, Ill., 1960), p. 159.
4. Robert W. Love, Jr., "Ernest Joseph King, 26 March 1942–15 December 1945," in Robert W. Love, Jr., ed., *The Chiefs of Naval Operations* (Annapolis, Md., 1980), p. 140.
5. Buell, *Master of Sea Power*, p. 107.
6. King and Whitehill, *King*, p. 293.
7. Ibid., p. 294.
8. Buell, *Master of Sea Power*, p. 139.
9. King and Whitehill, *King*, p. 355.
10. Buell, *Master of Sea Power*, p. 161.
11. King and Whitehill, *King*, p. 355.
12. Buell, *Master of Sea Power*, pp. 161–62.
13. King and Whitehill, *King*, pp. 306, 413.
14. Dwight D. Eisenhower, *The Eisenhower Diaries*, ed. Robert H. Ferrell (New York, 1981), p. 50.
15. Adm. Richard L. Conolly, Interview (1958), pp. 279, 280, OHC, NHC.
16. Turner Catledge to Lloyd J. Graybar, July 15, 1974, Turner Catledge Papers, MSU.
17. Vice Adm. Alan G. Kirk, Interview (1961), I: 231, CUOHC.
18. Adm. Thomas C. Hart, Interview (1961), I: 274–75, CUOHC.
19. Leahy, *I Was There*, p. 104.
20. Joseph W. Stilwell, *The Stilwell Papers*, ed. Theodore H. White (New York, 1948), p. 245.
21. Arthur Bryant, *The Turn of the Tide: A History of the War Years Based on the Diaries of Field-Marshal Lord Alanbrooke, Chief of the Imperial General Staff* (Garden City, N.Y., 1957), p. 279.
22. Hastings L. Ismay, *The Memoirs of General Lord Ismay* (New York, 1960), p. 253.
23. George H. Lobdell, "Frank Knox, 11 July 1940–28 April 1944," in Paolo E. Coletta, ed., *American Secretaries of the Navy*, 2 vols. (Annapolis, Md., 1980), II: 715.
24. King and Whitehill, *King*, p. 637.
25. Leahy, *I Was There*, p. 3.
26. Ibid., p. 4; Henry H. Adams, *Witness to Power: The Life of Fleet Admiral William D. Leahy* (Annapolis, Md., 1985), p. 89.

27. Vernon E. Davis, "The History of the Joint Chiefs of Staff in World War II: Organizational Development," vol. I, "Origins of the Joint and Combined Chiefs of Staff" (MS study, Historical Div., JCS, 1953), p. 257.
28. Ibid., p. 259.
29. King to Col. Thomas G. Dobyns, June 22, 1951, King Papers.
30. Leahy, *I Was There*, pp. 94, 96.
31. "William Daniel Leahy," in Graham and Wander, eds., *Roosevelt*, pp. 235–36.
32. James M. Burns, *Roosevelt: The Soldier of Freedom, 1940–1945* (New York, 1970), p. 452.
33. Kimball, ed., *Churchill and Roosevelt*, III: 88.
34. Davis, "Organizational Development," pp. 260–61.
35. Leahy, *I Was There*, pp. 347–48; Adams, *Witness to Power*, p. 282.
36. Harry S Truman, *Memoirs*, 2 vols. (Garden City, N.Y., 1955–56), I: 29.
37. Hart, Interview, pp. 44, 54, 55.
38. Conolly, Interview, pp. 278–79.
39. Winston S. Churchill, *The Second World War*, 6 vols. (Boston, 1948–53), II: 508.
40. Robert J. Donovan, *Conflict and Crisis: The Presidency of Harry S. Truman* (New York, 1977), p. 156.
41. Edward J. Marolda, "William Daniel Leahy," in *DAMB*, II: 598.

CHAPTER THREE
CRISIS IN COMMAND

1. Robert D. Heinl, Jr., comp., *Dictionary of Military and Naval Quotations* (Annapolis, Md., 1966), p. 47.
2. Gordon W. Prange, with Donald M. Goldstein and Katherine V. Dillon, *Pearl Harbor: The Verdict of History* (New York, 1986), p. xvi.
3. Eisenhower, *Eisenhower Diaries*, p. 42.
4. Rear Adm. Claude C. Bloch to Rear Adm. James O. Richardson, March 3, 1942, Claude C. Bloch Papers, LC.
5. Also in this category were Lt. Gen. George H. Brett and Vice Adm. Herbert F. Leary, the first commanders of Allied air and naval forces, respectively, in the Southwest Pacific Area; and Rear Adm. Robert A. Theobald, the first head of the North Pacific Area.
6. Brig. Gen. Ira C. Eaker to Col. Harold George, March 5, 1942, Carl A. Spaatz Papers, LC.
7. Buell, *Master of Sea Power*, pp. 178, 179.
8. Some ranking officers with longtime command experience were expected by their peers to get important wartime assignments—and did. Several of these men, together with their posts in early 1942, were Lt. Gens. Ben Lear and Walter Krueger, commanders of the Second and Third Armies, respectively; Lt. Gen. Frank Andrews, the gifted but controversial airman,

then heading the Caribbean Defense Command; and Rear Adms. H. Kent Hewitt, in charge of the Amphibious Force, Atlantic Fleet, and Thomas C. Kinkaid, an esteemed cruiser division leader in the early Pacific operations.

9. Douglas MacArthur, *Reminiscences* (New York, 1964), p. 145; Stilwell, *Stilwell Papers*, p. 106.
10. Samuel E. Morison, *The Two-Ocean War: A Short History of the United States Navy in the Second World War* (Boston, 1963), p. 115.
11. MacArthur, *Reminiscences*, p. 145.
12. Henry L. Stimson, Diary, entry of May 21, 1941, Henry L. Stimson Papers, Manuscripts and Archives Department, Sterling Library, Yale University, New Haven, Conn.
13. Marshall to Maj. Gen. Douglas MacArthur, June 20, 1941, OCS 20850-15, RG 165, NA.
14. MacArthur to Roosevelt, Feb. 11, 1942, RG 4, MMA.
15. Brig. Gen. Le Grande A. Diller, Interview with D. Clayton James (1977), p. 10, DMBP.
16. D. Clayton James, *The Years of MacArthur*, 3 vols. (Boston, 1970–85), II: 116.
17. MacArthur to Marshall, Dec. 17, 1944, RG 4, MMA.
18. George C. Kenney, *General Kenney Reports: A Personal History of the Pacific War* (New York, 1949), p. 533.
19. U.S. Joint Chiefs of Staff, Directive to the Supreme Commander for the Allied Powers, Aug. 15, 1945, RG 5, MMA.
20. MacArthur to Pres. Harry S Truman, Aug. 15, 1945, RG 9, MMA.
21. Field Marshal Viscount Alanbrooke to Randall, Aug. 14, 1962, RG 21, MMA; Bryant, *Turn of the Tide*, p. 560.
22. Gen. Henry H. Arnold, Diary, entry of Sept. 25, 1942, Henry H. Arnold Papers, LC.
23. King, Memorandum of Talk with Fleet Adm. William D. Leahy, Mar. 11, 1945, King Papers.
24. Adm. William F. Halsey to Charles Belnap, Oct. 8, 1943, William F. Halsey Papers, LC.
25. Turner Catledge, *My Life and the Times* (New York, 1971), p. 156.
26. E. B. Potter, *Nimitz* (Annapolis, Md., 1976), p. 61.
27. Bloch to Rear Adm. Chester W. Nimitz, Mar. 23, 1939, Bloch Papers.
28. Nimitz to Halsey, July 11, 1943, Halsey Papers.
29. Fleet Adm. Chester W. Nimitz, Interview (1965), IV: 60–61, CUOHC.
30. Potter, *Nimitz*, p. 9.
31. Ibid., p. 172.
32. Ibid., p. 17.
33. Edwin T. Layton, with Roger Pineau and John Costello, *"And I Was There": Pearl Harbor and Midway—Breaking the Secrets* (New York, 1985), p. 354.

34. W. J. Holmes, *Double-Edged Secrets: U.S. Naval Intelligence Operations in the Pacific During World War II* (Annapolis, Md., 1979), p. 42.
35. Potter, *Nimitz*, p. 1.
36. Steven T. Ross, "Chester William Nimitz, 15 December 1945–15 December 1947," in Love, ed., *Chiefs of Naval Operations*, pp. 184–85.
37. E. B. Potter, "Chester William Nimitz, 1885–1966," *U.S. Naval Institute Proceedings*, XCII (July 1966), p. 52.
38. Conolly, Interview, p. 257.
39. Potter, "Nimitz, 1885–1966," pp. 52–53.
40. King to Truman, Nov. 12, 1945, King Papers.

CHAPTER FOUR
TROUBLED BEGINNINGS IN
BRITAIN AND AFRICA

1. Allen Andrews, *The Air Marshals: The Air War in Western Europe* (New York, 1970), p. 178.
2. Richard W. Steele, *The First Offensive, 1942: Roosevelt, Marshall, and the Making of American Strategy* (Bloomington, Ind., 1973), p. viii.
3. George F. Howe, *Northwest Africa: Seizing the Initiative in the West. USAWWII* (Washington, D.C., 1957), p. 33.
4. Kenneth J. Macksey, *Crucible of Power: The Fight for Tunisia, 1942–1943* (London, 1969), p. 119; Robert E. Sherwood, *Roosevelt and Hopkins: An Intimate History* (New York, 1950), p. 293.
5. Omar N. Bradley, *A Soldier's Story* (New York, 1951), p. 41.
6. James M. Gavin, *On to Berlin: Battles of an Airborne Commander, 1943–1946* (New York, 1978), p. 10.
7. Martin Blumenson, *Kasserine Pass* (Boston, 1966), p. 307.
8. David MacIsaac, *Strategic Bombing in World War Two: The Story of the United States Strategic Bombing Survey* (New York, 1976), p. 14.
9. Edgar F. Puryear, *Nineteen Stars* (Washington, D.C., 1971), pp. 388–89.
10. Dwight D. Eisenhower, *At Ease: Stories I Tell to Friends* (Garden City, N.Y., 1967), p. 187.
11. Ibid., p. 213.
12. Eisenhower, Interview, p. 74.
13. Stephen E. Ambrose, *The Supreme Commander: The War Years of General Dwight D. Eisenhower* (Garden City, N.Y., 1970), pp. 7–8.
14. Mark W. Clark, *Calculated Risk* (New York, 1950), p. 20.
15. Eisenhower, *Eisenhower Diaries*, p. 62.
16. Ibid., p. 78.
17. Ray S. Cline, *Washington Command Post: The Operations Division. USAWWII* (Washington, D.C., 1951), p. 376.
18. Stephen E. Ambrose, "Dwight David Eisenhower," in *DAMB*, I: 302.
19. Arnold to Eisenhower, Dec. 12, 1942, Arnold Papers.

20. Dwight D. Eisenhower, *Crusade in Europe* (New York, 1979 [1st ed., 1948]), p. 197.
21. Maurice Matloff, *Strategic Planning for Coalition Warfare, 1943–1944. USAWWII* (Washington, D.C., 1959), p. 363.
22. Ambrose, *Supreme Commander*, p. 306.
23. Stephen E. Ambrose, *Eisenhower*, 2 vols. (New York, 1983–84), I: 271.
24. Eisenhower, *Crusade in Europe*, pp. 206–7.
25. Bernard L. Montgomery, *Memoirs* (Cleveland, 1958), p. 484.
26. Forrest C. Pogue, *The Supreme Command. USAWWII* (Washington, D.C., 1954), p. 34.
27. Francis W. de Guingand, *Operation Victory* (New York, 1947), pp. 436–37.
28. Gen. Lucius D. Clay, Interview (1967), III: 26, 40–41, CUOHC.
29. John J. McCloy, Interview (1970), III: 13–14, CUOHC.
30. Ambrose, *Supreme Commander*, p. 666.
31. Ambrose, *Eisenhower*, I: 271; Pogue, *Supreme Command*, p. 490.
32. Robert H. Ferrell, in Eisenhower, *Eisenhower Diaries*, p. xi.
33. Edgar F. Puryear, Jr., *Stars in Flight: A Study in Air Force Character and Leadership* (Novato, Calif., 1981), p. 76.
34. Wesley F. Craven and James L. Cate, eds., *Plans and Early Operations, January 1939 to August 1942. AAFWWII*, vol. I (Chicago, 1948), p. 649.
35. Eaker to Lincoln Barnett, Oct. 20, 1942, Spaatz Papers.
36. Copp, *Forged in Fire*, p. 225.
37. Eisenhower to Maj. Gen. Carl A. Spaatz, May 12, 1943, in *PDDE*, II: 1126.
38. Puryear, *Stars in Flight*, p. 89.
39. Sidney Shallet, "Nerveless Master of Our Superfortresses," *New York Times Magazine*, Aug. 5, 1945.
40. Gen. Carl A. Spaatz, Interview (1945), p. 4, Spaatz Papers.
41. Arnold, Diary, entry of Dec. 8, 1943.
42. Eaker to Asst. Sec. of War Robert A. Lovett, Jan. 8, 1944, Ira C. Eaker Papers, LC.
43. Eisenhower, Memorandum, Feb. 1, 1945, in *PDDE*, IV: 2466.
44. Brig. Gen. E. P. Curtis, Interview (1945), p. 6, Spaatz Papers.
45. Roger Beaumont, "Carl Andrew Spaatz," in *DAMB*, III: 1032.

CHAPTER FIVE
INTERSERVICE DIFFICULTIES IN
THE WAR AGAINST JAPAN

1. Herbert Merrilat, *Guadalcanal Remembered* (New York, 1982), p. 26.
2. In the First Marine Div. on Guadalcanal, the future generals included Cols. Clifton B. Cates and Gerald C. Thomas; Lt. Cols. Edwin A.

Pollock, Merrill B. Twining, and Samuel B. Griffith; and Maj. Lewis W. Walt. Cates would serve as USMC commandant in 1948–51.

3. Samuel E. Morison, *The Struggle for Guadalcanal, August 1942–February 1943. HUSNOWWII*, vol. V (Boston, 1949), p. 63.
4. Other future notables among the flag officers participating in the naval battles off Guadalcanal were Rear Adms. Willis A. Lee, Thomas C. Kinkaid, A. Stanton "Tip" Merrill, and Walden L. Ainsworth.
5. Brig. Gen. Nathan Twining, who was Harmon's chief of staff over Army forces in the South Pacific in 1942, later became the first commander of the Thirteenth Air Force, in the Solomons-Bismarck region; subsequently he headed the Fifteenth Air Force, in Italy, and then returned to the Pacific to command the Twentieth Air Force, rising in the postwar era to Air Force chief of staff and JCS chairman. Also playing a significant part was Rear Adm. Aubrey F. "Jake" Fitch, who led the Navy's land-based air command for two years in the South Pacific and then became deputy chief of naval operations (air).
6. Maj. Gen. DeWitt Peck, Interview (1967), p. 105, OHC, MCHC.
7. Lt. Gen. Clovis E. Byers, Interview with D. Clayton James (1971), p. 12, DMBP.
8. MacArthur, *Reminiscences*, p. 174; William F. Halsey and Joseph Bryan III, *Admiral Halsey's Story* (New York, 1947), p. 154.
9. Arnold, *Global Mission*, p. 331.
10. Louis Morton, *Pacific Command: A Study in Interservice Relations* (Colorado Springs, Colo., 1961), p. 11.
11. Brian Garfield, *The Thousand-Mile War: World War II in Alaska and the Aleutians* (Garden City, N.Y., 1969), p. 299.
12. Adm. Fletcher held the North Pacific command until the end of the war, King never allowing him to return to an active combat area after his wounding in Aug. 1942.
13. Frank O. Hough, Verle E. Ludwig, and Henry I. Shaw, Jr., *Pearl Harbor to Guadalcanal. HUSMCOWWII*, vol. I (Washington, D.C., 1958), p. 373.
14. Henry L. Stimson and McGeorge Bundy, *On Active Service in Peace and War* (New York, 1948), pp. 506–7.
15. Charles F. Romanus and Riley Sunderland, *Stilwell's Mission to China. USAWWII* (Washington, D.C., 1953), p. 387.
16. Ronald H. Spector, *Eagle Against the Sun: The American War with Japan* (New York, 1985), pp. 326, 333.
17. A. Archer Vandegrift, with Robert B. Asprey, *Once a Marine: The Memoirs of General A. A. Vandegrift* (New York, 1964), p. 29.
18. J. Robert Moskin, *The U.S. Marine Corps Story* (rev. ed., New York, 1982), p. 212.

19. Allan R. Millett, *Semper Fidelis: The History of the United States Marine Corps* (New York, 1980), p. 365.
20. Marc R. Fore, with *Newsweek* editors, *The Generals and the Admirals: Some Leaders of the United States Forces in World War II* (New York, 1945), p. 58.
21. Fletcher Pratt, *Eleven Generals: Studies in American Command* (New York, 1949), pp. 264–65, 294.
22. Vandegrift, *Once a Marine*, p. 212.
23. Don Cook, *Fighting Americans of Today* (New York, 1944), p. 99.
24. Vandegrift, *Once a Marine*, p. 183.
25. Hough, Ludwig, and Shaw, *Pearl Harbor to Guadalcanal*, pp. 373–74.
26. Vandegrift, *Once a Marine*, p. 216.
27. Gen. Gerald C. Thomas, Interview (1966), p. 430, OHC, MCHC.
28. Vandegrift, *Once a Marine*, p. 224.
29. Ibid., p. 237.
30. Thomas, Interview, p. 549.
31. Morison, *Struggle for Guadalcanal*, p. 66.
32. Robert Leckie, *Challenge for the Pacific: Guadalcanal—the Turning Point of the War* (Garden City, N.Y., 1965), p. 16.
33. Chief Warrant Officer E. S. Rust, quoted in John Foster, *Guadalcanal General: The Story of A. A. Vandegrift, USMC* (New York, 1966), p. 216.
34. Vice Adm. Theodore S. Wilkinson, Diary, entry of Oct. 13, 1943, Naval Historical Foundation Collection, LC.
35. William Shakespeare, *Henry IV*, part 1, act 1, scene 3.
36. Stilwell, *Stilwell Papers*, pp. 339, 346.
37. Ibid., p. x.
38. Ibid., p. 15.
39. Romanus and Sunderland, *Stilwell's Mission*, p. 62.
40. Pogue, *Marshall*, II: 357.
41. Romanus and Sunderland, *Stilwell's Mission*, p. 66.
42. Ibid., p. 70.
43. Gen. Joseph W. Stilwell, Diary, entry of Jan. 23, 1942, Joseph W. Stilwell Papers, HIWRP.
44. Stilwell, *Stilwell Papers*, p. 30.
45. Ibid., p. 36; Frank Dorn, *Walkout with Stilwell in Burma* (New York, 1971), p. 16.
46. Sherwood, *Roosevelt and Hopkins*, p. 513.
47. Dr. Lauchlin Currie to Marshall, Sept. 14, 1942, Lauchlin Currie Papers, HIWRP.
48. Barbara W. Tuchman, *Stilwell and the American Experience in China, 1911–45* (New York, 1970), p. 1.

49. Michael Schaller, *The U.S. Crusade in China, 1938–1945* (New York, 1979), p. 132.
50. Joseph W. Stilwell, *Stilwell's Personal File: China-Burma-India, 1942–1944*, eds. Riley Sunderland and Charles F. Romanus, 5 vols. (Wilmington, Del., 1976), V: 2422.
51. Roosevelt to Maj. Gen. Patrick J. Hurley, Aug. 18, 1944, Stilwell Papers.
52. Tuchman, *Stilwell*, p. 5.
53. Michael Schaller, "Joseph Warren Stilwell," in Graham and Wander, eds., *Roosevelt*, p. 404.
54. Stilwell, *Stilwell Papers*, p. 339.
55. Stilwell to T. V. Soong, Sept. 16, 1944, Stilwell Papers.
56. Charles F. Romanus and Riley Sunderland, *Stilwell's Command Problems. USAWWII* (Washington, D.C., 1956), p. 462.
57. Stilwell, *Stilwell Papers*, pp. 347–48.
58. Albert C. Wedemeyer, *Wedemeyer Reports!* (New York, 1958), p. 202; Gen. Albert C. Wedemeyer, Interview with D. Clayton James (1971), p. 19, DMBP.
59. Dorn, *Walkout with Stilwell*, p. vii.
60. John J. Sbrega, "Joseph Warren Stilwell," in *DAMB*, III: 1057.
61. Sec. of War Henry L. Stimson to Lt. Gen. Joseph W. Stilwell, June 17, 1942, in Stilwell, *Stilwell's Personal File*, I: 233.
62. Stimson and Bundy, *On Active Service*, p. 541.
63. Grace P. Hayes, *The History of the Joint Chiefs of Staff in World War II: The War Against Japan* (Annapolis, Md., 1982), p. 651.
64. Stilwell, *Stilwell's Personal File*, I: 191.
65. Maj. Gen. Haydon L. Boatner, Memorandum, n.d. [c. 1971], Haydon L. Boatner Papers, HIWRP.
66. Tuchman, *Stilwell*, p. 531.
67. Stimson and Bundy, *On Active Service*, pp. 540–41.

CHAPTER SIX
MEDITERRANEAN TROUBLES
AND NORMANDY WORRIES

1. Max Hastings, *Overlord: D-Day and the Battle for Normandy* (New York, 1984), pp. 24, 225.
2. Hanson W. Baldwin, *Battles Lost and Won: Great Campaigns of World War II* (New York, 1966), p. 235.
3. W. G. F. Jackson, *The Battle for Italy* (New York, 1967), p. 78.
4. Martin Blumenson, *Patton: The Man Behind the Legend, 1885–1945* (New York, 1985), p. 135.
5. Martin Blumenson, *Mark Clark* (New York, 1984), pp. 125, 130.
6. Ibid., pp. 171–72.

7. Clark, *Calculated Risk*, p. 309.
8. Martin Blumenson, *Anzio: The Gamble That Failed* (Philadelphia, 1963), p. 139.
9. Lucian K. Truscott, Jr., *Command Missions: A Personal Story* (New York, 1954), p. 328.
10. Blumenson, *Anzio*, p. 143.
11. Allan R. Millett and Peter Maslowski, *For the Common Defense: A Military History of the United States of America* (New York, 1984), p. 433; R. Ernest Dupuy and Trevor N. Dupuy, *The Encyclopedia of Military History: From 3500 B.C. to the Present* (New York, 1970), p. 1105.
12. Eisenhower to Marshall, Dec. 27, 1943, in *PDDE*, III: 1622–23, 1623n.
13. Erwin Rommel, *The Rommel Papers*, ed. B. H. Liddell Hart (New York, 1953), p. 496.
14. Blumenson, *Clark*, p. 1.
15. Puryear, *Nineteen Stars*, p. 72.
16. Pogue, *Marshall*, II: 83.
17. Ernest N. Harmon, with Milton MacKaye and William R. MacKaye, *Combat Commander: Autobiography of a Soldier* (Englewood Cliffs, N.J., 1970), p. 59.
18. Harry C. Butcher, *My Three Years with Eisenhower* (New York, 1946), p. 24.
19. Churchill, *Second World War*, IV: 385.
20. Eisenhower to Marshall, Aug. 17, 1942, in *PDDE*, I: 478.
21. William L. Langer, *Our Vichy Gamble* (New York, 1947), p. 370.
22. Pogue, *Marshall*, II: 424.
23. Clark, *Calculated Risk*, p. 132.
24. Howard M. Smyth and Albert N. Garland, *Sicily and the Surrender of Italy. USAWWII* (Washington, D.C., 1965), p. 55.
25. Eisenhower to Lt. Cdr. Harry C. Butcher, Dec. 10, 1942, in *PDDE*, II: 825.
26. Eisenhower, Memorandum for Diary, May 22, 1944, in ibid., III: 1880.
27. Trumbull Higgins, *Soft Underbelly: The Anglo-American Controversy Over the Italian Campaign, 1939–1945* (New York, 1968), p. 115.
28. Eisenhower to Marshall, Sept. 20, 1945, in Joseph P. Hobbs, *Dear General: Eisenhower's Wartime Letters to Marshall* (Baltimore, Md., 1971), p. 129.
29. Clark, *Calculated Risk*, p. 284.
30. W. G. F. Jackson, *The Battle for Rome* (New York, 1969), p. 183.
31. Gen. Lucian K. Truscott, Jr., to Brig. Gen. Don E. Carleton, Dec. 12, 1960, Don E. Carleton Papers, HIWRP.
32. Carleton to Chief of Military History, Jan. 12, 1961, Carleton Papers.
33. Clark, *Calculated Risk*, p. 357.

34. Martin Blumenson, *Salerno to Cassino. USAWWII* (Washington, D.C., 1969), pp. 348, 351.
35. Martin Blumenson, *Bloody River: The Real Tragedy of the Rapido* (Boston, 1970), p. 132.
36. Maj. Gen. Everett S. Hughes, Diary, entry of July 8, 1945, Everett S. Hughes Papers, LC.
37. Blumenson, *Clark*, p. 181.
38. Ibid., p. 185.
39. John Ellis, *Cassino: The Hollow Victory* (New York, 1984), p. 169.
40. Clark, *Calculated Risk*, p. 319.
41. Harold R. L. G. Alexander, *The Alexander Memoirs, 1940–1945*, ed. John North (New York, 1962), p. 126.
42. Harold Macmillan, *War Diaries: Politics and War in the Mediterranean, January 1943–May 1945* (New York, 1984), pp. 400, 400n, 405.
43. Kay Summersby, SHAEF Office Diary, entry of Oct. 31, 1944, Kay Summersby Papers, Dwight D. Eisenhower Library, Abilene, Kans.; copy in David Irving, comp., *Papers Relating to the Allied High Command, 1943–1945* (8 microfilm reels, Wakefield, U.K., c. 1981), reel IV, file 20 (*PRAHC* hereafter).
44. Maurine Clark, *Captain's Bride, General's Lady: The Memoirs of Mrs. Mark W. Clark* (New York, 1956), p. 160.
45. Eisenhower, Memorandum, Feb. 1, 1945, in *PDDE*, IV: 2466.
46. Michael Carver, "On Toward Rome," *New York Times Book Review*, Aug. 12, 1984.
47. Macmillan, *War Diaries*, pp. 269, 703.
48. Blumenson, *Clark*, pp. 283, 289.
49. Flint Dupre, *Hap Arnold: Architect of American Air Power* (New York, 1972), p. 78.
50. Eaker to Maj. Gen. Walter R. Weaver, Jan. 7, 1942, Eaker Papers.
51. Dupre, *Arnold*, p. 78.
52. Arnold to Eaker, Jan. 25, 1942, Arnold Papers.
53. Dupre, *Arnold*, p. 90.
54. Arthur Harris, *Bomber Offensive* (London, 1947), p. 246; Robert Saundby, *Air Bombardment: The Story of Its Development* (New York, 1961), p. 121.
55. Brig. Gen. Alfred R. Maxwell, Interview (1945), p. 27, Spaatz Papers.
56. Spaatz to Arnold, Aug. 27, 1942, Arnold Papers.
57. Eaker to Maj. Gen. George E. Stratemeyer, Dec. 6, 1942, Spaatz Papers.
58. Andrews, *Air Marshals*, p. 225.
59. Eaker to Arnold, June 29, 1943, Spaatz Papers.
60. Arnold to Eaker, July 7, 1943, Arnold Papers.
61. Maj. Gen. Follett Bradley to Arnold, June 14, 1943, Eaker Papers.
62. Copp, *Forged in Fire*, p. 452.

63. On the decision to transfer Eaker, see also Arnold, Diary, entry of Dec. 12, 1943; Arnold to Eaker, March 29, 1944, Arnold Papers; Gen. Carl A. Spaatz, Diary, entries of Dec. 9, 26, 1943, Spaatz Papers; Marshall to Eisenhower, Dec. 22, 1943, Walter B. Smith Papers, Eisenhower Library (copy in *PRAHC*, reel IV, file 8); Coffey, *Hap*, pp. 319–24; Butcher, *My Three Years*, p. 463; Lowell Thomas and Edward Jablonski, *Doolittle: A Biography* (Garden City, N.Y., 1976), pp. 257–60; Copp, *Forged in Fire*, pp. 447–52; Wesley F. Craven and James L. Cate, eds., *Europe: Torch to Pointblank, August 1942 to December 1943. AAFWWII*, vol. II (Chicago, 1949), pp. 745–51.
64. Copp, *Forged in Fire*, pp. 449, 452.
65. Lovett to Eaker, Sept. 19, 1944, Eaker Papers.
66. Eaker to Lt. Gen. Jacob L. Devers, Oct. 3, 1944, Eaker Papers.
67. Hanson W. Baldwin, *Great Mistakes of the War* (New York, 1949), p. 39.
68. Arnold to Eaker, June 8, 1945, Arnold Papers.
69. Copp, *Forged in Fire*, p. 483.

CHAPTER SEVEN
MOUNTING THE DUAL ADVANCE
TOWARD TOKYO

1. MacArthur, *Reminiscences*, pp. 172–73.
2. E. B. Potter and Chester W. Nimitz, *Triumph in the Pacific: The Navy's Struggle Against Japan* (Englewood Cliffs, N.J., 1963), pp. 102–3.
3. Layton, *"And I Was There"*, p. 468.
4. John Miller, Jr., *Cartwheel: The Reduction of Rabaul. USAWWII* (Washington, D.C., 1959), pp. 381–82.
5. Halsey and Bryan, *Halsey's Story*, p. 189.
6. Nimitz to King, Apr. 2, 1944, King Papers.
7. King-Nimitz Conference Notes, May 5, 1944, King Papers.
8. James R. Stockman, *The Battle for Tarawa* (Washington, D.C., 1947), p. ii.
9. Robert Sherrod, *Tarawa: The Story of a Battle* (New York, 1944), p. 148.
10. Robert D. Heinl and John A. Crown, *The Marshalls: Increasing the Tempo* (Washington, D.C., 1954), p. 1.
11. Samuel E. Morison, *Strategy and Compromise* (Boston, 1958), p. 93.
12. Potter and Nimitz, *Triumph in the Pacific*, p. 74.
13. Joseph Bryan III, "Four-Star Sea Dog," pt. 1, *Saturday Evening Post*, CCXVI (Dec. 25, 1943), p. 28.
14. Thomas, Interview, p. 426.

15. E. B. Potter, "The Command Personality: Some American Naval Leaders in World War II," *U.S. Naval Institute Proceedings*, XCV (Jan. 1969), p. 25.
16. Bryan, "Four-Star Sea Dog," pt. 2 (Jan. 1, 1944), p. 26.
17. Clark G. Reynolds, *The Fast Carriers: The Forging of an Air Navy* (New York, 1968), p. 24.
18. Halsey and Bryan, *Halsey's Story*, pp. 106, 107.
19. Potter, "Command Personality," p. 24.
20. E. B. Potter, *Bull Halsey* (Annapolis, Md., 1985), p. 176.
21. Halsey and Bryan, *Halsey's Story*, p. 109.
22. George C. Dyer, *The Amphibians Came to Conquer: The Story of Admiral Richmond Kelly Turner*, 2 vols. (Washington, D.C., 1972), II: 599.
23. James A. Merrill, *A Sailor's Admiral: A Biography of William F. Halsey* (New York, 1976), p. 70.
24. Clark Lee, *They Call It Pacific: An Eye-Witness Story of Our War Against Japan from Bataan to the Solomons* (New York, 1943), p. 358.
25. Potter, *Halsey*, p. xiii.
26. Halsey and Bryan, *Halsey's Story*, p. 129.
27. Wilkinson, Diary, entry of March 12, 1943.
28. Potter, "Command Personality," pp. 23, 24.
29. Nimitz to Halsey, Oct. 5, 1944, Halsey Papers.
30. Halsey to Nimitz, Oct. 6, 1944, Halsey Papers.
31. Holmes, *Double-Edged Secrets*, p. 184.
32. Halsey and Bryan, *Halsey's Story*, p. 200.
33. Charles E. Pfannes and Victor A. Salamone, *The Great Admirals of World War II*, vol. I, *The Americans* (New York, 1983), p. 86.
34. Reynolds, *Fast Carriers*, p. 484.
35. J. J. Clark, with Clark G. Reynolds, *Carrier Admiral* (New York, 1967), p. 237.
36. Halsey and Bryan, *Halsey's Story*, p. 129.
37. Rear Adm. Charles J. Moore, Interview (1964), pp. 682, 684, OHC, NHC.
38. Benis M. Frank, *Halsey* (New York, 1974), p. 159.
39. Merrill, *Sailor's Admiral*, p. 70.
40. Adm. Arleigh A. Burke, Interview with D. Clayton James (1971), pp. 5–6, DMBP.
41. Adm. Russell S. Berkey, Interview with D. Clayton James (1971), p. 15, DMBP.
42. Conolly, Interview, p. 183.
43. *Army Times* editors, *Famous American Military Leaders of World War II* (New York, 1963), p. 110.

44. Robert L. Eichelberger, with Milton MacKaye, *Our Jungle Road to Tokyo* (New York, 1950), p. xv.
45. Copp, *A Few Great Captains*, p. 478.
46. Copp, *Forged in Fire*, p. 412.
47. George C. Kenney, *Dick Bong: Ace of Aces* (New York, 1960), p. 9.
48. Arnold, *Global Mission*, p. 192.
49. Cato D. Glover, *Command Performance with Guts* (New York, 1969), p. 17.
50. Kenney, *Kenney Reports*, p. 29.
51. Ibid., p. 45.
52. Gen. George C. Kenney, Interview with D. Clayton James (1971), pp. 3–4, DMBP. Brig. Gen. Whitehead's biographer maintains that "it was Ennis C. Whitehead and not George Kenney who was the guiding force behind the great air victories in the Pacific." Donald M. Goldstein, "Ennis C. Whitehead, Aerospace Commander and Pioneer" (unpublished Ph.D. dissertation, University of Denver, 1970), p. 457.
53. U.S. Army Air Forces, *AAF: The Official Guide to the Army Air Forces; A Directory, Almanac and Chronicle of Achievement* (New York, 1944), p. 289.
54. Arnold, Diary, entry of June 17, 1945.
55. Arnold to Gen. George C. Kenney, March 15, 1945, Arnold Papers.
56. Kenney, *Dick Bong*, p. iii.
57. George H. Johnston, *Pacific Partner* (New York, 1944), p. 102.
58. Kenney, Interview, pp. 30, 32.
59. Excerpts from sundry interviews with senior SWPA officers by D. Clayton James, DMBP.
60. Adm. Thomas C. Kinkaid, Interview (1961), p. 361, OHC, NHC.
61. Potter, *Halsey*, p. 404.
62. Arnold, Diary, entry of Sept. 25, 1942.
63. Maj. Gen. Richard J. Marshall, Interview with D. Clayton James (1971), p. 11, DMBP.

CHAPTER EIGHT
LEADING THE FINAL CAMPAIGNS
AGAINST GERMANY

1. Churchill, *Second World War*, V: 426.
2. Martin Van Creveld, *Fighting Power: German and U.S. Army Performance, 1939–1945* (Westport, Conn., 1982), p. 167.
3. Russell F. Weigley, *Eisenhower's Lieutenants: The Campaign of France and Germany, 1944–1945* (Bloomington, Ind., 1981), p. 729.

4. Baldwin, *Battles Lost and Won*, p. 278.
5. Charles B. MacDonald, *The Mighty Endeavor: American Armed Forces in the European Theater in World War II* (New York, 1969), p. 518.
6. Bradley, *Soldier's Story*, p. 298.
7. Spaatz recommended Vandenberg to Arnold for the Ninth Air Force command without consulting Brereton or Doolittle. Gen. Hoyt S. Vandenberg, Diary, entry of July 16, 1944, Hoyt S. Vandenberg Papers, LC.
8. Ambrose, *Supreme Commander*, p. 346.
9. Maurice Matloff, "Allied Strategy in Europe, 1939–1945," in Peter Paret, ed., *Makers of Modern Strategy: From Machiavelli to the Nuclear Age* (Princeton, N.J., 1986), p. 694.
10. Matloff, "Allied Strategy," p. 702.
11. Forrest C. Pogue, "General of the Army Omar N. Bradley," in Michael Carver, ed., *The War Lords: Military Commanders of the Twentieth Century* (Boston, 1976), p. 538.
12. Omar N. Bradley and Clay Blair, *A General's Life: An Autobiography* (New York, 1983), p. 67.
13. Pogue, "Bradley," p. 539.
14. Charles Whiting, *Bradley* (New York, 1971), p. 13.
15. Bradley and Blair, *General's Life*, p. 112.
16. Ibid., p. 113.
17. Bradley, *Soldier's Story*, p. 19.
18. Eisenhower to Marshall, Feb. 11, 1943, in *PDDE*, II: 951.
19. Bradley and Blair, *General's Life*, 131.
20. Eisenhower to Marshall, March 11, 1943, in *PDDE*, II: 1024.
21. Pogue, *Marshall*, II: 409.
22. Weigley, *Eisenhower's Lieutenants*, p. 81.
23. Eisenhower to Marshall, Aug. 27, 1943, in *PDDE*, II: 1357, 1358.
24. Ladislas Farago, *Patton: Ordeal and Triumph* (New York, 1963), p. 131.
25. Weigley, *Eisenhower's Lieutenants*, p. 84.
26. Pogue, "Bradley," p. 543.
27. Bradley and Blair, *General's Life*, p. 394.
28. J. Lawton Collins, *Lightning Joe: An Autobiography* (Baton Rouge, La., 1979), p. 192.
29. John Colville, *The Fringes of Power: 10 Downing Street, 1939–1955* (New York, 1985), pp. 506–7.
30. De Guingand, *Operation Victory*, pp. 135, 136.
31. Kay Summersby, *Eisenhower Was My Boss* (New York, 1948), p. 211.
32. Gen. George S. Patton, Jr., Diary, entry of Feb. 10, 1945, George S. Patton, Jr., Papers, LC (quoted from copy in *PRAHC*, reel IV, file 10).

33. Pogue, *Marshall*, III: 516.
34. Eisenhower to John S. D. Eisenhower, Jan. 31, 1944, in *PDDE*, III: 1700.
35. Pogue, "Bradley," p. 550.
36. Bradley and Blair, *General's Life*, p. 13.
37. Gen. Lucius D. Clay, Interview (1971), III: 712, CUOHC.
38. Maj. Gen. Elwood R. Quesada, Interview (1960), III: 45, CUOHC.
39. Eisenhower to Gen. Walter B. Smith, Dec. 10, 1947, in *PDDE*, IX: 2129.
40. Col. W. H. S. Wright, Report to the Secretary of War on His Activities from 26 May to 8 July 1944, Stimson Papers (copy in *PRAHC*, reel II, file 7).
41. Martin Blumenson, *The Patton Papers*, 2 vols. (Boston, 1972–74), I: 230.
42. Fore, *The Generals and the Admirals*, p. 26; Blumenson, *Patton Papers*, I: 232.
43. Martin Blumenson, "General George S. Patton," in Carver, ed., *War Lords*, p. 556.
44. Blumenson, *Patton Papers*, I: 432.
45. Harry H. Semmes, *Portrait of Patton* (New York, 1955), p. 47.
46. Martin Blumenson, *The Many Faces of George S. Patton, Jr.* (Colorado Springs, Colo., 1972), p. 12.
47. Farago, *Patton*, p. 112.
48. Blumenson, *Many Faces*, p. 14.
49. Farago, *Patton*, p. 130.
50. Blumenson, *Patton Papers*, I: 956.
51. Ibid., pp. 74, 75.
52. Blumenson, "Patton," p. 559.
53. Farago, *Patton*, pp. 177–78.
54. Semmes, *Portrait of Patton*, p. 90.
55. Blumenson, *Patton Papers*, II: 390.
56. Ibid., pp. 392, 393.
57. Hughes, Diary, entry of Jan. 9, 1944.
58. Robert S. Allen, *Lucky Forward: The History of Patton's Third Army* (New York, 1947), p. 20.
59. Eisenhower to Marshall, Apr. 30, 1944, in *PDDE*, III: 1840, 1841.
60. Blumenson, *Patton Papers*, II: 445, 446, 447.
61. Blumenson, "Patton," p. 561.
62. George S. Patton, Jr., *War As I Knew It* (Boston, 1947), p. 331.
63. Hughes, Diary, entry of Feb. 16, 1945.
64. Marshall to MacArthur, June 19, 1945; MacArthur to Marshall, June 19, 1945, RG 4, MMA.
65. Jay Luvaas, ed., *Dear Miss Em: General Eichelberger's War in the Pacific, 1942–1945* (Westport, Conn., 1972), p. 237.

66. Gen. Omar N. Bradley, Efficiency Report on Gen. George S. Patton, Jr., June 30, 1945, Patton Papers (copy in *PRAHC*, reel IV, file 9).
67. Handy, Interview, p. 28.
68. Maj. Gen. John H. Chiles, Interview with D. Clayton James (1977), p. 44, DMBP.
69. Alexander, *Alexander Memoirs*, pp. 44, 45.
70. Hubert Essame, *Patton: A Study in Command* (New York, 1974), pp. 258–59.
71. Blumenson, *Patton: The Man Behind the Legend*, p. 189.
72. Paul D. Harkins, with *Army Times* Editors, *When the Third Cracked Europe: The Story of Patton's Incredible Army* (Harrisburg, Pa., 1969), p. 14.
73. Charles R. Codman, *Drive* (Boston, 1957), pp. 158–59.
74. Blumenson, *Many Faces*, p. 26.

CHAPTER NINE
THE LAST FIFTEEN MONTHS
OF THE PACIFIC WAR

1. Spector, *Eagle Against the Sun*, p. 560.
2. Robert W. Coakley and Richard M. Leighton, *Global Logistics and Strategy, 1943–1945. USAWWII* (Washington, D.C., 1968), p. 564.
3. Luvaas, ed., *Dear Miss Em*, p. 99.
4. Robert G. Albion and Robert H. Connery, *Forrestal and the Navy* (New York, 1962), p. 179.
5. The new Eighth Air Force, as reconstituted under Doolittle in July 1945, was built from the XX Bomber Command of B-29s and stationed in the Ryukyus. The XXI Bomber Command of B-29s, in the Marianas, became the nucleus of the Twentieth Air Force. Spaatz established his Strategic Air Force headquarters on Guam.
6. Morton, *Pacific Command*, p. 28.
7. Schaller, *U.S. Crusade in China*, p. 217.
8. Hayes, *History of the Joint Chiefs of Staff*, pp. 728, 729.
9. U.S. Strategic Bombing Survey, *Summary Report (Pacific War)* (Washington, D.C., 1946), p. 26.
10. Thomas M. Coffey, *Iron Eagle: The Turbulent Life of General Curtis LeMay* (New York, 1986), p. 179.
11. Kent R. Greenfield, *American Strategy in World War II: A Reconsideration* (Baltimore, Md., 1963), p. 120.
12. Holland M. Smith and Percy Finch, *Coral and Brass* (New York, 1948), p. 32.
13. Fore, *The Generals and the Admirals*, p. 60; Norman V. Cooper, "The Military Career of General Holland M. Smith, USMC" (unpublished Ph.D. dissertation, University of Alabama, 1974), p. 3.

14. Cooper, "Military Career," p. 179.
15. Maj. Gen. Omar T. Pfeiffer, Interview (1968), p. 230, OHC, MCHC.
16. Smith and Finch, *Coral and Brass*, pp. 104, 105.
17. Cooper, "Military Career," p. 200.
18. Millett, *Semper Fidelis*, p. 392.
19. Cooper, "Military Career," pp. 202–03.
20. Harry A. Gailey, *Howlin' Mad vs the Army: Conflict in Command, Saipan 1944* (Novato, Calif., 1986), p. 240.
21. Philip A. Crowl, *Campaign in the Marianas. USAWWII* (Washington, D.C., 1960), p. 201.
22. Moskin, *U.S. Marine Corps Story*, p. 359.
23. Millett, *Semper Fidelis*, p. 415.
24. Cooper, "Military Career," p. 7.
25. Norman V. Cooper, "Holland McTyeire Smith," in *DAMB*, III: 1015.
26. Sherrod, *Tarawa*, p. 133.
27. Smith and Finch, *Coral and Brass*, p. 193.
28. Cooper, "Military Career," p. 133.
29. Ibid., p. 295.
30. Gen. Clifton B. Cates, Interview (1967), p. 224, OHC, MCHC.
31. Potter, *Nimitz*, p. 250.
32. Dyer, *Amphibians Came to Conquer*, II: 600.
33. Thomas, Interview, p. 570.
34. Cooper, "Military Career," p. 405.
35. Jeter A. Isely and Philip A. Crowl, *The U.S. Marines and Amphibious War: Its Theory and Its Practice in the Pacific* (Princeton, N.J., 1951), p. 62.
36. Cooper, "Military Career," pp. 481, 482.
37. Thomas B. Buell, *The Quiet Warrior: A Biography of Admiral Raymond A. Spruance* (Boston, 1974), pp. 14, 16.
38. Ibid., p. 49.
39. Thomas B. Buell, "Raymond Ames Spruance," in *DAMB*, III: 1033.
40. Pfannes and Salamone, *Great Admirals*, p. 180.
41. Buell, *Quiet Warrior*, p. 121.
42. Emmet P. Forrestel, *Admiral Raymond A. Spruance, USN: A Study in Command* (Washington, D.C., 1966), p. 50.
43. Ibid., pp. 56, 57.
44. Nimitz, Interview, IV: 70.
45. Forrestel, *Spruance*, p. 60.
46. Ibid., p. 59.
47. Buell, *Quiet Warrior*, p. 165.
48. King and Whitehill, *King*, p. 491n.
49. Potter, *Nimitz*, p. 239.
50. Reynolds, *Fast Carriers*, p. 70.
51. Nimitz to Adm. Raymond A. Spruance, Feb. 23, 1944, Raymond A. Spruance Papers, HIWRP.

52. Spector, *Eagle Against the Sun*, p. 312.
53. Buell, *Quiet Warrior*, p. 339.
54. Ibid., pp. 356–57.
55. Moore, Interview, p. 906.
56. Potter, *Halsey*, p. 350.
57. Pfannes and Salamone, *Great Admirals*, p. 238; Reynolds, *Fast Carriers*, p. 387.
58. Richard Hough, *The Greatest Crusade: Roosevelt, Churchill, and the Naval Wars* (New York, 1986), p. 197.
59. Forrestel, *Spruance*, p. v.
60. Morison, *Two-Ocean War*, p. 581.
61. Buell, *Quiet Warrior*, p. 435.
62. Buell, "Spruance," p. 1035.
63. Potter, "Command Personality," p. 25.

CHAPTER TEN
POLITICS?

1. *Webster's Third New International Dictionary of the English Language* (unabridged ed., Springfield, Mass., 1982), p. 1755; *American Heritage Dictionary* (2d college ed., Boston, 1982), p. 960; *The Random House Dictionary of the English Language* (unabridged ed., New York, 1981), p. 1113.
2. Mylander, *The Generals*, pp. 48–49.
3. Eisenhower to Butcher, Dec. 10, 1942, in *PDDE*, II: 824.
4. S. L. A. Marshall, *The Officer as Leader* (Harrisburg, Pa., 1966), pp. 223, 224–25.

BIBLIOGRAPHY

The notes provide an indication of the manuscript riches available to those who wish to undertake research in the unpublished sources on the United States high command of 1941–45. The following highly selective bibliography gives the general reader some of the best works by or about the top wartime commanders. See the notes for other published materials.

ARNOLD

Arnold, Henry H. *Global Mission.* New York, 1949.
Coffey, Thomas M. *Hap: The Story of the U.S. Air Force and the Man Who Built It, General Henry H. "Hap" Arnold.* New York, 1982.

BRADLEY

Bradley, Omar N. *A Soldier's Story.* New York, 1951.
Bradley, Omar N., and Clay Blair. *A General's Life: An Autobiography.* New York, 1983.

CLARK

Blumenson, Martin. *Mark Clark.* New York, 1984.
Clark, Mark W. *Calculated Risk.* New York, 1950.

EAKER

Parton, James. *"Air Force Spoken Here": General Ira Eaker and the Command of the Air.* New York, 1986.

EISENHOWER

Ambrose, Stephen E. *Eisenhower*. 2 vols. New York, 1983–84.
————. *The Supreme Commander: The War Years of General Dwight D. Eisenhower*. Garden City, N.Y., 1970.
Eisenhower, Dwight D. *At Ease: Stories I Tell to Friends*. Garden City, N.Y., 1967.
————. *Crusade in Europe*. New York, 1979 (1st ed., 1948).
————. *The Papers of Dwight David Eisenhower: The War Years*. Edited by Alfred D. Chandler, Jr. 5 vols. Baltimore, Md., 1970.
Pogue, Forrest C. *The Supreme Command. United States Army in World War II: European Theater of Operations*. Washington, D.C., 1954.

HALSEY

Halsey, William F., and Joseph Bryan III. *Admiral Halsey's Story*. New York, 1947.
Merrill, James A. *A Sailor's Admiral: A Biography of William F. Halsey*. New York, 1976.
Potter, E. B. *Bull Halsey*. Annapolis, Md., 1985.

KENNEY

Kenney, George C. *General Kenney Reports: A Personal History of the Pacific War*. New York, 1949.

KING

Buell, Thomas B. *Master of Sea Power: A Biography of Fleet Admiral Ernest J. King*. Boston, 1980.
King, Ernest J., and Walter M. Whitehill. *Fleet Admiral King: A Naval Record*. New York, 1952.

LEAHY

Adams, Henry H. *Witness to Power: The Life of Fleet Admiral William D. Leahy*. Annapolis, Md., 1985.
Leahy, William D. *I Was There: The Personal Story of the Chief of Staff to Presidents Roosevelt and Truman Based on His Notes and Diaries Made at the Time*. New York, 1950.

MACARTHUR

James, D. Clayton. *The Years of MacArthur*. 3 vols. Boston, 1970–85.

MacArthur, Douglas. *Reminiscences*. New York, 1964.
————. *Reports of General MacArthur*. Edited by Charles A. Willoughby. 2 vols. in 4 pts. Washington, D.C., 1966.

MARSHALL

Marshall, George C. *The Papers of George Catlett Marshall*. Edited by Larry J. Bland. 2 vols. to date. Baltimore, Md., 1981–86.
Pogue, Forrest C. *George C. Marshall*. 3 vols. to date. New York, 1963–73.

NIMITZ

Potter, E. B. *Nimitz*. Annapolis, Md., 1976.

PATTON

Blumenson, Martin. *Patton: The Man Behind the Legend, 1885–1945*. New York, 1985.
————. *The Patton Papers*. 2 vols. Boston, 1972–74.
Essame, Hubert. *Patton: A Study in Command*. New York, 1974.
Farago, Ladislas. *Patton: Ordeal and Triumph*. New York, 1963.
Patton, George S., Jr. *War as I Knew It*. Boston, 1947.

SMITH

Cooper, Norman V. "The Military Career of General Holland M. Smith, USMC." Unpublished Ph.D. dissertation, University of Alabama, 1974.
Gailey, Harry A. *Howlin' Mad vs the Army: Conflict in Command, Saipan 1944*. Novato, Calif., 1986.
Smith, Holland M., and Percy Finch. *Coral and Brass*. New York, 1948.

SPAATZ

Davis, Richard G. "The Bomber Baron: Carl Andrew Spaatz and the United States Army Air Forces in Europe, 1942–1945." Unpublished Ph.D. dissertation, George Washington University, 1986.

SPRUANCE

Buell, Thomas B. *The Quiet Warrior: A Biography of Admiral Raymond A. Spruance*. Boston, 1974.
Forrestel, Emmet P. *Admiral Raymond A. Spruance, USN: A Study in Command*. Washington, D.C., 1966.

STILWELL

Romanus, Charles F., and Riley Sunderland. *Stilwell's Command Problems. United States Army in World War II: China-Burma-India Theater.* Washington, D.C., 1956.

—— and ——. *Stilwell's Mission to China. United States Army in World War II: China-Burma-India Theater.* Washington, D.C., 1953.

Stilwell, Joseph W. *The Stilwell Papers.* Edited by Theodore H. White. New York, 1948.

——. *Stilwell's Personal File: China-Burma-India, 1942–1944.* Edited by Riley Sunderland and Charles F. Romanus. 5 vols. Wilmington, Del., 1976.

Tuchman, Barbara W. *Stilwell and the American Experience in China, 1911–45.* New York, 1970.

VANDEGRIFT

Vandegrift, A. Archer, with Robert B. Asprey. *Once a Marine: The Memoirs of General A. A. Vandegrift.* New York, 1964.

MISCELLANEOUS

Army Times editors. *Famous American Military Leaders of World War II.* New York, 1963.

Barbey, Daniel E. *MacArthur's Amphibious Navy: Seventh Amphibious Force Operations, 1943–1945.* Annapolis, Md., 1969.

Bell, William G. *Commanding Generals and Chiefs of Staff, 1775–1983: Portraits and Biographical Sketches of the Army's Senior Officers.* Washington, D.C., 1983.

Blumenson, Martin, and James L. Stokesbury. *Masters of the Art of Command.* Boston, 1975.

Brereton, Lewis H. *The Brereton Diaries: The War in the Air in the Pacific, Middle East, and Europe, 3 October 1941–8 May 1945.* New York, 1946.

Bryant, Arthur. *Triumph in the West: A History of the War Years Based on the Diaries of Field-Marshal Lord Alanbrooke, Chief of the Imperial General Staff.* Garden City, N.Y., 1959.

——. *The Turn of the Tide: A History of the War Years Based on the Diaries of Field-Marshal Lord Alanbrooke, Chief of the Imperial General Staff.* Garden City, N.Y., 1957.

Buck, James H., and Lawrence J. Korb, eds. *Military Leadership.* Beverly Hills, Calif., 1981.

Burns, James M. *Leadership.* New York, 1978.

——. *Roosevelt: The Soldier of Freedom, 1940–1945.* New York, 1970.

Carver, Michael, ed. *The War Lords: Military Commanders of the Twentieth Century.* Boston, 1976.

Churchill, Winston S. *The Second World War*. 6 vols. Boston, 1948–53.

Collins, J. Lawton. *Lightning Joe: An Autobiography*. Baton Rouge, La., 1979.

Copp, DeWitt S. *A Few Great Captains: The Men and Events That Shaped the Development of U.S. Air Power*. Garden City, N.Y., 1980.

———. *Forged in Fire: Strategy and Decisions in the Air War Over Europe, 1940–45*. Garden City, N.Y., 1982.

Davis, Burke. *Marine! The Life of Lt. Gen. Lewis B. (Chesty) Puller, USMC (Ret.)*. Boston, 1962.

Dyer, George C. *The Amphibians Came to Conquer: The Story of Admiral Richmond Kelly Turner*. 2 vols. Washington, D.C., 1972.

Eichelberger, Robert L., with Milton MacKaye. *Our Jungle Road to Tokyo*. New York, 1950.

Eisenhower, John S. D. *Allies: Pearl Harbor to D-Day*. Garden City, N.Y., 1982.

Forrestal, James V. *The Forrestal Diaries*. Edited by Walter Millis, with E. S. Duffield. New York, 1951.

Gavin, James M. *On to Berlin: Battles of an Airborne Commander, 1943–1946*. New York, 1978.

Glover, Cato D. *Command Performance with Guts*. New York, 1969.

Greenfield, Kent R., ed. *Command Decisions*. Washington, D.C., 1960.

Harmon, Ernest N. with Milton MacKaye and William R. MacKaye. *Combat Command: Autobiography of a Soldier*. Englewood Cliffs, N.J., 1970.

Hayes, Grace P. *The History of the Joint Chiefs of Staff in World War II: The War Against Japan*. Annapolis, Md., 1982.

Hays, Samuel H., and William N. Thomas, eds. *Taking Command: The Art and Science of Military Leadership*. Harrisburg, Pa., 1967.

Huntington, Samuel P. *The Soldier and the State: The Theory and Politics of Civil-Military Relations*. Cambridge, Mass., 1957.

Irving, David. *The War Between the Generals*. New York, 1981.

Ismay, Hastings L. *The Memoirs of General Lord Ismay*. New York, 1960.

Janowitz, Morris. *The Professional Soldier: A Social and Political Portrait*. Glencoe, Ill., 1960.

Johnson, Allen, Dumas Malone, and John A. Garraty, eds. *Dictionary of American Biography*. 27 vols. New York, 1928–81.

Kahn, E. J., Jr. *McNair: Educator of an Army*. Washington, D.C., 1945.

Krueger, Walter. *From Down Under to Nippon: The Story of Sixth Army in World War II*. Washington, D.C., 1953.

LeMay, Curtis E., with MacKinlay Kantor. *Mission with LeMay: My Story*. Garden City, N.Y., 1965.

Love, Robert W., ed. *The Chiefs of Naval Operations*. Annapolis, Md., 1980.

Luvaas, Jay, ed. *Dear Miss Em: General Eichelberger's War in the Pacific, 1942–1945*. Westport, Conn., 1972.

Macmillan, Harold. *War Diaries: Politics and War in the Mediterranean, January 1943–May 1945*. New York, 1984.

Marshall, S. L. A. *The Officer as Leader*. Harrisburg, Pa., 1966.

May, Ernest R., ed. *The Ultimate Decision: The President as Commander-in-Chief*. New York, 1960.

Montgomery, Bernard L. *Memoirs*. Cleveland, 1958.

Morison, Elting E. *Turmoil and Tradition: A Study of the Life and Times of Henry L. Stimson*. Boston, 1960.

Morton, Louis. *Pacific Command: A Study in Interservice Relations*. Colorado Springs, Colo., 1961.

————. *Strategy and Command: The First Two Years. United States Army in World War II: The War in the Pacific*. Washington, D.C., 1962.

Mylander, Maureen. *The Generals: Making It, Military Style*. New York, 1974.

Pfannes, Charles E., and Victor A. Salamone. *The Great Admirals of World War II*. Vol. 1, *The Americans*. New York, 1983.

Puryear, Edgar F., Jr. *Nineteen Stars*. Washington, D.C., 1971.

————. *Stars in Flight: A Study in Air Force Character and Leadership*. Novato, Calif., 1981.

Reynolds, Clark G. *Famous American Admirals*. New York, 1978.

————. *The Fast Carriers: The Forging of an Air Navy*. New York, 1968.

Ridgway, Matthew B. *Soldier: The Memoirs of Matthew B. Ridgway*. New York, 1956.

Sherman, Frederick C. *Combat Command: The American Aircraft Carriers in the Pacific War*. New York, 1950.

Sherwood, Robert E. *Roosevelt and Hopkins: An Intimate History*. New York, 1950.

Spector, Ronald H. *Eagle Against the Sun: The American War with Japan*. New York, 1983.

Spiller, Roger J., ed. *Dictionary of American Military Biography*. 3 vols. Westport, Conn., 1984.

Steele, Richard W. *The First Offensive, 1942: Roosevelt, Marshall, and the Making of American Strategy*. Bloomington, Ind., 1973.

Stimson, Henry L., and McGeorge Bundy. *On Active Service in Peace and War*. New York, 1948.

Stoler, Mark A. *The Politics of the Second Front: American Military Planning and Diplomacy in Coalition Warfare, 1941–1943*. Westport, Conn., 1977.

Taylor, Maxwell D. *Swords and Ploughshares*. New York, 1972.

Tedder, Arthur. *With Prejudice: The War Memoirs of Marshal of the Royal Air Force Lord Tedder, G.C.B*. London, 1966.

Truman, Harry S. *Memoirs*. 2 vols. Garden City, N.Y., 1955–56.

Truscott, Lucian K., Jr. *Command Missions: A Personal Story*. New York, 1954.

U.S. Department of the Army. *Field Manual 22-100: Military Leadership*. Washington, D.C., 1983.

Van Creveld, Martin. *Fighting Power: German and U.S. Army Performance, 1939–1945*. Westport, Conn., 1982.

Wavell, Archibald. *Generals and Generalship: The Lees Knowles Lectures Delivered at Trinity College, Cambridge, in 1939.* Toronto, 1941.
Wedemeyer, Albert C. *Wedemeyer Reports!* New York, 1958.
Weigley, Russell F. *Eisenhower's Lieutenants: The Campaign of France and Germany, 1944–1945.* Bloomington, Ind., 1981.

INDEX

Submarine warfare, 28–29, 37–38, 56–57, 173
Sultan, Daniel I., 21, 132
Sulzberger, Arthur H., 68
Sutherland, Richard K., 200
Swanson, Claude A., 44

Tarawa assault, 174, 179, 250
Tedder, Arthur, 100, 101, 147, 165, 166
Teheran Conference, 92–93
Theobald, Robert A., 111, 112
Thomas, Gerald C., 120, 122, 182, 253–254
Tinian, 241, 250
Tojo, Hideki, 180
Tokyo raid, 55, 184, 197
Torrey, Philip, 118
Towers, John H., 75, 183, 261, 264
Trident Conference, 114, 115
Truk, 179, 180
Truman, Harry S, 24, 103, 192, 244, 246
  King and, 41
  Leahy and, 48, 49
  MacArthur and, 65–67, 241
  on Marshall, 22
Truscott, Lucian K., 82, 139, 143, 145, 159, 216, 231, 233, 234
  in Italian campaign, 143, 155–156
  Operation Anvil (Dragoon) and, 146, 208
  in Sicilian campaign, 139
Tulagi, 73, 118
Turner, R. Kelly "Terrible," 56, 174, 180, 186, 187, 242, 251, 261, 264
  Nimitz and, 75
  Pearl Harbor and, 56
  Savo Island, Battle of, 107
  Smith and, 249, 250, 253, 254
  Spruance and, 256, 257
  Vandegrift and, 112, 120
Twining, Nathan F., 102, 103, 148, 165, 176, 199, 242, 244

Ultra system, 172

Vandegrift, A. Archer, 6, 116–124, 176, 250, 252, 253, 269
  background of, 116–117
  as commandant of the Marine Corps, 120, 122–123
  court martial of, 117
  Guadalcanal campaign and, 106, 112, 118–120, 185, 187, 248
  postwar career of, 123
  Turner and, 112, 120
  Wilkinson on, 123–124
Vandenberg, Hoyt S., 201, 210
Vella Lavella, 121
Vinson, Carl, 192
Vogel, Clayton B. "Barney," 121, 248

Wainwright, Jonathan M., 54, 58
Wake, 53, 184
Walker, Fred L., 156
Walker, Kenneth N., 197
Watson, Edwin "Pa," 21, 64
Wavell, Archibald P., 27, 115, 116, 126, 133
Wedemeyer, Albert C., 32, 113, 132–133, 245
Westover, Oscar, 9–12
Weyland, Otto P., 232
Wheeler, Raymond A., 32
Whitehead, Ennis C., 111, 198, 199, 239, 240
Wilkinson, Theodore S. "Ping," 121, 174, 177, 242
  Halsey and, 187, 188
  on Vandegrift, 123–124
Willoughby, Charles A., 173
Wilson, Henry M. "Jumbo," 29–30, 143, 155–159, 167
Wilson, Walter K., 125
Wood, Leonard, 224
Woodring, Henry H., 9, 11, 19–21
Wright, W.H.S., 222–223
Wurtsmith, Paul B., 198

Yalta Conference, 49
Yamamoto, Isoroku, 180, 184, 259

★ 317 ★